P9-CLS-133

10 Smart Ways to Invest in Mutual Funds

1. **Zero in on your investment goals.** Understand what you want to accomplish before you get involved with mutual funds. Are you saving for your child's future college education or your retirement? Are you looking for a temporary place to park your cash so you can earn more than a bank account?

2. **Understand your tolerance for risk before you invest.** Determine whether you are an aggressive, moderate, conservative, or least-risk-minded investor. Then you can make the right investment decision.

3. **Invest in mutual funds for the long term.** You need to invest through thick and thin. Because you can lose when you invest in mutual funds, you need time to make back any losses. Invest for a minimum of five years.

4. **Pay yourself first.** Invest regularly. That way, you'll buy more shares of your fund when the price is down. Over the long term, you build your wealth.

5. **Reinvest any income you get from your fund to buy more shares.** The profits will pile up over the years.

6. **Diversify.** Own different types of mutual funds, such as stock, bond, and money funds. One type of mutual fund will zig while the other zags—losses in one fund can be offset by gains in another.

7. **Compare fund fees, charges, and commissions before you invest.** Make your money work for you, not your stockbroker. Check the cost of several funds before you plunk down your hard-earned cash.

8. **Investigate before you invest.** Do your homework. Compare the performance, risks, investment objectives, and costs of several funds before you invest. That way you're sure to find the best deal.

9. **Open an IRA retirement savings account.** You'll invest for the long haul and your profits grow tax-deferred until you retire.

10. **Make sure you've taken care of your insurance needs before you invest in mutual funds.** Do you have adequate life insurance to protect your family in the event of an untimely death? Do you have disability insurance coverage to protect your wages in case you get injured or incapacitated? If not, consider obtaining life and disability insurance coverage first. Then start a mutual fund investment program.

5 Ways to Mutual Fund Profits

1. **Invest in no-load mutual funds.** These funds charge no commissions, so 100 percent of your money is invested in the fund of your choice.

2. **Invest in common stock mutual funds for long-term growth.** Over the past 30 years, the average diversified common stock fund grew at an 11 percent annual rate.

3. **Take advantage of mutual fund families that have a wide variety of funds to pick.** As your financial condition or needs change, you can find the fund that's right for you.

4. **Invest early and often.** Don't procrastinate. If you're investing annually, make your investment at the beginning of each year. Investing monthly? Do it at the start of each month. That way your money will grow faster and longer over the years.

5. **Invest to beat the taxman.** If you avoid paying Uncle Sam taxes on your investment earnings, you have more money in your pocket. Consider tax-free bond and money funds if you pay at least 28 percent of your income to the IRS.

tear here

Mutual Fund Risk/Reward Chart

Investor Risk Level/Objective	Type of Fund	Risk/Reward
Stock Funds		
Speculative	Precious metals	Highest/Big gains
Speculative	Most sector	Higher/Big gains
Aggressive	Aggressive growth	High/Maximum capital growth
Aggressive	International growth	High/Maximum capital growth
Aggressive	Small company	High/Maximum capital growth
Aggressive	Growth	High/Longer-term growth
Moderate	Growth & income	Moderate/Growth plus income
Moderate	Equity income	Low-moderate/Income plus growth
Conservative	Income	Lower/Long-term income
Conservative	Utility	Lower/Long-term income
Conservative	Balanced	Lower/Income plus growth
Bond Funds		
Aggressive	High-yield	High/High income
Aggressive	Long-term government	High/Income
Aggressive	Long-term tax-free	High/Income
Aggressive	International	High/Income
Moderate	Intermediate-term	Moderate/Income
Moderate	Intermediate tax-free	Moderate/Income
Conservative	Short-term	Lower/Income and less risk
Conservative	Short-term tax-free	Lower/Income and less risk
Other Funds		
Safety-minded	Money market	Lowest/Income and least risk

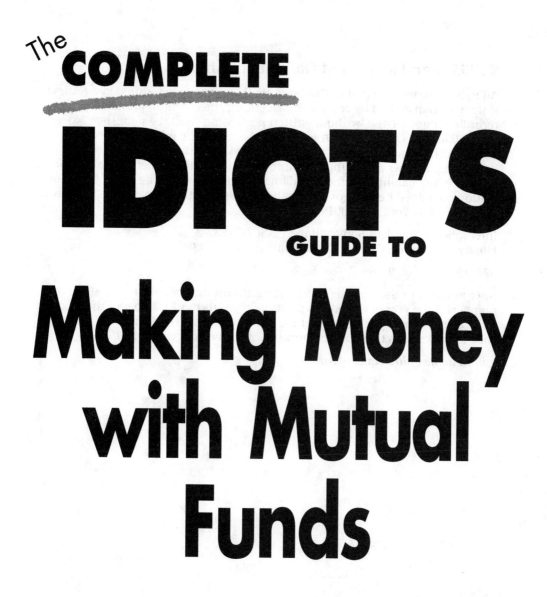

The COMPLETE IDIOT'S GUIDE TO

Making Money with Mutual Funds

by Alan Lavine and Gail Liberman

alpha books

A Division of Macmillan General Reference
A Simon & Schuster Macmillan Company
1633 Broadway, New York NY 10019-6785

International Standard Book Number: 1-56761-637-2
Library of Congress Catalog Card Number: 95-075739

97 96 95   9 8 7 6 5 4 3 2 1

Interpretation of the printing code: the rightmost number of the first series of numbers is the year of the book's printing; the rightmost number of the second series of numbers is the number of the book's printing. For example, a printing code of 95-1 shows that the first printing of the book occurred in 1995.

Printed in the United States of America

Publisher
Theresa H. Murtha

Associate Publisher
Lisa A. Bucki

Manuscript Editor
Nancy Albright

Designer
Kim Scott

Illustrations
Judd Winick

Indexer
Chris Cleveland

Production Team Supervisor
Laurie Casey

Production Team
*Heather Butler, Angela Calvert, Kim Cofer,
Tricia Flodder, Beth Rago, Gina Rexrode,
Erich J. Richter, Christine Tyner*

Contents at a Glance

Contents

Foreword

Time was, up until the early 1980s really, when it was relatively easy for sophisticated, average, and not-so-sophisticated investors to make money in mutual funds. Back then, there were relatively few mutual funds to buy and even fewer places from which to buy stock, bond, and money market mutual funds.

But that was then and this is now. And today, there are thousands of mutual funds of every type imaginable from which to choose and an even greater number of institutions and investment professionals from which any kind of investor (novice or expert) can buy such investments.

Alan Lavine and Gail Liberman demystify the world of mutual funds in such a way that it no longer intimidates, that it no longer leads to inaction and inertia. Alan and Gail , both of whom I have known for as long as I have been writing about mutual funds, are two of the most, if not the most, knowledgeable experts on the subject of personal finance—and especially mutual funds.

If you follow their advice, you'll learn how to establish your investment goals, your tolerance for risk, and your time horizon—that is, the time in which you would like to achieve your goals. Equally important, you'll learn how to match the right fund and the right amount of funds to you, given your goals, risk tolerance, and time horizon.

What's more, you'll learn an easy way to evaluate your fund's performance. You'll also get the low-down on the disadvantages of dollar-cost averaging, the practice of buying a set dollar amount of mutual fund shares on a regular basis.

Gail and Alan also tell how to adjust your mix of funds. Sure, many investors buy and hold and many investors buy and sell a lot, but few have a game plan regarding how to fine-tune their portfolio as their objectives, personal circumstances, and performance of the underlying funds change over time.

The Complete Idiot's Guide to Making Money with Mutual Funds includes a favorite topic of mine, especially given the recent rush of bank customers into bond mutual funds. Gail and Alan explain just what the major mistakes are that bond fund investors make.

Truly, there's something for everyone: great low-risk retirement savings strategies, how to save and invest for a college education, and a primer on whether you should own mutual funds at all.

As a personal finance journalist, I always felt it was my obligation to write about a subject in such a way that readers could either "do it" themselves, or that they would have enough knowledge to talk intelligently with a financial advisor. Alan and Gail have done just that in page after page, chapter after chapter. Hats off to them and to you for buying this book!

Robert Powell

Robert Powell is editor-in-chief of DALBAR, Inc., a Boston-based mutual fund publishing and research firm. Among other things, DALBAR publishes *Mutual Fund Market News*, the industry's only single-source, weekly trade publication of record, *Variable Annuity Market News*, and *The Journal of Mutual Fund Services*.

Introduction

You've heard about mutual funds. Maybe you've read about them. Or you might know someone who has invested in them. Getting started is easier said than done, however. Invest your hard-earned savings based on what your friends, neighbors, or that ultra-friendly stock broker or insurance salesman down the street say is hot, and you're sure to get stung. In fact, you probably have friends who already are crying in their beer over their ill-fated investment decisions.

We whole-heartedly can relate to your need to avoid these scenarios. We know first-hand—both as mutual fund investors and as husband-wife journalists. We spent a combined 30 years with our hands on the pulse of both the mutual fund and banking industries. For your benefit, we've also combined our marital temperaments of conservatism (fear) and aggressiveness (speculation) to present to you the *complete* unbiased story of how you can both win and lose at mutual fund investing.

It is by assessing the pros and cons of the investments that you can determine what is right for you.

With *The Complete Idiot's Guide to Making Money with Mutual Funds*, you easily can locate all the information you need— both before and long after you take your first venture into mutual funds. And once we help you determine whether mutual fund investing is right for you, we'll present you with quick and safe ways of managing your stash.

For your benefit, we've taken all the jargon out of investing and spelled things out in plain English so that learning to invest is as easy as learning to ride a bike. Consider this book our gift to you so that you can reap the most possible out of your hard-earned money for both yourself and family. It's just a matter of doing a little homework, learning exactly how these things work, and making your own decisions based only on sound financial planning and a little research—not on the word of somebody else looking to make a buck.

This book is a starting point. It will help you

> ➤ Learn how mutual funds work and what they invest in

> ➤ Understand the stock and bond markets

> ➤ Find the mutual fund investment that's best for you

> ➤ Avoid losses

> ➤ Build your wealth long-term

> ➤ Invest for your child's college education

➤ Invest for retirement

➤ Manage your investments

➤ Save on taxes

How to Use This Book

The Complete Idiot's Guide to Making Money with Mutual Funds zeros in on all the important things you need to know to invest in mutual funds. Start now. Read this book and learn the keys to a happy and healthy financial future. The important details about mutual funds are covered in five parts.

Part 1, "Mutual Funds: What Are They? What Are They Not? Are They for You?" explains how mutual funds work. This section nails down the dos and don'ts of mutual fund investments and shows you how to develop a savings plan. You'll learn all about stocks and bonds, as well as the pluses and minuses of mutual fund investing. You'll also get a rundown of the different types of mutual funds and learn how to tell whether a fund is a winner or loser.

Part 2, "Getting Started," helps you discover exactly what types of investing you can handle without hitting the Maalox bottle. Then you'll learn how to locate funds that are right for you. You'll also learn where to get mutual funds and how much you'll pay for them. You'll learn how to track down the best fund deals. You'll also learn about the resources available to help you pick your mutual funds.

Part 3, "Zoning In on the Picks," gets to the nitty gritty. You'll learn how money funds work and *exactly* how safe they are. You'll learn about the different types of bond funds available to investors and the risks they carry. Chapter 15, on stock funds, looks at all the types of stock funds—from aggressive, small company, growth, and growth and income to international—and what they invest in. You'll also learn about stock funds for special situations.

Part 4, "The One-Hour-a-Year Investment Plans," gives you time-saving tools to manage your money like a pro. This section reviews several easy-to-use investment strategies to build your wealth. You'll learn how to invest regularly so that you automatically keep buying fund shares at low prices. You'll also learn a couple of easy ways to buy low and sell high—just in case you prefer to take your profits and run. You'll learn how to slice your mutual fund investment pie to get the best returns with the least risk. You'll also find out a real low-risk way to invest your retirement savings in mutual funds and beat the performance of the old bank account.

Part 5, "Special Considerations: Taxes, Retirement, College, and Estate Planning," reviews important issues you need to know when you invest in mutual funds.

Unfortunately, you have to pay the taxman on your mutual fund profits. In this part, you'll learn the most painless ways to do it. Chapter 23, on saving for important life goals, shows how to determine the amount of money you'll need for your child's college education and your retirement.

Extras

We built a launch pad for you to get started with mutual funds. To make it as simple as flipping your car's ignition switch, *The Complete Idiot's Guide to Making Money with Mutual Funds* is chock full of tips to ensure that you have a successful trip into the world of mutual funds. Look for these elements in the book to point you in the right direction:

Sidelines

This is your coach sitting on the sidelines telling you how to navigate through the investment maze. You learn extra little details to make even better investment decisions.

Technobabble

WHAT?

Want to talk the same language as the investment pros? No problem. It's all highlighted for you as a quick reference in these little boxes.

Look Out!

Watch these potholes on the road to successful mutual fund investing! These tips tell you what to avoid so you can save money in the long run.

Hot Tip

Hot tips help you invest. We cut through the red tape and tell you straight out the wisest moves. You'll learn quickly the best route to take on your mutual fund journey.

Acknowledgments

We'd like to thank the following people who helped us along the way.

Special thanks to Theresa Murtha, publisher with Macmillan Publishing Company, not only for making this book possible, but for always taking time out of her busy schedule to respond!

We also would like to thank our editors at various publications for their support throughout the years. Robert K. Heady, founder and publisher of *Bank Rate Monitor*, brought us together in more ways than one. Also, a word of gratitude to the *Boston Herald* for running Alan Lavine's column for 12 years and giving him a forum to develop his mutual fund expertise. Special thanks to Mary Helen Gillespie, business editor of the *Boston Herald*, who, as our wedding present, gave us our first husband-wife newspaper column together! Thanks also go to Evan Simonoff, editor of *Financial Planning Magazine*; Tom Siedell, editor of *Your Money*; John Wasik, editor of *Consumer's Digest*; Susan Postlewaite, managing editor of the Miami, Fort Lauderdale, and Palm Beach *Daily Business Review*; and Charles DeRose, host of the "Financial Advisor" syndicated radio program.

Gail Liberman would like to acknowledge all the folks at the Associated Press, UPI, the Asbury Park Press, and the Courier Post in New Jersey for launching her career. She'd also like to thank her husband, Alan Lavine, for his undying support and continuous education on the subject of mutual funds.

We can't forget Alan Lavine's Mom, Doris Lavine, who kept us well-fed through an especially long summer, and Si and Dorothy Liberman for all their support.

Most of all, we'd like to dedicate this book to Gail Liberman's grandparents: Ruth Gold, who taught her how to read, and the late Jacob Gold, who taught her how to save.

Special Thanks

The Complete Idiot's Guide to Making Money with Mutual Funds was reviewed by Marla Brill, an expert in the field who not only checked the technical accuracy of what you'll learn here, but also provided insight and guidance to help us ensure that this book gives you everything you need to know to begin building your investment portfolio.

Formerly an editor at *Kiplinger's Personal Finance Magazine*, Ms. Brill is a personal finance writer specializing in mutual funds. She's written hundreds of articles for such general circulation publications as *USA Today* and *Mutual Funds Magazine*. Ms. Brill is the principal of Brill Editorial Services and publishes **The Mutual Funds Home Page** on the World Wide Web.

You can access The Mutual Funds Home Page at http://www.brill.com.

Part 1
Mutual Funds: What Are They? What Are They Not? Are They For You?

Once you read this part of the book, you'll be richer than you are. After all, you've got to have money before you can invest in mutual funds, right?

In this part, you discover ways to come up with money you didn't know you had. You learn what's involved in becoming an investor.

You also learn about the advantages and disadvantages of mutual funds in particular. There are a tremendous variety of mutual funds to choose. When you know what options are out there, you can zero in on what is right for you.

Chapter 1

The Ten Commandments of Mutual Fund Investing

In This Chapter

➤ How mutual funds work

➤ Who runs the funds?

➤ How mutual funds are regulated

➤ Ten rules to live by

Let's face it. You had good reason to pick up this book. After all, *everybody's* talking about mutual funds these days.

If you're like most of us, you have the bulk of your money in bank savings accounts because you're afraid you'll make the wrong move. Your biggest investment probably is your home. Some of you might have an interest in company pension plans. Aside from that, and maybe some money tucked away each paycheck in a 401(k), investing is a mystery.

Get ready! A whole new world of investing is about to unfold before your eyes. Fear no more. Mutual funds, once you know the ropes, can be your ticket to a whole variety of money-making opportunities. This chapter introduces you to the option of mutual fund investing.

Welcome to the World of Investing

When you were younger, chances are you had a piggy bank. When you filled it up, you took the next big step. You carted it to the bank and opened a savings account. You knew your savings account was safe. You couldn't lose money. Every once in a while, assuming you left your money in there, you'd notice it was growing in value.

With your savings account, you couldn't lose any money because it was federally insured. You paid dearly for this sense of security, though. About the most you could earn as long as your money stayed in your savings account was 5.50 percent.

Investing is the next big step on the ladder to financial growth for those who want to make more.

When you enter the world of investing, you're giving yourself a promotion. You're taking a more active role in building your wealth and stand to make more as a result. By putting your money in a mutual fund, however, you're also giving up some of the safety and security of your piggy bank and savings account. If you learn what makes mutual funds tick, you can make educated investment decisions that can help your nest egg grow that much more.

What Is a Mutual Fund and How Does It Work?

Think of a mutual fund as an investment company that pools the money of people just like you for one common reason—to make more. Not all pots of money, though, are alike. Each mutual fund has its own strategy and investment objective for making money. It's up to you to select the right mutual fund for you based on your own needs.

There are two types of mutual funds. The most common, which this book primarily talks about, is *open-end* funds. In essence, they are open—money flows directly into the fund when investors buy and goes directly out when they sell. The other type is *closed-end* funds, which technically are not mutual funds. You'll learn about them in Chapter 16.

With a mutual fund, the big pool of money we talked about previously is managed by a company, which is frequently the organization that started the fund. This management company either serves as or hires the fund's investment advisor. The advisor employs a portfolio manager and his or her research staff to select investments for the mutual fund.

Mutual funds are subject to strict federal regulations. The fund broker or other salesperson is required to give you a prospectus before you invest. The *prospectus* is an important document that spells out the investment objectives of the fund, risks, fees, and other important information. You'll learn more about what's in a prospectus and what you should look for in Chapter 9. The *Securities and Exchange Commission (SEC)* is the U.S. government agency in charge of regulating mutual funds.

Generally, mutual funds continuously offer new shares to the public. They also are required legally to buy back outstanding shares at the shareholder's request. When you sell shares in a fund, you receive a check based on its share's price or *net asset value* (less any sales charges, if applicable). The net asset value is obtained when the fund figures the value of its investments, less liabilities, divided by the number of shares outstanding at the end of the day.

> **Technobabble**
>
> WHAT?
>
> The *investment advisor* is an organization hired by the mutual fund company to manage a mutual fund's investments. A *portfolio manager* is the professional who actually manages the fund. The *investment objective* describes what your mutual fund hopes to accomplish. *Assets* represent any investment that the mutual fund holds, including stocks, bonds, and cash reserves. A mutual fund *share* is a unit of ownership in the fund. A mutual fund investor who owns shares is called a *shareholder* and has voting rights.

Introducing: The Cast of a Mutual Fund

Like any company, the mutual fund management company is an organization with a number of people that run the show. You want to understand how this company works because you've entrusted it with your hard-earned cash. Although mutual funds are set up under state law, usually as corporations, they differ from other companies.

First, they are legally entitled to hire companies to handle the bulk of their services. They typically hire the investment advisor, also known as an *investment advisory firm*, to manage your mutual fund. They also may make arrangements to have the fund sold through a brokerage firm.

The following sections review the cast of characters who make a mutual fund work.

The Investment Advisor

The investment advisor is one—or in some cases, a group—of the key people in a mutual fund, including the portfolio manager(s) and his/her/their staff. You've probably seen some portfolio managers on TV's "Wall Street Week," spotted their quotes in magazines, or read some of their books. This person selects, buys, and sells the investments based on the fund's investment objective. The investment advisor is paid an annual fee based on a percentage of the value of the fund's cash and investments, or assets.

The Board of Directors

A mutual fund has a board of directors to make major policy decisions and oversee management. These are important people. The directors steer the fund's course, determining investment objectives and hiring out help.

The directors keep tabs on investment performance, as well as that of investment advisors and others who work for the fund.

The Shareholder

Mutual fund investors are known as shareholders. When you invest in a mutual fund, you actually buy a share or portion of a mutual fund. Each share has a price tag. If a fund sells for $10 a share and you invest $1,000, you're the proud owner of 100 shares of the fund! Mutual funds, like many other companies, are very democratic. Because you own shares in the fund, you have voting rights. As part owner, a shareholder gets to vote in the election of the board of directors. The shareholder also must approve many operational changes within the fund, including accounting procedures and the investment objective.

Custodians and Transfer Agents

As you can imagine, the millions of mutual fund transactions executed each year require a gargantuan behind-the-scenes record-keeping effort. The securities a mutual fund invests in are kept under lock and key by an appointed custodian, usually a bank. The custodian may respond only to instructions from fund officers responsible for dealing with the custodian. The custodian safeguards the fund's assets, makes payments for the fund's securities, and receives payments when securities are sold.

Fund *transfer agents* maintain shareholder account records, including purchases, sales, and account balances. They also authorize the payments made by the custodian (referred to previously), prepare and mail account statements, maintain a customer service department to respond to account inquiries, and provide federal income tax information, shareholder notices, and confirmation statements.

The Underwriter

The underwriter is an organization with a staff of salespeople who either administers sales directly to the public or meets with the brokerage firms to convince them to sell the fund. Brokers sell fund shares to the public and collect a commission for the sale. Chapter 8 goes into more detail about what you pay for a mutual fund and who sells them.

Mutual Funds Make It EZ to Invest

Boy, there are a lot of important people and ingredients that go into the making of a mutual fund. The end result, however, is that mutual funds provide one of the simplest ways to invest—especially if you count yourself among us working stiffs, and lack time and training to manage money like the Wall Street big boys.

The major difference between investing in a mutual fund and investing in an individual stock or bond is that with a mutual fund, instead of buying just one stock or bond, you really buy a portion of a variety of investments. Exactly how much money you make or lose in your mutual fund can change daily, as you'll learn in later chapters. It all depends on how many shares you own and how well your mix of investments perform. As Chapter 3 explains, owning a lot of different investments helps to protect you against losing money. If one investment in your mutual fund does poorly, you have a number of others to cushion the blow.

Sidelines

There are approximately 6,000 mutual funds, but not all are alike. Depending on your particular needs, you can find a mutual fund that's right for you. In Chapters 3 and 5, you'll learn more about the different types of mutual funds.

Here They Are: The 10 Commandments

Have we whetted your appetite? Good. Let's get ready to proceed. However, we don't want you to invest one penny in a mutual fund until you read and thoroughly digest these 10 critical rules of mutual fund investing:

1. **Always understand exactly what you're investing in.** You can lose a bundle if you pick the *wrong* kind of mutual fund. Read carefully the *free* literature that mutual fund companies provide on their funds.

2. **Don't rush out and buy the first mutual fund that looks good.** You first have to identify your investment goals, determine how much you need from your investment (*see Chapter 2*), and figure out how much you're willing to risk losing (*see Chapter 6*).

3. **Don't try to make quick profits.** Always invest for the long term. You should plan to keep some of your mutual funds an absolute minimum of 5 to 10 years.

4. **Mix up your investments.** You can cut your chances of losing money by putting your money in different types of investments. Chapter 6 shows you how.

5. **Invest regularly with each paycheck—before you have a chance to spend all your money.** Mutual funds have automatic investment programs. Money is electronically taken out of your checking account and invested in the fund.

6. **Do your homework.** Once you determined how much money you need and by when—as well as how much you can afford to lose—research the best investments to meet your goals. Most library business sections carry information on mutual funds.

7. **Avoid paying high commissions and fees for mutual funds.** Make your money work for you, not for your stockbroker. Read about this in Chapter 7.

8. **Make sure your mutual fund investment earns enough so that your nest egg at least keeps pace with rising prices.** Chapter 5 discusses this further.

9. **Know when to sell your mutual funds.** Chapter 16 explains ways to evaluate how a fund is doing. You'll learn when to get rid of a mutual fund that's a lemon.

10. **Invest to beat the tax man.** Take advantage of Individual Retirement Accounts (IRAs) and other tax shelters. Chapter 22 discusses how you can make tax-deductible contributions and watch your money grow tax-free until you retire.

Sidelines

You can buy mutual funds either directly from the mutual fund company or from stockbrokers or financial planners licensed to sell them. Chapter 7 explains how much you pay in each case.

The Least You Need to Know

➤ With a mutual fund, investors pool their money with one common goal—to make more.

➤ A mutual fund's investment decisions are made by the portfolio manager, or a team of managers, who is an investment advisor hired by the mutual fund.

➤ When you invest in a mutual fund, you own share(s) of the fund, which gives you certain voting rights.

➤ Invest for the long term. Don't try to make quick profits in mutual funds.

that is the question...

Chapter 2

Mutual Funds: To Own or Not to Own?

In This Chapter

➤ Zeroing in on your goals

➤ Starting a savings plan

➤ Scrounging up enough money to invest

Do you need extra cash in time for your next rent payment? Are you a teen-ager looking to start saving for college? Or are you a retiree who wants to increase your very limited income over the next five years?

Regardless of who you are, it never hurts *anybody* to raise a little extra cash for the cause—and nobody wants to lose their shirts in the markets, right?

We hear ya' on both counts. In this chapter, you learn how to figure out how much you'll need and by when. As Thomas A. Edison would testify if he were here today, a plan is Step One toward getting where you want to go. That's what this chapter is all about.

Is Father Time on Your Side?

Your age has a lot to do with how you save. Unless you're a Rockefeller, 20- and 30-year-olds typically don't have as much money to invest as people who have been working for 20 years.

Nevertheless, younger investors do have an important advantage when it comes to investing. They have more time for their money to grow. Big-ticket events such as retirement and children's educations are further away, so it's all right for them to put a little less away on a regular basis. Plus, they have all those years to watch their money grow.

If you're in your 40s and just getting into mutual funds, you have a shorter period to save for retirement, so you might need to save more. Get into your 60s, and it may be more important to keep what you already have to meet your everyday living expenses.

How does all this relate to mutual funds?

Probably the most critical factor in figuring out how or whether to invest in mutual funds is determining when you need your money. It also influences which mutual funds you choose. You will learn in the following chapters the advantages of investing in mutual funds and what funds are right for your situation. If there is one thing for sure, depending on your needs, mutual fund investing should be a long-term affair. History has shown repeatedly that over the long term—say, 20 years—most mutual funds perform substantially better than bank savings accounts or CDs. History also has proven that the longer you have to invest in a mutual fund, the slimmer your chance of losing money. That's why it's important to get a fix on your investment goals and how long you have to invest.

Setting Your Goals

If you're like most American families, this part of our exercise will astound you. When you see on paper the money you're going to need throughout your life, there's a good chance you'll want to hop right on a space shuttle and move to another planet!

Don't get discouraged. Fortunately, mutual funds and other types of investments are here to help you achieve your goals. The sooner you start planning, the better off you'll be. As astounded as you are at the staggering costs most people encounter in their lifetimes, you'll be just as surprised when you see how quickly your money can grow.

Huh? Why Do I Need to Invest?

First, find a comfortable chair. Then sit down with a pad and pencil and jot down all the reasons you'll need more money in the future. Rank those goals from most to least important.

The next step is to figure how much each will cost. The Investment Goals Worksheet in this section will help.

To organize your thoughts, first zero in on every money worry you have. Cars, unfortunately, need to be repaired. Teeth need to be fixed. No doubt, you've got out-of-town guests that need to be taken out to dinner. What about emergency trips or medical emergencies? And don't forget the dentist and eye doctor.

Next, list your short-term goals. Most people buy a car about every five years. That's going to cost you some big bucks. The way new car prices are rising, in a few years the average new car will cost us $20,000 to $25,000. Ah, what if you've been dreaming about buying a house in five or six years? You may need $20,000 to $25,000 for a down payment. You'll also need money—$2,000 plus—to furnish it.

Once you cover emergencies and the stuff you need, it's time to focus on longer-term needs. If you're going to send a child who is now an infant to college in some 18 years, expect to pay a whopping $30,000 to $40,000 a year by the time Junior's ready. Looking to retire? If you're making $35,000 annually now, you need about $500,000 earning 7 percent interest annually to make the same amount, discounting the impact of inflation. Chapters 13, 14, and 15 of this book will help you find the right mutual funds to help you meet long-term needs. Chapter 23 goes into more depth in helping you figure exactly how much you'll need for college and retirement.

Next, think about those little luxuries. Sure, you don't *have* to have it, but wouldn't it be nice to have a yacht and a winter home in Florida?

Now that you've got your financial necessities and desires down on paper and ranked in order of importance, attach a price tag to each. Figure out how much each is likely to cost.

Finally, look at the time frame you have to invest for each of your goals. For example, if you've just had a baby, chances are you have 18 years before your child will be ready for college. That's 18 years you have to come up with the cash. If you're driving an old clunker, you may have to shell out that $20,000 for a new car in one year. That's not much time at all!

Once you have your financial plan mapped out, you can start socking away your cash. You can take advantage of mutual funds to invest in tax-advantaged savings plans for your child, such as the Uniform Gifts to Minors Act (discussed further in Chapters 22 and 23), and retirement plans, such as IRAs, SEPs, or Keoghs (discussed further in Chapter 23).

If you've never saved much before, it's time to start. You'll also need to find a particularly safe place to do it. You've got to have a cash reserve of three to six months of your income to meet emergencies. This money needs to be in a very secure place where you can tap it right away. You don't want to be forced to take losses on your investments because you need quick cash. In Chapter 12, you'll learn all about money market mutual funds. These are less risky mutual fund investments that come with a checkbook.

If you've already saved six months of income, you might be ready to try some new investments. In Chapter 6, you'll also learn to determine your *risk tolerance*, which is how much money you can stomach losing in any given year. Then, you'll be able to put both pieces of information together to make the right kinds of mutual fund investments.

Investment Goals Worksheet

Goal	Amount You Need	When You Need It
Cash reserves		
Retirement		
Child's college education		
Second home down payment		
Travel		
Estate		
Other		

Create a worksheet like this to help set your investment goals.

Starting a Savings Plan

You want to invest in mutual funds to meet your goals. "But I have no money," you balk. Regardless of whether you have money to invest, it always pays to squeeze as much as you possibly can out of your budget for investing.

This needn't be as painful as it sounds. We're willing to bet you have more cash than you think sitting right under your nose.

To figure out exactly where you stand, first list and then add up your monthly income from your paycheck, savings, and other sources. Then, get your checkbook register and list all your monthly expenses. The worksheet in this section called Finding Money to Invest will help you do this.

Technobabble
Your *goals* are all your future desires. A *spending plan* is a strategy to help cut wasteful spending so you can invest.

Subtract your expenses from your income to determine the amount of cash you should have available to invest monthly.

Things to Attack Right Away

Whether the money you have left for investing is a large sum or a big fat zero, it's time to set up a spending (and savings) plan for next year—including, without fail, money to invest!

Even before you look for big ways to cut your expenses, we bet you can save $20 a month on little items—such as the gum, candy, and coffee you buy every day. If you put the $20 a month into a bank account that pays a piddling 5 percent, you have an extra $3,100 of savings in 10 years. Imagine what it can be in a mutual fund!

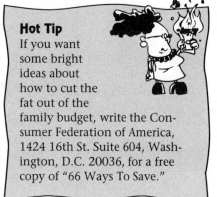

Hot Tip
If you want some bright ideas about how to cut the fat out of the family budget, write the Consumer Federation of America, 1424 16th St. Suite 604, Washington, D.C. 20036, for a free copy of "66 Ways To Save."

Now, let's examine each item in your income and expenses line by line to find any areas you might cut to free even more money.

Credit card debts are a good place to start. You may pay as much as 18 percent interest on your credit card bills. If you can first pay those off, that's a better return than you'll get on many mutual funds.

Vacations are another expense worth reviewing. Rather than going to Aruba, maybe you can find a nice resort close to home. You still can have a good time and save a bundle.

Finding Money to Invest

Monthly Income

Paycheck (after taxes)   _____

Other   _____

Total Income: _____

Monthly Spending

Rent or mortgage   _____

Utilities   _____

Groceries   _____

Entertainment   _____

Vacations   _____

Car payments   _____

Car repairs   _____

Gas   _____

Car insurance   _____

Health insurance   _____

Life insurance   _____

Disability insurance   _____

Child care   _____

Child support or alimony   _____

Gifts   _____

Educational expenses   _____

Pet expenses   _____

Newspapers and magazines   _____

Hobbies   _____

Miscellaneous expenses   _____

Savings   _____

Credit cards and loans   _____

Total Expenses: _____

**Monthly Cash
(Income - Expenses)**   _____

Use this worksheet to get a better handle on the cash you might have available for investing and to see whether there are any areas where you may be spending too much.

Sidelines

Looking for ways to reduce your credit card bills? You can get information on low-rate credit cards for a small fee from the following companies:

➤ Bank Rate Monitor, Box 08888, North Palm Beach, FL 33408. 800-327-7717.

➤ Bankcard Holders of America, 524 Branch Dr., Salem, VA 24153. 540-389-5445.

➤ RAM Research Corp., P.O. Box 1700, Frederick, MD 21702. 800-344-7714.

Manage Your Money like a Pro

You'd be surprised what a little savvy cash management can do for your long-term financial picture. Why not take some tips from professional money managers, whose job it is to use efficient cash-management tactics to make their money work for them?

Here are a few ways to manage your cash like a pro. By following these guidelines, you can free as much as $150 a year for investing. That annual investment, earning just the pedestrian rate of 5 percent, can grow over 20 years to an extra $4,960 for retirement—not a bad reward for no lifestyle cutbacks.

Hot Tip
Want ideas on how to save money? Pick up the newsletter, *The Tightwad Gazette*, RR1, Box 3570, Leeds, Maine, 207-524-7962 ($12 a year) or books by Amy Dacyczyn: *The Tightwad Gazette* and *The Tightwad Gazette II*, Villard Books, New York.

The key to cash management is to invest your money right away and pay your bills at the end of the month. You may already have an interest-bearing checking account, but you also can take advantage of higher interest rates and invest in a money market fund (discussed in Chapters 4 and 12 of this book). Then, follow this plan:

➤ Deposit all your checks as soon as you receive them; then you will earn interest right away if you have a NOW account.

➤ Avoid all bank fees. When you withdraw money from ATM machines other than your own bank's machines, for example, you pay as much as $1.50 on every transaction.

17

➤ Make use of your employer's payroll direct-deposit program. The money is electronically credited to your interest-bearing checking account and earns interest immediately. Some institutions waive checking fees if you direct-deposit your paycheck.

➤ Along the same lines, if you automatically have money taken out of your interest-bearing checking account to pay life insurance or disability insurance premiums, do it at the end of the month. That way your money earns interest for a full month before you pay your life and health insurance bills.

➤ Charge smart. As long as you have no outstanding balance on your Visa or MasterCard, for example, you have a 25-day grace period each month before the bill is due. Try to make your purchases at the very beginning of the billing cycle (just after the monthly closing date). Then you'll have 25 days before the credit card company bills you, plus 10 days or more before you have to pay the bill.

The Least You Need to Know

➤ Always know how much you'll need and by when.

➤ Monitor your monthly income and expenses.

➤ Make adjustments to the way you spend to free extra cash for investing.

➤ Look for ways to cut everyday expenses to free money to invest.

Chapter 3

Investing: Your Options, Your Risks, Your Rewards

In This Chapter

➤ What's inside mutual funds?

➤ What is a stock?

➤ What is a bond?

➤ What is a money market or cash investment?

Are you getting ready to join the club? Nearly one out of three American families now owns a mutual fund, but before you join this select fraternity, it's important to understand the investments that mutual funds make.

Mutual funds come in a variety of flavors. You wouldn't buy a car without checking the tires and looking under the hood.

This chapter pops open the hood on mutual fund investments. It explains what mutual funds invest in and the advantages mutual funds have to offer you as potential investors.

Stocks vs. Bonds vs. Cash

Congrats! In Chapter 2 you probably came up with money you didn't even know you had. Before you get excited and plunk down all the cash you just worked so hard to dig up, you need to know about all the critters that can hang out in a mutual fund.

Earlier, we mentioned stocks, bonds, or cash investments that you normally can buy directly from a stockbroker. Stockbrokers have one word for all this stuff—*securities*.

Look Out!
Unlike with an FDIC-insured bank CD, you're not guaranteed to receive your original investment, or *principal*, back with a mutual fund. So, before investing, it's critical to investigate the quality of a mutual fund's investments.

A mutual fund may invest in one type of security or a mix of different kinds of securities. A mutual fund's value may rise or fall quite rapidly—or slowly—depending on the types of securities investments it makes. The exception is money market mutual funds, which are designed to maintain a constant $1 per share value.

The following sections offer a rundown of the kinds of securities you're apt to find in a mutual fund and how each affects how much money you may make from your mutual fund investment.

Stocks

Stocks provide a way for a company to raise money. The company sells stock shares in exchange for money to use to grow the business—by buying new equipment or performing research and development, for example. If you or your mutual fund own shares of a company's stock, you're a big shot. Not only are you part owner of that company, but you may get to share in its earnings, which may be distributed to shareholders in the form of *dividends*. If the mutual fund owns shares of a particular dividend-paying stock, it pays these dividends to you, based on the number of mutual fund shares you own.

If the company profits, it's good news. The share price of the stock can increase, which in turn, hikes the value of its shares. The company's board of directors may vote to increase dividends they pay shareholders.

Unfortunately, the opposite also can happen. If the company does poorly, the value of the stock may decline, and dividends may be cut or eliminated entirely.

Stocks probably are one of the riskiest investments for individuals and mutual funds. Not only might the fund earn a ton of money in stocks before you have a chance to blink your eye, but the fund also can lose just as much just as quickly.

Sidelines

There are two major types of stocks—*common* and *preferred*. If you own preferred stock, you receive the dividends before common stockholders. You also get preferred treatment over common stockholders when it comes to getting your investment back if the company goes under. Preferred stocks tend to pay slightly higher dividends than common stock, but the share price usually doesn't rise as much. Most individual stockholders and mutual funds own common stock.

Bonds

A *bond* is an I.O.U. issued by a company or a city, state, or federal government or its agencies. When you buy a bond, you're the lender. In exchange for a loan, the borrower or *issuer* promises to repay the money on a specific date, known as the *maturity date*. If you or your mutual fund own a bond, you, as lender, receive fixed periodic interest payments. Bonds require a minimum investment of at least $1,000, which is also know as the *face value* or principal. After you buy your bond, you or your mutual fund can hold it to maturity and get the principal back, or you can sell it before maturity.

Bonds can be tricky little devils to understand. There are three ways that describe how much interest income you will receive from a bond. It's important to understand the distinctions so that you don't get it mixed up later when you begin to invest in bond mutual funds.

The *coupon* rate, which we will call the stated interest rate, tells you the interest payment in dollars that you will receive from the bond as a percentage of the bond's face value. Suppose for example, you buy a newly issued bond for $1,000 and it has a coupon rate of 9 percent. That means you receive a total of $90 in interest income from the bond for the year. Year in and year out you will collect $90 from the bond until it matures. Then you get your $1,000 back.

Bonds have two yields: The *current yield* is based on the current market price of the bond rather than the face value. If a bond with a face value of $1,000 declines in value to $900, it still earns $90 a year in interest income, based on the bond's stated interest rate. As a result, the current yield of the bond is $90 divided by $900, or 10 percent.

You also have to consider a bond's *yield to maturity*. Bonds typically pay semi-annual interest over a specific time period. The interest compounds twice a year as long as you own the bond until it matures. The yield to maturity of a bond includes not only this semiannual compounding of interest, but also the capital gain, or profit or loss, on the security itself.

How Bonds Are Classified

Bonds issued by the United States government are backed by the full faith and credit of Uncle Sam. Corporate bonds are not. Once you go beyond Uncle Sam, you have to make sure you invest in financially strong companies. That's why it's important to look at bond credit ratings.

Companies, such as Standard & Poor's and Moody's, rate the financial strength of bond issuers, based on the ability of companies to repay principal and interest on time. The highest quality bonds are rated AAA. Bonds rated below single A stand a greater chance of failing to repay their debts during tough economic times. Unless you're a seasoned investor, you might want to stay clear of investing in bonds with lower ratings or mutual funds that invest in them.

Other Bond Risks

When you buy bonds or invest in bond funds, you not only have to look at the issuers' financial strengths, but you also must deal with changing bond prices. Chapters 13 and 14 discuss the risks and ratings of bonds in more detail, but it is important to note that you can get into trouble even with the highest-quality bonds if you're not careful. Interest rates and bond prices move in opposite directions, so it's not always a time for rejoicing if interest rates head up. It means that your bonds are losing value if their coupon rates (stated interest rates) are less than the going rates.

Put yourself in a bond-buyer's shoes. If you could buy a newly issued bond paying a stated interest rate of 10 percent by investing $1,000, you certainly wouldn't offer Joe Biddle the same $1,000 for his bond paying a stated rate of 9 percent, would you? Unless you can buy the bond for less money, it's simply not worth putting up your hard-earned cash for a lower yield.

That's exactly how the big bond traders think. Moreover, the longer the term (time to maturity) of the bond, the riskier it appears to the bond investor and the less it is valued. Why? The longer the term, the greater the period an investor has to worry about the threat of rising interest rates.

If interest rates rise 1 percent, a two-year Treasury *note*, which is just another word for a short-term bond, loses nearly 2 percent in value. By contrast, a 30-year Treasury bond loses about 12 percent in value. Chapter 14 shows you exactly how much rate shifts can affect bond prices.

Believe it or not, bond investors also might get their principal back faster than they'd like. That's because issuers may have the right to *call* their bonds or return the bondholder's principal. Bonds get called when interest rates fall. The issuer then sells lower-yielding bonds and reduces its interest payments.

Kinds of Bonds a Fund May Own

You typically can find the following variety of bonds in your mutual fund if it invests in bonds:

➤ U.S. Treasury bonds, issued by Uncle Sam.

➤ U.S. government agency bonds, issued by agencies of our national government.

➤ Municipal bonds, issued by state and local governments.

➤ Corporate bonds, issued by companies.

➤ International bonds, issued by foreign corporations or governments.

Money Market or Cash

Cash or *money market investments* are short-term loans to banks, governments, or companies. Although they're considered the least risky types of securities, there's still a chance with a cash investment that you might not get back your principal, or original investment. One of the most common cash investments is a CD or time deposit, like the type you might already have at your local bank. However, unlike most of us, mutual funds generally invest in these at $1 million at a shot.

Risk of Going It Alone

The good news is that any of the securities just discussed has the potential to do better (and in some cases much better!) than your old faithful savings account.

The bad news, as we warned you earlier, is that none of these securities is quite as low-risk as FDIC-insured savings accounts and CDs.

You've probably heard the horror stories yourself. Joe Biddle's stockbroker has inside information on a company that makes 3D video games. "Buy the stock," the stockbroker whispers. "Double your money in a couple of days. Buy now and sell when everybody gets wind of this deal."

WHAT?

Technobabble

Diversified means funds are spread out among a large number of different investments. *Distributions* are dividends and capital gains distributed by mutual funds to their shareholders. *Interest income* represents earnings you receive from bonds and/or the fixed income securities. *Capital gains* are profits on the sale of securities. A variety of funds available to investors from one investment management company may be known as a *fund family*.

Aha! Joe empties his bank account and buys 500 shares at $10 a share for a total investment of $5,000. The next day he opens the newspaper. "Video Games Cause Creepy Slime Disease," the headline blares. Wham! The next day, everyone sells. The stock's price plunges to $5 a share. Worried that it soon could drop to zero, he also sells. Joe's loss: $2,500 or half of his investment.

A similar situation could happen with a bond if Joe happens to invest in a weak company that falls on tough times. Suppose Joe, based on his stockbroker's advice, invests $5,000 in a new bond issued by the same 3D video game company. Investors get wind of the fact that the company may have a tough time paying back interest and principal to the bondholders. Bondholders tie up the stockbroker's phone lines all day trying to sell their bonds in the secondary market. The price of the bonds drop and Joe is worried it could get worse. Joe sells his bond for $4,000—$1,000 less than he paid for it.

Advantages of Mutual Funds

The following sections explore the advantages of mutual funds.

Mutual Funds Are Diversified

When you're investing in a mutual fund, you needn't worry so much that you're investing in one dud. As mentioned earlier in this book, most funds own a large number of investments. In other words, they're diversified. If one investment owned by the fund performs poorly, there's still hope that the others might rally. At least, you're less likely to lose as much.

A federal law gives you some added protection. It sets a 5 percent limit on your mutual fund's investment in any one stock or bond issuer. Suppose a fund owns 50 different stocks, including Computer Chip Inc. One day there is terrible news about Computer Chip Inc., and the stock price drops 5 percent. That's a big loss for a stock! The other 49 stocks don't drop in price, however. In fact, some rise. At the end of the day, that Computer Chip Inc. loss didn't put a dent in the value of the fund.

Mutual funds also relieve you of a major workload. Who has time nowadays to play the stock market or find a company with a great credit record? Not only that, but by the time we peons hear about a great investment, it's generally too late to profit from it. The Wall Street pros sell us the hot tips and bank *their* whopping profits. Where does that leave us? In the hole.

Enter mutual funds...

You Get Your Own Investment Pro

With a mutual fund, you get your own highly trained hired gun or guns working full-time to ensure that you make money. The fund manager, or portfolio manager, has all the investment research at his or her fingertips, and even visits companies before investing. This individual often earns a high salary plus a bonus at year's end if a fund performs better than similar funds. This gives the fund manager a high level of incentive to ensure that the fund does well. Some funds are managed by a team of portfolio managers.

Higher Returns on Your Investment Are Possible

With a mutual fund, you have greater potential to grow your money over the long term than you do in a bank. The value of your mutual fund fluctuates with changing market conditions.

Mutual Funds Pay You Back

What a mutual fund earns on its investments ultimately is passed on to you as distributions. There are three types of distributions you can receive from a fund. When the fund owns bonds, it earns interest income. When a fund owns stocks it earns dividends. The dividends are a share of company profits that are paid periodically to its shareholders. When the fund sells either stock or bond investments at a profit, the profits are called capital gains. You can

25

receive your distributions in cash, or you can have your mutual fund reinvest the money to buy more shares in the fund.

You Get Your Money Whenever You Want It

You can buy and sell all or part of your mutual fund whenever you want. Just call the fund or your stockbroker, toll-free, and give your directions on a tape-recorded line. You generally can get your cash in a couple of days. In fact, many funds even give you a book of checks with their funds.

You Have a Fund Family

Many mutual fund families offer investors a wide variety of mutual funds. The funds may invest in different kinds of stocks, bonds, or cash equivalents based on different investment objectives. When one investment company owns a number of mutual funds, those funds are considered part of a fund family. The T. Rowe Price Group of Funds, Baltimore, for example, has more than 20 different stock and bond funds in its family of funds. Mutual fund families make investing easy. As your money situation or the markets change, you can switch from one fund to another.

Mutual Funds Have Toll-Free Numbers and Automatic Exchange Privileges

If you're investing within a fund family, you can call toll-free and switch from one fund to another, generally at no charge, as investment conditions or your financial needs change. It's easy.

You Don't Have to Be Rich to Invest

As we told you earlier, you don't need much money to invest in a mutual fund. Although you may need several thousand dollars to invest in individual stocks and bonds, you can get started in a mutual fund with as little as $100. With most funds, though, you need $500 to $1,000. Minimums may be lower for IRA accounts. Chapter 11 discusses how to fill out the forms to open a mutual fund account. When you open an account, you are on record as a shareholder of the fund. You get periodic statements from the fund showing how many shares of the fund you own, the distributions you have received, and how much your holdings in the fund are worth.

Look Out!
If you want to sell fund shares, some mutual fund companies require you to put your directions in writing, and you may have to get a notary at your bank to guarantee your signature.

Mutual Funds Are Highly Regulated

Mutual funds are regulated by both the SEC and your own state's regulators. The funds are required to report their financial activities to these agencies. Meanwhile, mutual funds also are required to send shareholders financial reports. Often, reports are consolidated for a fund group or family. Therefore, if you own more than one mutual fund in a fund group or family, you won't necessarily have to keep track of a hundred different pieces of paper.

Sidelines

Even if the company managing a fund bites the dust, no creditor will have access to your investment. Your money is deposited in an account in your name at a custodian bank, which is responsible for the safekeeping of your account. The fund group can't touch your account.

You Can Save for Your Retirement

Mutual funds are a great way to save for retirement. On your application to open your mutual fund account, you merely arrange to have it specially set up as an Individual Retirement Account (IRA). With this retirement plan, which you learn more about in Chapter 23, you not only get the benefits of mutual fund investment profits, but you may get to deduct annual contributions from your income on your federal tax return. Meanwhile, you pay no taxes on your earnings until you retire. If you open your IRA with one fund family, you can switch your money back and forth between that family's funds. Not a bad deal!

Mutual funds also work similarly in other retirement plans. Self-employed individuals may use mutual funds in their Simplified Employee Pension Plans (SEPs) or Keogh plans. Companies may set up 401 (k) investment plans for their employees. Your 401 (k) retirement plan contribution, which often is matched by an employer, is taken off the top of your salary. With a 401 (k) plan, you might be able to lower the income tax you pay on your wages, and the earnings grow tax-deferred.

You can have as many mutual funds as you want in your retirement account, and you can switch back and forth between those funds. You must keep your money in your retirement account mutual funds, however. If you try to move it into mutual funds outside the account, the IRS considers it a withdrawal from your retirement plan and you pay taxes on the amount withdrawn. If you're under 59-1/2, you also pay a 10 percent fine on the amount withdrawn; whatever is withdrawn gets added to your annual income.

You Get Automatic Investment and Withdrawals

You know how you can have your paycheck automatically sent by your employer to your checking account? You can do the same with your mutual fund. As little as $50 a month can be automatically taken out of your checking account and invested in your mutual fund. If you're retired and need income, you also can arrange to receive monthly checks from your mutual fund, in addition to having your mutual fund automatically reinvest distributions to buy more shares in your fund. You also can arrange to invest the distributions of one fund automatically into another fund, provided that it is in the same family.

Free Information and Advice Are Available

Most fund families will send you free "how-to" booklets to help you invest wisely. The material is educational, but don't forget the fund families want your business. It always pays to do your own independent homework.

The Least You Need to Know

➤ The kinds of securities a mutual fund invests in affects the value of the mutual fund.

➤ Mutual funds invest in either stocks, bonds, or cash equivalents. Some invest in all three.

➤ Unlike a typical FDIC-insured account, there's always a chance you can lose much of your original investment in a mutual fund.

➤ With stocks, you own a piece of a company. You can quickly make a lot of money, but you also can lose big.

➤ Bonds are like loans to companies or governments.

➤ Even if you invest in high-quality bonds, you can lose if you're not careful. If interest rates head up, the bond price falls, so you can suffer a loss of much of your original investment if you sell. A bond's interest payments don't increase when interest rates do.

➤ Mutual funds are diversified. They own a large number of securities. If you have one dud in your mutual fund, the others still can rally.

➤ Mutual funds also offer professional management and easy access via a toll-free line.

Chapter 4

Mutual Funds for Everyone

In This Chapter

➤ Mutual funds come in several flavors

➤ Spotting a fund with a good batting average

➤ Investing in mutual funds for a long time

As someone once said, there's a mutual fund for all seasons. To help zero in on the right fund or funds for you, you first need to know which categories to examine.

Would you like a fund that takes risks in the hopes of big gains? Do you want a fund that invests in small companies or a fund that invests in large companies? Do you want a fund that invests overseas?

There also are funds specifically for the more squeamish investor that enable you to earn a decent return on investment with little risk. Part 3 of this book discusses in more detail the different types of mutual funds and the investments they make. In this chapter, you get acquainted with the different ways mutual funds are classified.

What Flavor Is Your Fund?

Now that you know about all the critters roaming around *inside* mutual funds, you're ready to get to the real meat of the matter—the funds themselves. As we mentioned before, there are more mutual funds than you can shake a stick at. Before you can determine which mutual funds are right for you (more about that later in Part 2), you need to review the menu.

It's easy to find mutual funds that invest in any one of the securities we discussed in Chapter 3—stocks, bonds, or cash—or a mishmash of any of these securities.

Sidelines

Different types of funds pay different types of distributions, so your need for regular income is an important key to determining what type of fund you select. Chapter 3 presents all the different kinds of distributions—dividends from stocks, interest income from bonds, and capital gains from the fund's sale of either stock or bond securities at a profit.

The type of fund you select determines the distributions you get, if any. For example, stock fund distributions may come from capital gains and from dividends. A bond fund distribution also may come from capital gains. In addition, bond fund distributions come from interest income. Some funds, such as income funds, own both stocks and bonds. They may pay distributions from all three sources—dividends, capital gains, and interest income.

Mutual funds might invest in stocks of one particular type of company. Some specialize, for example, in small new companies. There also are funds for middle-size companies and some for larger companies.

Certain funds invest in companies based in one particular type of industry, such as utilities or technology. Still others invest in companies that mine gold bullion. It's also possible a fund could invest in the stocks or bonds of companies overseas.

Whenever you're considering a mutual fund, it's important first to pin down a mutual fund's investment objective. Fund objectives tell you exactly what the fund manager hopes to accomplish with your money.

Often the fund objective is smack-dab in the fund's name, but to double-check, always locate the fund objective, which tells the fund's main goal or goals, in the fund's prospectus. You can also double-check things with the salesperson for the fund.

It's only by learning about a fund's investment objective that you can determine whether it matches your own.

Look for These Clues

Now, put on your Sherlock Holmes hats and get out your magnifying glass. You're going to learn about a couple of clues to help you decipher what's in a mutual fund and what it all means.

Please note that the high, low, and average total returns of the fund groups discussed in the next sections are based on the Morningstar Mutual Fund Performance Report. The average annual returns discussed are based on the 10-year performance ending in 1994.

Clue No. 1: Growth

See the word "growth" in the name or investment objective of a mutual fund, and chances are that fund investments largely are in stocks. By growth, we mean that fund is designed to register big increases in the share price. You also may be in for a roller-coaster ride because the fund's share price can go up and down. Based on historical performance, investors tend to make great profits with growth funds over the long term, but they also risk losing the most. Funds with the word "growth" in the fund objective are apt to fall into one of the following categories:

> *Aggressive growth funds,* also known as *capital appreciation funds*, are among the most speculative funds. The fund manager often seeks to make quick gains. Although these funds have the potential to give you very large returns on your investment, they also

Technobabble
Income refers to periodic interest or dividend distributions from a fund. *Growth* means long-term appreciation in value as a result of increases in share price. *Blue-chip* stocks are issued by well-established companies that typically pay a lot of dividends. *Equity* is another word for stock.

can rack up the heaviest losses. For example, aggressive stock funds as a group delivered an average annual total return of 13.3 percent over the past 10 years, reaching a high of 53.6 percent in one year, but also hitting a low of –8.3 percent in another. Examples of aggressive growth funds include AIM Equity-Aggressive Growth Fund, IDS Strategy Aggressive Equity Fund, and USAA Mutual Aggressive Growth.

➤ *Small company stock funds* also are aggressive investments. These funds invest in younger companies whose stocks are traded over the counter. Small companies plow profits back into the company to grow their businesses and eventually become larger outfits. This is what you bank on as an investor. Typically, there are fewer shares of a small company stock traded. As a result, small company stock prices can be volatile. Heavy buying or selling of a small company's stock can send it soaring or plunging at a moment's notice. Over the past 10 years, small company stock funds as a group have delivered an average annual total return of 13.2 percent, with the high reaching 50.1 percent and the low, –9.6 percent. Examples of small company stock funds include Acorn Fund, John Hancock Emerging Growth Fund, and Berger Small Company Growth Fund.

Sidelines

Stock fund portfolio managers use different strategies that they hope will make their shareholders richer. There are two basic investment styles that are used to select stocks.

Stock funds that buy on *value* tend to invest in overlooked stocks that appear as if they could increase in price. The funds gain when the companies register unexpected profits and other investors start buying the stock in droves. By contrast, fund managers who invest for *growth* want to own companies whose earnings are growing rapidly, often at more than 25 to 30 percent or more a year.

Does it matter which style a fund manager uses? Over 10-year periods, there has been little difference in the returns on funds that invest for growth or value. However, over a shorter period, three months to three years, for example, it is possible for one investment style to outperform the other. You can hedge your bets by owning stock funds that invest for growth and value, or you can stick with one style and invest regularly for the long term.

➤ *Growth funds,* which are a tad less risky than aggressive growth funds, invest in the stocks of companies that have been around a while and should be profitable for years to come. These funds have the potential to appreciate in value, but they also can suffer big losses. Over the past 10 years, long-term growth funds as a group have delivered an average 12.9 percent annual total return, with the high reaching 37.1 percent and the low, –4.7 percent. Examples of growth funds are T. Rowe Price Growth Stock Fund, Strong Growth Fund, and Twentieth Century Growth.

➤ *Specialty funds,* also known as *sector funds,* invest in the stock of one specific industry. These funds generally are among the riskiest because the fund manager puts all the eggs in one basket. Not all specialty funds are alike. Some are riskier than others. It is also possible to find some specialty funds, such as utility stock funds, that are considered relatively low in risk. Utility stock funds invest in businesses such as electric utilities, telephones, or telecommunications. They tend to have high yields because the firms whose stocks they own pay out most of their profits in dividends, which is a nice benefit for retirees living on fixed income. They also are used by many as a defensive investment. These stocks perform relatively well during an economic recession. After all, everyone uses electricity—even in a recession. Over the past 10 years, utility stock funds had an average annual total return of 10.9 percent. The high was 14.7 percent and the low was 3.2 percent. Examples of utility stock funds include ABT Utility Income Fund, Fidelity Utilities Income, and Prudential Utility Fund.

Gold and precious metals are another popular type of specialty fund. Gold and precious metals, such as platinum and silver, tend to soar in value when the prices for necessities zoom. For that reason, some investors routinely keep a little money in gold funds. Recall that in the late 1970s, around when the price of oil shot up 40 percent, the price of gold also hit $800 an ounce. Mutual funds that invested in gold mining stocks gained a whopping 100 percent! Gold funds, however, are volatile investments and can lose big when the prices of goods and services stagnate or fall. Over the past 10 years, gold funds as a group experienced an average annual total return of 4.3 percent, with a high of 11.8 percent and a low of –5.6 percent. Examples of Gold funds include U.S. World Gold Fund, Lexington Gold Fund, and IDS Precious Metals.

Look Out!
Invest in an aggressive growth, growth, small company or sector fund for just one or two years, and you could lose your shirt! Over the past 50 years, the worst return for speculative stock funds was -27 percent. In 1973 and 1974, the average stock fund lost a total of 45 percent.

There are other specialty funds, including those that limit their investments to chemicals, financial services, health care, real estate, technology, and so forth. These funds can be high-risk gambits. Investors can earn whopping returns on investment or they can lose their shirts if they invest at the wrong time. For example, the average technology stock fund delivered a 12.5 percent annual return rate over the past 10 years, with a high of 23.6 percent and a low of –12.7 percent for an entire year. Examples of specialty funds are the Evergreen Global Real Estate, Fidelity Select Biotechnology, and Invesco Strategic Financial Services.

Clue No. 2: Income

The word "income" in the name or investment objective of the fund means the fund pays periodic dividends. These funds tend to be less risky than growth or aggressive growth funds because the periodic income helps make up for any future potential declines. Be prepared, though, for lower overall returns long-term than you might get with a growth or aggressive-growth fund. You normally do not get the increase in share price and thus increase in the value of the investment that you would get from investing in aggressive growth or growth stock funds. Funds with the word "income" listed somewhere as the investment objective probably fall into one of these categories:

➤ *Growth* and *income funds* own primarily stocks of well-established companies that pay out a lot of *dividends* to their shareholders. They strive first for growth or long-term gains over income. These funds can pay off handsomely, and they are less risky than aggressive stock funds. For example, over the past 10 years, growth and income funds as a group experienced a 12.02 percent annual total return, with a high of 28.7 percent and a low of –4.6 percent. Examples of growth and income funds are Scudder Growth and Income Fund, Neuberger & Berman Guardian Fund, and Babson Value Fund.

➤ *Equity income funds,* which also invest in stocks, are similar to growth and income funds, but they tend to favor income a bit more than growth. As a result, they can be less risky than other types of stock funds. For example, over the past 10 years, equity income funds have delivered an average annual total return of 11.5 percent, with a high of 27.4 percent and a low of –6.4 percent. Examples of equity income funds include Franklin Equity Income, Vanguard Equity Income, and Oppenheimer Equity Income.

➤ *Income funds* invest in higher-yielding stocks plus bonds. You get income first along with some growth. These funds usually invest in utility, telephone, and *blue-chip* stocks. Investors do not get as much growth out of income funds as they do by investing in growth or growth and income funds. Over the past 10 years, income funds had an average annual total return of 10.2 percent, with a high of 24 percent and a low of –4.5 percent.

Examples of income funds are Vanguard Wellesley Income Fund, Income Fund of America, and Pioneer Income Fund.

Sidelines

Some stock funds pay very little, if anything, in the way of distributions. Small company stock funds, for example, don't distribute much dividend income to shareholders at all.Why? These funds invest in smaller companies that are busy pumping all their profits back into their businesses. A fund, however, that invests in small company stocks may sell the stock at a gain, so it's possible for a small company stock fund to produce capital gains.

At the opposite end of the spectrum are funds that trade stocks frequently. The typical aggressive stock fund, for example, owns each stock for a relatively short period of time, so an aggressive growth fund may pay lots of distributions that come from both stock dividends and capital gains.

Mutual funds by law are required to distribute 98 percent of their earnings from dividends, interest, and capital gains to its shareholders, but they don't necessarily all do it at the same time. Most funds distribute income from interest monthly and income from stock dividends every three months. Capital gains are distributed once a year, usually in December. You can find out when a fund pays distributions by reading the fund's prospectus, which you learn more about in Chapter 9.

When you open an account with a fund, you have a choice. You can elect to receive the distributions from the fund by check, have them automatically deposited into a fund family's money fund, or have the fund reinvest the distributions into new shares of your existing fund. If you don't need the income, it's generally best to reinvest.

Another Type of Income Fund

Don't be surprised if your mutual fund salesperson calls a fund a *fixed-income* fund even though you can't necessarily find those exact words in the fund's investment objective. Fixed-income fund is another term for a bond fund. Bond funds are considered among the least risky mutual funds because bond-holders have first priority for payoff if a company goes under. However, as we mentioned in Chapters 13 and 14, these funds can rise and fall in value as interest rates fluctuate. Inflation also can erode the purchasing power of the money.

Until now in this chapter, we've explored primarily stock funds. Of course, there are a dizzying array of bond mutual funds to sift through as well. Recall that bond funds may invest all or part of their money in issues of corporations, foreign governments, U.S. Treasury securities, or U.S. government agencies. Municipal bond funds pay income that is free from federal, and, in some cases, state taxes.

Bond funds also are identified by the types of bond investments they make. For example, if the fund invests in bonds of Uncle Sam or affiliated agencies, the bond fund usually has the words "government securities," in its title. Be advised: Read the prospectus because you can't always go by the name of the fund.

Some bond funds also are identified by their bonds' terms. A fund that invests in bonds that mature in 10 to 30 years is known as a *long-term bond fund*. *Intermediate-term bond funds* invest in bonds that mature in 5 to 10 years. *Short-term bond funds* invest in bonds that mature in less than 5 years.

The longer the bond fund's term, the greater your chances of losing money if interest rates rise (*see Chapter 3*). Of course, on the upside, when interest rates fall, bond prices rise. There are a slew of bond categories to consider. Chapters 13 and 14 take a closer look at bond funds that may be right for you based on your income needs and tolerance for risk. Chapter 14 also takes a closer look at why long-term bond funds show greater changes in price when interest rates change.

There are a slew of bond fund categories to consider. Chapters 13 and 14 take a closer look at bond funds that may be right for you based on your income needs and tolerance for risk. Bond funds also generally are broken down into two broad groups—taxable and tax-free.

Taxable Bond Funds

Think of it. High yields and low risk. An investor's dream.... That's what a number of mutual fund companies and promoters would have you believe. Unfortunately, in the mutual fund world, these two investment objectives don't, as a rule, go hand in hand.

Taxable bond funds are a good example of this. Some corporate bond funds invest in high-quality corporate bonds issued by companies rated double A and triple A by Standard and Poor's and Moody's. Others, called high-yield bond funds invest in bonds of companies with lower credit ratings. High-yield bond funds, as you've probably already deducted, have higher yields. You'll learn more about bond ratings in Chapter 14.

Some funds invest a small percentage of the assets in nonrated bonds. The outfits that issue these bonds are not rated for creditworthiness by Standard & Poor's and Moody's. That does not mean the bonds are bad deals. The fund manager and his or her research staff evaluate the financial strength and the ability of the issuers to pay back principal and interest.

Essentially, here's the deal. A bond *has* to pay more interest if it has a lower credit rating or no one would invest in it. Suppose *you* had the choice. You could buy a bond issued by Scurvy Inc., which is B-rated by Standard & Poor's and Moody's, or you could invest in a Hope-to-Succeed Corp. bond, rated AAA by Standard & Poor's and Aaa by Moody's. If they both have the same current yield, Hope-to-Succeed Corp. clearly is sure-to-be the better choice.

As we reported in Chapter 3, there are a wide range of bonds that are backed by Uncle Sam. There are an even greater variety of bond funds. U.S. Treasury bond (T-bond) funds, which invest only in U.S. Treasury bonds, have less credit risk than other bond funds because the interest is paid by the United States Treasury.

Government mortgage bond funds, which invest in bonds issued or guaranteed by U.S. government agencies to help finance mortgages, pay higher yields than plain old T-bond funds. These funds sport higher interest rates than 100 percent U.S. Treasury bond funds because the

Look Out!
The words "high-yield" tacked onto a corporate or tax-free bond fund's name means this is a higher-risk investment. The fund invests in bonds from issuers with lower credit ratings.

Hot Tip
Is your mind boggled by all the bond funds available? Here's a good investment rule of thumb: The higher the interest rate, the riskier the investment.

agencies technically are private, rather than a direct branch of the least risky bond issuer, the U.S. government. In other words, they're one notch higher on the risk ladder. Then there are funds that invest in both U.S. Treasury bonds and U.S. government agency mortgage bonds.

In most cases, you won't get the capital appreciation from a bond fund that you get from a stock fund over the long term. These funds are designed to pay investors monthly income.

Tax-Free Bond Funds

As mentioned in Chapter 3, tax-free bond funds invest in municipal bonds, or bonds issued by states, cities, and towns and paid through taxes or project revenues. These are considered tax-free investments. There are several types of tax-free bond funds available. Funds with "municipal bond" in their names typically invest in bonds throughout the United States. This enables the fund manager to find the best investments nationwide with the least risk. Interest income from these bonds is exempt from federal taxes, but not state taxes. Investors residing in high-tax states such as New York, Massachusetts, California, and Pennsylvania, also can invest in *single-state municipal bond funds*. As the name implies, these funds invest in the bonds of a single state so residents of these states avoid paying both state and federal taxes on their interest income.

As with taxable bonds, there also are high-yielding tax-free municipal bond funds that invest in lower-rated municipal bond issuers. Investors may get

Hot Tip
Insured municipal bond funds have been some of the best-performing tax-free bond funds over the past several years. These bonds are insured against default by insurance companies that specialize in municipal bonds.

more interest income from high-yield municipal bond funds, but there also is a greater risk that they can lose if an issuer has problems paying back its principal and interest.

A word to the wise: Investors may find themselves paying some taxes on their municipal bond fund's earnings. Although the interest income isn't taxed, investors pay taxes on capital gains distributions. If a fund manager sells a bond at a profit, those profits must be passed on to the shareholders. Investors pay tax on long-term capital gains distributions from the sale of bonds held in the portfolio for more than one year. Short-term capital gains from the sale of bonds held less then one year are taxed at the shareholder's tax rate.

Balanced Funds

Balanced funds bridge the gap between stock funds and bond funds; that is, they split their investments relatively equally between stocks and bonds. Most of these funds invest 60 percent in blue-chip stocks and 40 percent in U.S. government and/or high quality corporate bonds. Some funds, however, may invest 10 percent to 15 percent of their money in small company or foreign stocks. Balanced funds are less risky than stock funds but a little more risky than certain bond funds. For example, balanced funds have experienced an average annual return of 11.4 percent over the past 10 years, with a high of 27.7 percent and a low of –2.8 percent. You might not necessarily find the word "balanced" in the title of these types of funds, so you'll have to check the fund's investment objective. Examples of balanced funds include the Dodge & Cox Balance Fund, Fidelity Puritan Fund, CGM Mutual Fund, and American Balanced Fund.

International Funds

International funds invest in stocks or bonds worldwide. There are a wide variety of international funds to pick from—international growth, growth and income, and small company stock funds. There are funds that invest in a specific region of the world such as Europe, Asia, or Latin America. Then there are funds that invest in a single country. Some funds invest worldwide, excluding the U.S. Those funds that invest in both the U.S. and foreign countries are known as *global funds* or *world funds*.

The more countries a fund invests in, the less risky it is. That's because the financial markets of different countries don't always move the same way. When the Japanese market may be dropping in value, the European markets may be moving higher. As a result, losses in one country may be offset by gains in another. Over the past 10 years, foreign funds have grown at an average annual rate of 14.8 percent, with the high being 47.3 percent and the low, –11.5 percent.

Regional funds or *single-country funds* are riskier than diversified international funds—all your eggs are in one basket. Your fortune may rise and fall within one country or area of the world. If there is a political uprising in the Far East, for example, the Asian stock markets may tumble. If one country, such as Japan, falls on economic tough times, Japan fund investors can lose investment value.

Regional or single-country fund investing can be a boom or bust proposition. Over the past 10 years, for example, the funds that invested in the countries of the Pacific Basin had an average annual return of 14.8 percent—but the high was a whopping 72 percent and the low was –20 percent.

On the bond side, there are funds that invest in corporate and government bonds worldwide. These are the least risky of the international bond fund group.

Someone who invests in international bond funds should not expect to earn a whopping amount more than they would by investing here at home. Bond funds that invest worldwide, for example, had an average annual total return of 9.8 percent over the past 10 years. By contrast, on average, U.S. bond funds gained 9 percent over same period. However, by investing in international bond funds, you get diversification. A U.S. bond fund may zig, and a bond fund that invests worldwide may zag. For example, in 1987, on average, T-bond funds lost almost 1 percent in value for the year. By contrast, on average, world bond funds gained 16 percent that year.

For Even Less Risky Returns...

As we told you in Chapter 3, money market funds invest mostly in money market or cash equivalent investments—typically short-term government and company debt and CDs. These tend to be lower-yielding, and have lower total returns, but they are less risky than the other types of funds described earlier in this chapter. There are several types of money funds available. Government-only money funds invest in Treasury bills and short-term U.S. government debt. These are the least risky money funds because the investments are backed by Uncle Sam. General purpose money funds invest in bank CDs, short-term corporation I.O.U.s (called commercial paper), and other short-term debt. Because their investments are not backed by the U.S. government, these funds pay higher yields. There also are tax-free money funds that invest in short-term municipal obligations, and single-state money funds are both federal and state tax-free.

Hot Tip
Directing Your Own Mutual Fund Investments is a handy three-part book and audio tape that sells for $15.00. For a copy, write The Mutual Fund Education Alliance at 1990 Erie Street, Suite 120, Kansas City, MO 64116.

The Least You Need to Know

➤ Some mutual funds aim for growth in the value of your investment; others may aim for income from interest and dividends.

➤ Bond funds or fixed-income funds pay you income and may invest both here and abroad.

➤ Balanced funds invest in both stock and bonds for more conservative investors.

Chapter 5

Is a Fund a Winner or Loser?

In This Chapter

➤ Betting on the *right* mutual fund

➤ Deciphering those performance figures

➤ Knowing what the averages are

Before you invest in a mutual fund, you need to act like a schoolteacher and give it a cool, objective evaluation. Once you know the A,B,C's, you can make a solid lifetime investment.

To evaluate a fund, you first have to know what to look for and what all this financial stuff means. There are several measurements to determine how well a fund has performed, how much it's likely to lose, and what you can expect to earn today.

You can get information about a fund's total return, yield, and measures of risk, which are discussed later in this chapter, from several sources of information, including the fund's prospectus, local newspaper mutual fund tables, or papers such as *The Wall Street Journal*. Chapters 9 and 10 show you how to find all the information you need to make wise investment decisions.

Then, once you finally invest, it's important to keep your eye on the ball. In this chapter, you'll learn all the important signals.

Where to Get the Risk Information

There are several sources of information on mutual fund risk measures. You can ask the mutual fund service representative or a stockbroker for the beta of a particular stock fund or the duration of a bond fund (more on beta and duration later in this chapter). In Chapter 10, you'll find a list of sources of information you can tap.

What's a Fund's Batting Average?

Chances are you can figure out that a baseball player with 25 home runs and a .350 batting average will be named to the All Star Team.

Just think if you had the same insight in advance about your mutual fund! There's no reason why you can't if you simply check on how a mutual fund is doing *before* you buy it. You certainly don't want to bet on a loser.

Luckily, you don't have to be Albert Einstein to figure things out. The rest of this chapter explains the basic ways to evaluate funds, which you'll learn even more about in later chapters.

Check Out the Yield

There are a lot of numbers associated with mutual funds, and it's important to be sure you're comparing apples to apples.

As discussed in Chapter 3, a mutual fund pays distributions based on dividend income from stocks, interest income from bonds, and capital gains from the profitable sale of both.

The yield, expressed as a percentage of the fund's current net asset value or price per share, tells how much income you get from these sources. It measures the interest income, in the case of bonds, or dividend income, in the case of stock funds. This figure is particularly useful if you need to have steady money coming in. It allows you to compare the periodic income each fund generates.

The yield is expressed as an annual number—it represents a yield for a full 12 months. Suppose, for example, a fund paid out 60 cents in dividends for the year and the fund's net asset value is $10. Sixty cents divided by 10 equals 6 percent.

Some bond mutual funds report 30-day SEC yields. That yield is calculated by dividing the net income per share during the period by the maximum offering price (MOP) on the last day of the period.

Check Out Operating Expenses—They Can Cost You

Fund expenses are taken out before the mutual fund distributes income or dividends. Like any company, the mutual fund must pay for the normal cost of doing business—including, for example, costs associated with the management of the fund, custody of the fund's assets, and servicing of the fund's shareholders. These operating expenses are not paid directly by the investor. They are paid by the fund from its assets before distributions are made to the investor. The higher the operating expenses the fund has, the lower the amount of distributions to shareholders. Chapter 8 discusses mutual fund costs in greater detail.

The Whole Ball of Wax: Total Return

In a mutual fund, you don't just profit from distributions in the form of interest and dividends. You also stand to make money if the market price of your mutual fund rises. Total return figures in the whole kit and caboodle.

What good is it to invest in a high-yielding fund only to find that the market value of the investment has dropped? Total return measures how well the fund is doing overall. If a fund manager is making the right investments, buying the right securities, adjusting the fund's investments to avoid large losses, and letting the profits roll in, the fund will have a positive total return.

Simply put, total return represents the change in the fund's share price plus the amount of money generated from reinvested income and capital gains distributions. Divide this by the original share price to calculate your total return rate.

You don't need to worry about fund expenses when you calculate the total return. As mentioned previously, the mutual fund deducts expenses before paying you distributions. As a result, the fund's yield already reflects the expenses that were taken out.

If all you know is that the total return of a fund over three years is 52 percent, you're stuck! That doesn't tell you the average annual return. You have to do some complicated algebra to come up with this number, which, by the way, is 15 percent.

Let's make life easier for you. Table 5.1 shows the annual average return based on the total return you've calculated. Simply look to the right for your total return under the column that represents the number of years you figured. Your annual return is to the left.

Table 5.1   Figuring the Average Annual Return

Annual Return	Number of Years of Total Return		
	3	5	10
5%	15.8%	27.6%	62.9%
6%	19.1	33.8	79.1
7%	22.5	40.3	96.7
8%	26.0	46.9	96.7
9%	29.5	53.9	136.7
10%	33.1	61.1	159.4
11%	36.8	68.5	183.9
12%	40.5	76.2	210.6
13%	44.3	84.2	239.5
14%	48.2	92.5	270.7
15%	52.1	101.1	304.6
16%	56.1	110.0	341.1
17%	60.2	119.2	380.7
18%	63.3	128.8	423.4
19%	68.5	138.6	469.5
20%	72.8	148.8	519.2

The annual return is the most frequently reported number on mutual funds. A number of mutual fund reporting services (discussed in Chapter 10) list the annual average returns—so do your local newspapers.

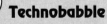

Technobabble

A stock fund's *beta* tells you how risky the fund tends to be in relation to the stock market. A fund with a low beta is less risky than the stock market in general. *Duration* tells you what percentage the value of your bond fund will rise or fall with a 1 percent change in interest rates. *Annual return* or *average annual return* is the total return translated into an annual average.

Checking Out the Fund's Long-Term Batting Average

Got the hang of it? A good fund has a good long-term batting average, but over the short term, like a baseball player, the fund can have some off years.

Perhaps a fund manager had a bad case of the hiccups in 1995. That doesn't necessarily mean you give up your Mickey Mantle or Hank Aaron of the mutual fund world. In Chapter 6 you will learn to pick the funds that are right for you based on your investment comfort level.

With all this talk about total returns and the growth in the share value of mutual fund investments, what could an investor expect to earn over the long term? Past performance is no indication of future returns, but history does give us an indication of what we can expect. To help zero in on your mutual fund choices, here are average annual total returns on stocks, bonds, and cash investments over the past 70 years, according to Ibbotson Associates, a Chicago-based research firm:

➤ **Common stocks.** 10 percent annually over the past 70 years. In any given year, you had a good chance of earning between –11 percent and +21 percent.

➤ **Corporate Bonds.** 5.5 percent annually over the past 70 years. In any given year, you had a good chance of making between –3 percent and +14 percent.

➤ **U.S. Government Bonds.** 5 percent annually over the past 70 years. In any given year, you had a good chance of making between –3.6 percent and +13.6 percent.

➤ **T-bills (cash).** 3.7 percent annually over the past 70 years. In any given year, you had a good chance of making between just under 1 percent or +7 percent.

Gauging a Fund's Risk

There are a couple of easy ways to figure out how risky a fund is. The more volatile a fund, the greater chance you'll see wide swings in total return and the share value of a fund. The swing in performance as measured by the fund's total return is known as *volatility*. In bad years, a volatile fund will lose a lot more money than other funds. However, in good years you can see double-digit returns.

Rate Your Stock Fund's Volatility

By looking at one simple number, you can tell how risky your stock fund is. The fund's beta tells you how much volatility, and therefore, risk, there is within the fund's portfolio in relation to the stock market average. Ask a fund service representative for the beta, or look it up in several reports discussed in Chapter 10.

If this all sounds like Greek to you, it's really simple. The lower the beta of your stock fund, the lower your risk. The beta measures stock fund performance in relation to the *S&P 500*, an index of 500 stocks, that is considered a standard measure of how the overall stock market performs. The S&P 500 has a beta of 1, so a mutual fund with a beta greater than 1 should both win more and lose more than the stock market average. By contrast, a fund with a beta of less than 1 won't gain as much as the S&P 500, but it also should lose less when the stock market heads south.

A fund's beta may help you decide on the type of stock fund that fits your tolerance for risk. If you are investing for long-term growth, you want to be sure you have a fund with a beta that's more than 1. That way, you know that the fund can perform well in a rising stock market. You may want to avoid a fund with an excessively high beta. It may be a hot-performing fund, but it can also lose a lot of money.

By contrast, even if you are a conservative stock fund investor, you don't want to invest in a stock fund that has a real low beta. Funds with betas below .5 may keep a lot of money in cash investments and bonds. These are very low-risk stock funds. Typically, funds with betas below .5 or .6 do well when the stock market declines in value. These funds register higher total returns compared with higher beta stock funds during bear markets when stocks drop. Consequently, you may not get the share value growth that you need to meet your financial goals over the long term.

Joe Biddle was considering two mutual funds for his retirement, which was 20 years away. One, the "Grow Like Crazy Stock Fund," had a beta of 1.2. Another, the "Steady As You Go" stock fund, had a beta of .85.

Although Joe wanted the "Grow Like Crazy Fund," his wife, Bertha, was a little nervous. Because the "Grow Like Crazy" fund had a beta of 1.2, if the stock market plunged, the fund could be down 20 percent more than the market!

They finally decided on the "Steady As You Go" fund.

How Did a Fund Do in Bad Years?

If looking for betas is not your cup of tea, there's an easier way to gauge a stock fund's risk. Compare how a number of stock funds did in bad years, such as 1973, 1974, 1981, 1987, 1990, and 1994. Suppose you're seriously considering three stock funds and they've all performed about the same. Here's what to consider:

Hot Tip
The Morningstar Mutual Fund Report and the Value Line Mutual Fund Survey, which are available in public libraries, also evaluate a fund's risk. These reports look at how funds do in down markets, then they rank the funds. These ratings automatically show how one fund stacks up against another.

➤ Growth Stock Fund A has grown at an annual rate of 13.25 percent over the past 10 years, stock Fund B gained 12.98 percent, and C was up 13.4 percent.

➤ Compare the funds' returns in 1987, 1990, and 1994. As you can see from Table 5.2, Fund B lost the least in the most recent bad years. It gained a little less than the others, but it wasn't far off the mark. Fund C gained the most, but it also seemed to lose the most in bad years.

Table 5.2 How Example Funds Did in Bad Years

Fund	1987	1990	1994
A	−6.0%	−9.0%	−12.0%
B	−3.0	−6.0	−5.5
C	−8.0	−9.5	−9.5

How to Gauge a Bond Fund's Risks of Losing Money

There are a couple of ways to tell whether a bond fund is too hot to handle. These measures, duration and average maturity, can help you assess the riskiness of a bond fund.

As discussed in Chapter 3, bond prices move in the opposite direction as interest rates. When interest rates rise, prices for bonds with lower rates fall. By contrast, when interest rates fall, prices for bonds with higher interest rates rise.

Look Out!
You can lose a lot of money in a bond fund that has a duration of 10 or more. These funds invest in long-term bonds. If interest rates rise 1 percent, the fund will lose 10 percent.

Duration measures how much your bond fund will increase or decrease in value with a 1 percent change in interest rates. A fund with a duration of 4, for example, drops about 4 percent in value if interest rates rise 1 percent, but it increases 4 percent in value if interest rates drop 1 percent. By contrast, a fund with a duration of 10 loses 10 percent in value if interest rates rise 1 percent, but increases 10 percent in value if interest rates drop 1 percent.

There's another easy way to measure a bond fund's risk: Look at its average maturity. The lower the average maturity, the less money the fund loses when interest rates rise. The higher the average maturity, the more money the bond fund loses if rates increase. By contrast, the higher the average maturity, the more the bond fund will make if interest rates fall.

Bond mutual funds typically own a lot of different bonds that mature in different years. How do you tell the average maturity of the bonds owned by a bond fund? Ask the fund rep or check the prospectus or semiannual and annual reports.

Tips on Spotting a Winning Fund

Chapter 17 will show you how to evaluate a fund or several funds' performances after you already own them. You will learn when to dump the losers and keep the winners.

The Least You Need to Know

➤ Even if you need regular income basis from a mutual fund, be sure to look at the fund's SEC yield *and* compare its total return with similar funds.

➤ If you need growth from a stock fund, take these steps:

1. Compare a fund's total return over at least three, five, and 10 years.

2. Check a fund's beta to see how it will do compared to the overall stock market.

3. Look at how the fund did in bad years.

Your objective is to find the fund with the best total return, the lowest beta, and the least amount of losses in bad years.

➤ Don't choose the funds with the hottest short-term track records. Last year's winners could be this year's laggards.

➤ Find out who the fund's portfolio manager is. Make sure the person responsible for a fund's strong track record is still running the show.

Part 2
Getting Started

Now we're getting serious, folks. The most important part of mutual fund investing is in the coming chapters—before you fill out the application. You need to make sure you're picking the right funds.

Don't worry—you don't need an MBA to do this. All you need are a few tricks. Believe it or not, the key to mutual fund investing is not necessarily knowing any major secrets about the direction of interest rates or major industry trends. It's knowing yourself and then knowing what to look for based on your own unique nature.

We're not talking major brain surgery here, so just sit back in a comfortable chair and relax. Consider this part the matchmaking part of the book. It will help you figure out your own personal investment profile and steer you in the direction of funds that may be right for you.

Chapter 6

What Kind of Investor Are You?

Are you ready to invest? Get on your mark, get set... Wait a minute. Stop the music!

Stock and bond prices sure bounce up and down a lot. Are you *really* ready to rock and roll? Pick up the business section of your local newspaper any day of the week and you'll see what we mean. Sure, you might be inspired because of a newspaper and magazine report that some mutual fund investors are making big profits. Wow! ABC mutual fund gained 20 percent so far this year. Joe Biddle invested $1,000 and now six months later it's up to $1,200! Then again, none of us needs to get fried by investing our life savings in a hot stock fund only to have it nosedive over the following few weeks.

Although you now have a clear picture of your savings goals and how to free the money to invest, that's not enough to get started.

Take it from one member of this team, a former diehard CD investor: You have to be sure you understand what you're getting into before committing your hard-earned cash to anything that fails to move consistently in a northerly direction.

That's why we're here, so read on...

What Are Ya in For?

Unfortunately, there are some pain-in-the-neck risks you need to contend with when you invest in mutual funds. The one that's most likely to trigger a headache is losing money. You also can make a killing, however. Your success as a mutual fund investor depends largely on how you handle the downside of this otherwise attractive investment.

Take John and Mary, who just retired to sunny West Palm Beach, Florida. They live on John's pension, Social Security, and some savings. Before John retired, he put the bulk of their life savings—$25,000—in a mutual fund.

Three months later, the value of his fund had plunged $3,000. Before John had time to regret his investment decision, he managed to crack his tooth on a cashew nut while eating dinner with Mary in a local Chinese restaurant.

Hot Tip
Mutual funds are long-term investments. The longer you invest, the less chance you have of losing. Based on financial history, stocks never have lost money over any 20-year period, according to Ibbotson Associates, Chicago. If you invest for just one year, you could lose money close to one-third of the time. Invest for five years and expect at least one bad year. This will give you a good idea of why it's important to invest in stock funds for the long term.

Because he had no dental insurance, he was forced to spend $3,000 for a bridge. He had to sell his mutual fund at precisely the wrong time.

That's what we mean by risk—investing in a mutual fund when you really can't afford to lose.

What's risky for John and Mary, however, may not be risky for somebody else.

Tad, a 35 year-old dentist, makes 100 grand a year. Tad is comfortable investing in mutual funds because he is aware that the $10,000 he invested today can drop in value over the short term. But he also knows that mutual funds are great investments for the long term. Tad has a good job. He can afford to invest for 25 to 30 years and build a nest egg. He won't be upset if his $10,000 investment is worth $9,000 at the end of this year because there's a good chance it could be worth $12,000 at the end of the following year.

There are a few reasons a mutual fund can fall in value. We already discussed many of these in Chapter 3. Mutual funds invest generally in stocks, bonds, or both. When tons of investors all over the country buy stocks, stock prices head up. If those same investors sell stocks, stock prices can take a dive. Because a mutual fund may own the stocks all these investors are buying or selling, the value of a fund changes based on what these people do. You should make sure that your investment decisions take into account anticipated market trends.

Believe it or not, there's also a risk that your investment can be *too* safe. Stay in an FDIC-insured savings account, for example, and your money may not grow fast enough to keep up with the prices of food and utilities. This is known as *inflation*.

True, your bank account is federally insured. You can't lose any money if your friendly banker goes out of business. Have you checked the interest banks pay on savings accounts, though? It's 3 percent.

What good is it if a few years down the road, you live on an investment that makes 100 bucks a week, but it costs $104 for groceries? You still have to reach into your pocketbook because you are $4 short.

Suppose you're saving for your child's college education. The cost of college is rising about 6 percent a year, and you estimate you need $100,000 for four years of tuition at Home Town State College in 18 years.

If you earn too little on your child's college savings kitty and it grows to $85,000, you're in the hole. Where are you going to get the rest of the money?

Now, we don't want you to get overly upset about these Chicken Little stories. As mentioned at the beginning of the book, mutual fund managers are fully aware of these bugaboos and take steps to limit losses.

Hot Tip
Over the past 20 years, stock mutual funds have been the best way to beat inflation. Bond mutual funds have come in second.

Zeroing in on Your Comfort Level

By asking yourself a few basic questions, you'll develop a better idea of the risk you're willing to assume when investing in mutual funds. You'll learn whether you're a conservative investor or a risk-taker. You don't want to invest in risky funds if you are a safety-minded investor. By the same token, if you like to invest aggressively, conservative funds aren't for you. Once you have this information in hand, you can move on to Chapter 7 to explore the kinds of mutual funds that fit in with your risk profile. You'll also learn how to divide your investments.

WHAT?

Technobabble
Conservative investors like less risky investments that lose little money. *Moderate investors* are willing to see the value of their mutual funds drop slightly in return for long-term profits. *Aggressive investors* want to earn big gains, but also are willing to accept big losses.

Risk Acceptance Quiz

To help determine your risk tolerance, select (circle) the letter that best expresses your answer to the following questions.

1. How old are you?

   A. Over age 65 (1)

   B Between age 55 and 65 (2)

   C. Between age 35 and 55 (3)

   D. Under age 35 (4)

2. How much are you willing to lose in mutual fund investments in any given year?

   A. 1 percent (1)

   B. 3 percent (2)

   C. 10 percent (3)

   D. 15 percent (4)

3. How important is regular income from your investments (that is, do you need to use the interest and dividends from your investments to cover expenses now)?

   A. Not important (1)

   B. Somewhat important (2)

C. Important (3)

D. Very important (4)

4. How important is regular income from your investments?

    A. Very important (1)

    B. Important (2)

    C. Somewhat important (3)

    D. Not important (4)

5. How important is it to avoid losses and know your money is safe?

    A. Very important (1)

    B. Important (2)

    C. Somewhat important (3)

    D. Not important (4)

6. How important is it that your money grow faster than the prices you pay for the things you need?

    A. Not as important as getting regular income (1)

    B. I want it to grow as fast as the cost of things I need (2)

    C. I want it to grow more than the cost of things (3)

    D. I want it to grow much faster than the cost of things (4)

Now add up the numbers in parentheses to the right of each of your answers to determine your total risk tolerance score:

➤ If your score is 10 or less, you are a conservative investor. This means that safety is as important as seeing your money grow in value over the years.

➤ If you score between 10 and 20, you are a moderate investor. You are willing to see your mutual funds decline in value a little bit in return for long-term growth.

➤ If you score 20 or more, you are an aggressive investor. You are willing to accept larger short-term losses than most people in return for substantial gains long-term.

The Least You Need to Know

➤ Mutual funds can lose money.

➤ The money you make on your savings or mutual funds should grow at least as fast as the prices of food and other necessities.

➤ Before you invest, understand what kind of risk-taker you are.

Chapter 7

Which Funds Are Right for You?

In This Chapter

➤ Matching your tolerance for risk with the right funds

➤ How to split up your investments

➤ Avoiding common fund selection mistakes

➤ How to avoid funds that are too risky

You might consider this chapter the Culinary Institute of Mutual Funds. You have the ingredients lined up: How much risk you can stand, how much money you need by when, and the types of mutual funds from which to select. Now you're going to mix it all together.

The general rule is: The higher the yield in the case of bond funds or the higher the total return in the case of stock funds, the more risky the mutual fund. (Unfortunately, even the most savvy investors can't necessarily have everything!) Investing for the long term is key to reaping any benefits from an aggressive or growth-oriented mutual fund. Invest for a year or two and you can lose. Investors with just a couple of years to invest also need to protect what they have in less risky investments.

This chapter takes what you already learned about yourself and mutual funds and helps put it into a format to help meet your needs. You'll see which funds are for which types of investors. You'll also discover how to split up your money among different types of funds to get the best return with the least amount of risk.

You already know how much heat you can stand. The time has come to select the funds that match your risk temperature. If you took the short quiz in Chapter 4, you now know whether you are an aggressive, moderate, or conservative investor. You know how much you can stomach losing in a year's time in return for the long-term profits. You also know whether anything short of an FDIC-insured investment makes you queasy.

Let's take a minute to review the investments available. Think of investing in funds based on a pyramid of risk, such as the one illustrated in this chapter. At the top are the riskiest funds, the funds that can lose or gain a lot of money over a short time. The riskiest funds often pay the highest returns. For instance, funds that invest in just one sector of an industry can gain 70 percent or lose 30 percent in any given year.

Next in line, in level of risk, are aggressive growth funds and small company stock funds. You also can win big or lose a lot with these. Although speculators often move in and out of aggressive growth and small company stock funds, they also are excellent long-term investments. Sock money into one of these babies for 20 years and you could have a nice retirement nest egg.

Next in line are growth funds, which also are considered good investments for the long term. These funds tend to invest in larger, well-established companies, but they also can be risky.

There are many well-managed growth funds to pick. Moderate and conservative investors may look at the middle of the investment pyramid. Growth and income funds and balanced funds are sleep-at-night stock funds. You can get rich slowly and with relative low risk with these funds.

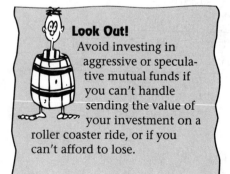

Look Out!
Avoid investing in aggressive or speculative mutual funds if you can't handle sending the value of your investment on a roller coaster ride, or if you can't afford to lose.

Corporate bond funds are next on the pyramid. You'll earn higher yields, but typically you won't get the kind of growth you get from stock funds. Funds that invest in Treasury bonds are less risky than their corporate counterparts because the bonds are backed against default by Uncle Sam. At the bottom of the pyramid are the least risky funds—short-term bond funds and money market funds.

If you have a short-term investment time span, it's best to stick with the lowest-risk funds.

Pyramid of Risk

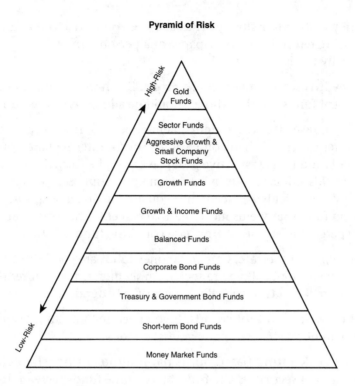

How mutual fund risk stacks up.

Matchmaker, Matchmaker, Make Me a Match

Investing in mutual funds is a long-term affair. Pick out the right types of funds and you can stick with 'em for life. In our travels, we've talked to people who've been investing the same funds for more than 10 years. They've made them part of their family and love them. After all, these investors are trusting an investment company with their life savings. The funds may not always be top-performing, but they're not the worst either. As long as their funds do better than 50 percent of similar funds, they just keep socking away the money to meet future goals.

Avoid a Fistful of Mistakes

Make yourself happy by picking the right funds. Unfortunately—and you've probably heard all too many of these horror stories—many mutual fund investors don't. Here are the mistakes many fund pickers make:

1. **They chase after the hot funds.** Once you read about a hot fund with a sizzling return in the newspaper or a personal finance magazine, it's usually too late to invest!

2. **They invest to make a quick profit.** Do that and you could lose big. Mutual funds, on the whole, should be a long-term investment.

3. **They chase after high yields.** Remember, the higher the yield, the greater the risk. When comparing a short-, intermediate-, or long-term bond fund to its respective group averages, be suspicious if a fund outyields similar funds by a wide margin. Suppose the average long-term bond fund yields 7 percent and you are looking at a specific long-term bond fund that yields more than 10 percent. The fund that yields over 10 percent is high-risk. How else could the fund pay those yields?

4. **They play it too safe.** CDs and money funds are good short-term places to park your money. If you're socking away money for your retirement, how-ever, stock funds historically have been a better deal for the long term.

5. **They pick unsuitable funds.** If you need income and lower risk, you should not be investing in aggressive stock funds.

6. **They pick a fund based on its name alone, rather than checking on the actual securities the fund buys.** Some funds have more flexibility than others to invest in different kinds of stocks or bonds. You can't always tell by the name of the fund.

7. **They panic and sell when the market goes down.**

Getting a Good Fit

Just try wearing the wrong size shoes for a day and see how you feel. There's nothing worse for your lovely disposition. The same goes for mutual funds. Chapter 4 discussed the different kinds of funds in which you can invest. Now let's try on a fund for size. Table 7.1 ranks stock and bond funds by their risk level, as well as the potential for the following types of rewards:

➤ Big gains refer to potential for very high total returns because the objec-tive of the fund is to speculate for the purpose of rapid and large in-creases in the share value of the fund.

➤ Maximum growth refers to the potential of producing the highest total returns from funds that invest most aggressively in stocks.

➤ Growth refers to higher-than-average total returns because the funds invest in stocks for long-term growth in the share value of the fund.

➤ Income refers to the potential ability of the fund to provide investors with regular interest and/or dividends.

➤ Low risk and least risk refer to the potential capability of the fund to preserve your principal.

Table 7.1 Getting Comfortable with a Fund

Investor Risk Level/Objective	Type of Fund	Risk/Reward
Stock Funds		
Speculative	Precious metals	Highest/Big gains
Speculative	Most sector	Higher/Big gains
Aggressive growth	Aggressive growth	High/Maximum capital
Aggressive growth	International growth	High/Maximum capital
Aggressive growth	Small company	High/Maximum capital
Aggressive growth	Growth	High/Longer-term
Moderate income	Growth & income	Moderate/Growth plus
Moderate plus growth	Equity income	Low-moderate/Income
Conservative income	Income	Lower/Long-term
Conservative income	Utility	Lower/Long-term
Conservative growth	Balanced	Lower/Income plus
Bond Funds		
Aggressive	High-yield	High/High income
Aggressive	Long-term government	High/Income

continues

Table 7.1 Continued

Investor Risk Level/Objective	Type of Fund	Risk/Reward
Bond Funds		
Aggressive	Long-term tax-free	High/Income
Aggressive	International	High/Income
Moderate	Intermediate-term	Moderate/Income
Moderate	Intermediate tax-free	Moderate/Income
Conservative	Short-term	Lower/Income and less risk
Conservative	Short-term tax-free	Lower/Income and less risk
Other Funds		
Safety-minded	Money market	Lowest/Income and least risk

Getting the Best Returns with the Least Amount of Risk

There is one more step to nailing down your mutual fund investments. Once you know your risk level, you can invest in different types of funds so that you can get the best possible return with the least risk.

Diversification Helps Limit Losses

Earlier in this book, we told you that the major advantage of mutual funds is that they diversify their investments. They might, for example, buy stocks of several different companies. This way if one performs poorly, the others might not. Gurus say it could pay to take a similar strategy when you pick your mutual funds. They call this diversification.

All diversification means is that if you divide your investments the right way, gains in one type of mutual fund can offset losses in other types of funds. One kind of fund may zig when the other zags.

Look at it this way. Suppose you're graphing the performance of a couple of mutual funds. Over several years, Fund A's performance looks just like an M. It goes up and it goes down. Fund B's performance looks like a W. It goes down, then up, then down and back up again.

If you own just one of these funds, you're in for a wild ride. Put them together and you get an entirely different picture. Losses in one fund are offset by gains in the other. You get a less bumpy ride. Look at the performance of C. The gains and losses of A and B give you C.

> **WHAT?**
>
> **Technobabble**
> When you *diversify* your mutual fund investments, you own different kinds of funds so that losses in one fund can be offset with gains in the others. Diversification is designed to give you the best returns with the least possible risk. *Hedging* is selecting investments so that the losses in one or more investments are offset by gains in others and vice versa. To hedge, you look for investments that perform at odds with each other. When one is gaining value, the other is losing value, and vice versa.

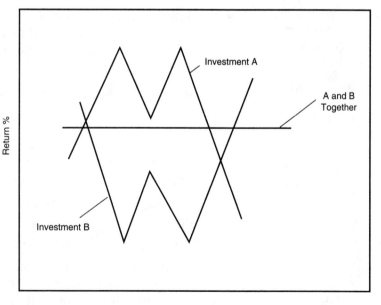

How diversification works to smooth out the bumps.

Slicing Up Your Investment Pie

How do you know how many of your available investment dollars to invest in each kind of mutual fund? One easy way to figure it out is to subtract your age from 100; the number you get is how much to invest in stocks. If you are 40 years old, 100–40 = 60. Based on this calculation, you put 60 percent of your money in stocks and 40 percent in bonds and money funds. Your stockbroker or financial planner also can help you find the best mix of funds. Many offer computer software that can analyze your goals and risk tolerance to come up with a mix of investments that's right for you. You can do it yourself by using material that investment companies, mentioned throughout this book, will send you upon request. You can call these fund families toll-free and ask for the information. You're not obligated to invest in their funds, but keep in mind that their material is designed to help get your business. You need to do your own research, which we'll help you through in Chapter 10.

The Main Ingredients

You need four major ingredients to diversify your mutual fund recipe:

Hot Tip
Mutual fund families have excellent booklets or computer software to help you find the right funds based on your comfort level. Call

T. Rowe Price, 800-638-5660

Vanguard, 800-662-7447

Scudder, 800-225-2470

Fidelity Investments, 800-544-8888

Dreyfus, 800-645-6561

Neuberger & Berman, 800-877-9700

➤ **Stock funds.** Invest in stock funds for growth and inflation protection. Recall that stocks historically have earned 6 to 7 percent more than the rate of inflation.

➤ **Bond funds.** Invest in bond funds for income and to hedge against stock fund losses. Stock fund and bond fund prices don't always move in the same direction, so if you own a bond fund, it could cushion the blow of losses in your stock funds or other investments.

➤ **Money funds.** Money funds generally are a stabilizer, and when interest rates rise, you earn higher yields from a money fund.

➤ **International stock or bond funds.** Foreign stock markets don't always perform like ours. Often, but not always, international bond or stock funds gain in value while U.S. funds perform poorly.

There are some funds that do the diversification for you. They are known as asset allocation funds (*see Chapter 15*).

Simple Mixes

Here are some suggested mixes of different kinds of mutual funds, based on your age and risk tolerance, that should give you solid returns while helping to protect you if the market nosedives:

➤ **Aggressive investors.** When you are young and just starting out in the work world or have built up a nest egg and still have a long time to invest before you retire, you can afford to invest aggressively. There is plenty of time for losses to be offset by gains in the share value of your mutual fund. That's why aggressive investors between the ages of 20 and 49 can invest 80 percent in stock funds and 20 percent in bond funds.

➤ **Moderate investors.** Investors between the ages of 50 and 59, who want to see the share value of their mutual fund or funds grow but want to protect their principal because they are nearing retirement, should invest 60 percent in stocks and 40 percent in bonds. Ages 50 through 59 are key savings and investing years when money is socked away for retirement a few years down the road. Because retirement is more than 10 years away, growth in the value of the investments is important to building a retirement nest egg. This group invests in stock funds for growth in the share value of their investments, but they also need to temper the risk of losing a lot of money.

➤ **Conservative investors.** Investors between the ages of 60 and 74 still need some growth so that the share value of their investments keeps pace with inflation. Then they can protect the purchasing power of their money. Consider a mix of 40 percent stocks, 40 percent bonds, and 20 percent money funds.

➤ **Senior citizens.** These investors, 75 and older, who need income but also need to preserve their principal, should keep 20 percent in stocks to help maintain the purchasing power of the money, 60 percent in bond funds, and 20 percent in money funds. The biggest fear senior citizens face is the fear of outliving their money. That's why it's still important to keep a small percentage of investments in a well-managed stock fund.

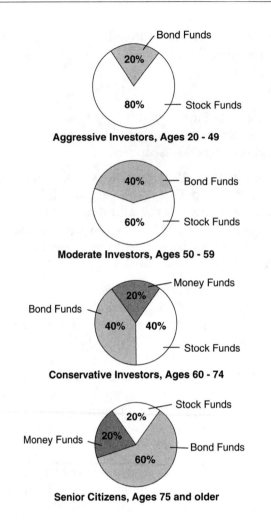

Suggested ways to slice the investment pie.

Spicing It Up

Want even more diversification? Invest in different kinds of stock and bond funds. A really aggressive investor can divide stock funds among aggressive growth funds, small company stock funds, or similar funds that invest overseas.

More moderate investors can split stock fund investments between growth and income funds and international funds or keep a teeny-weeny bit in a well-diversified growth stock fund.

Conservative investors can invest in U.S. and overseas growth and income funds, equity income funds, and short- or intermediate-term bond funds. A wide variety of bond funds are discussed in Chapter 4 and Part 2 of this book. It's always a good idea to mix and match your bond funds. If you need easy access to cash, you might want to have a money fund. Long-term bond funds typically pay higher yields than short- or intermediate-term bond funds, but the short/intermediate funds are less risky because their share value fluctuates less when interest rates change. For high yields, look at government mortgage bond funds, as well as corporate and international bond funds.

If you're really thoroughly diversified, you might have several kinds of funds. How much you invest in each type, as mentioned before, depends on your goals, how long you have to invest, and your risk tolerance.

Here are several types of funds you should consider when you want to diversify:

➤ A small company stock fund or aggressive stock fund

➤ A growth or a growth and income fund

➤ An international stock fund

➤ A corporate bond fund

➤ An international bond fund

➤ A money fund

The Least You Need to Know

➤ Learn how much risk you can tolerate.

➤ Match the investment objectives of the funds with your tolerance for risk.

➤ Diversify your investments. By splitting up your investments among different types of mutual funds you are comfortable with, you can lower your overall risk, even though you may be investing in some riskier funds.

➤ Almost everybody should have some money invested in stock funds. Why? Stock fund share values grow more than the rate of inflation over the longer term.

What Does All This Investment Stuff Cost?

In This Chapter

➤ Who sells mutual funds?

➤ What do these funds cost?

➤ Loads and no-loads

How much do you pay for mutual funds? Good question. Unlike with your bank checking account, your sales rep may not necessarily spout off *all* the fees charged by your mutual fund up front. Just because there are no fees or commissions to open a mutual fund, it doesn't mean that they don't exist.

What you pay for a mutual fund largely depends on who you buy it from and what types of securities you're buying. You need to balance the level of professional service you require with how much you're willing to spend.

Keeping your fees under control definitely is a key ingredient to investing profitably. To do this, you need to decipher a mutual fund's charges and know when you're paying too much. In this chapter, you will learn what mutual funds cost, how you can save a bundle, and how to get your money's worth when you must pick a financial advisor.

Who Peddles Mutual Funds?

Too many people have the mistaken idea that the only place to buy mutual funds is through a stockbroker. Wrong! Today, you can get mutual funds from a fistful of sources. You can open a mutual fund account at your local bank, through an insurance agent or financial planner, or deal directly with a mutual fund. Stockbrokers, financial planners, insurance agents, and SEC-registered investment advisors all sell mutual funds.

Regardless of which sales rep you choose, you can rest assured that anyone selling mutual funds must have a certain amount of training. The rep selling mutual funds must pass a test called an NASD (National Association of Securities Dealers) Series 6 examination. This exam tests a person's knowledge of mutual funds, as well as the rules for buying and selling investments. If the financial professional you select also sells individual securities, he or she also must have passed the even-tougher NASD Series 7 exam.

As we indicated earlier, it's possible today to buy mutual funds directly from the mutual fund company and save the commission or load charged by a broker or other licensed pro. By telephoning the mutual fund company directly, you skip the middleman. Mutual fund investment companies already have a trained staff on hand to help.

On the other hand, this can be pretty complicated stuff. Perhaps you want a little more handholding. In that case, it's important to get your money's worth. You want to hire someone who has a lot of experience and knows his or her stuff!

Want a Pro? Look for These Blue Ribbons

There are more than 30,000 financial planners in this country. Many also are stockbrokers, insurance agents, or registered investment advisors. When you do business with these people, you're supposed to get an extra layer of service, for which you pay. A financial planner will look at your whole financial picture and help you set up investment goals and a game plan. A financial planner also can help with insurance coverage and handle tax and estate planning.

When you check out financial planners or other investment professionals, it's important to see whether they have certain qualifications. If they do, they'll proudly display the certificates on their office walls and the acronyms on their business cards.

➤ **Certified Financial Planner (CFP).** The CFP's course work includes training in employee benefits, insurance investments, and tax and estate planning. To keep the CFP license—awarded by the International Board of Standards and Practices for Certified Financial Planners (IBCFP), Denver—the financial planner must stick to a code of ethics and meet continuing education requirements. CFP candidates have completed six intensive financial planning courses and passed a national examination.

➤ **Chartered Life Underwriter (CLU) and Chartered Financial Consultant (ChFC).** These designations, issued by the American College, Bryn Mawr, PA, generally go hand-in-hand. The CLU program requires a candidate to take courses with a specialty in life insurance and personal insurance planning. The ChFC adds a 10-course program in financial, estate, and tax planning, in addition to investment management. Both designations require candidates to pass national examinations.

➤ **Accredited Personal Financial Planning Specialist (APFS).** The APFS designation is given to Certified Public Accountants (CPAs) who pass a stringent financial planning examination administered by the American Institute of Certified Public Accountants. A CPA has passed a national examination, but is licensed by the state where he or she sets up practice. A CPA candidate must have a bachelor's degree and must have worked for an accounting firm for at least two years.

➤ **Registered Investment Advisors (RIA).** RIAs must register with the Securities and Exchange Commission. They must disclose their educational backgrounds, the type of investments they manage, and generally must file a financial statement revealing how their business is doing.

➤ **Brokers.** Stockbrokers take a training program, often through their brokerage firms. They also must pass the Series 6 and 7 exams.

Checking 'em Out

Before you hire anyone to give you financial advice, check his or her educational background and the number of years in business. You want someone with at least three years of experience, but the more years, the better. If you're hiring someone who manages money in addition to peddling insurance, ask your state's division of securities whether any complaints have been filed against that person. If the person is a registered investment advisor, ask to see the *ADV form,* which contains important financial information about the advisor's money management company. Registered investment advisors

Look Out!
Seeking a referral? Be sure to ask whether the people giving the referrals are receiving finders' fees. Be cautious if they are.

must file this form with the Securities and Exchange Commission. You can get the telephone number of your state's division of securities in the telephone book under listings for state government departments. Look under either Department of Securities or Division of Securities. Chapter 30 in the Appendix lists the State Securities Agency phone numbers.

For more information on financial planners write: The Institute for Certified Financial Planners, 7600 East Eastman Avenue, Suite 301, Denver, CO 80231. Ask for the booklet, "Selecting a Qualified Financial Planning Professional: Twelve Questions to Consider." You also can call the Institute for Certified Financial Planners at 800-282-7526 for names of qualified financial planners in your area. Another source of free information on how to pick a financial planner is the American Association of Retired Persons Consumer Affairs Section, 1909 K Street, NW, Washington, DC 20049. The International Association for Financial Planning (IAFP), 2 Concourse Parkway, Atlanta, GA 30328, has a consumer referral program. You can get a list of planners in your area by calling 800-945-IAFP.

What's the Price Tag?

There's no free lunch when you invest in mutual funds. You pay several kinds of fees when you invest. How much depends on how the fund is sold.

Load Funds

When you buy a mutual fund from a stockbroker, financial planner, or insurance agent who is registered to sell mutual funds, you'll pay a commission, which also is called a load. Loads generally range from as little as 3 percent to as much as 8.5 percent. The load is a percentage of the amount you invest. The average load on a fund sold by a broker is about 5 percent.

Look Out!
If your salesperson calls a fund a no-load fund, double-check. We've heard bankers use this incorrect terminology for funds that actually have back-end loads.

You might not realize you're paying this commission because of all the different ways you can be zapped. So, get out the Sherlock Holmes hat. In the old days, investors always paid a front-end load. Management companies have come up with a number of ways to sell their load funds. Here's the lowdown.

➤ Some funds charge *front-end loads*, in which the commission is taken out before the money is invested. Front-end loads range from 3 percent to 8.5 percent.

➤ There are funds with *back-end loads*. This load kicks you in the rear. The back-end loads usually start at 5 to 6 percent. You pay this commission only if you take money out over the first five or six years. On the other hand, if you keep your money invested longer, you're not charged.

➤ Funds also may charge a *level load*. You pay a flat ongoing annual fee, typically 1 percent, deducted from your fund's earnings. The 1 percent annual charge is broken down in two components: a 12b-1 fee that pays for the fund's advertising and marketing expenses and, by regulation, can't exceed .75 percent (three-quarters of 1 percent), and a .25 percent (one-quarter of 1 percent) service fee.

Technobabble

A *management fee* is the charge for running the fund. The *expense ratio* tells you the total charges on the fund, excluding commissions. An *ADV Form*, on file with the Securities and Exchange Commission, contains important financial information about a registered investment advisor's (RIA's) money management company.

You will not pay a front-end or back-end load with a level load.

What's the Best Way to Get Stiffed on Your Load?

What's the best way to pay? If you think you're going to hold on to the fund for longer than six years, pay the back-end load. Why? After the six years have expired, you can take money out of your fund free of charge and you avoid paying that dreaded front-end load.

If you don't know how long you're going to hold the fund and you must pay a load, it's better to pay the commission up front and be done with it. That way, if you have to cash out, you won't have to pay an exit fee. Why don't we like back-end loads? Most people panic when the fund declines in value, and they sell. Then they get double-whammied because they not only lose money, but they also must pay the back-end load.

The worst choice is the level load fund. Pay 1 percent a year over 20 years and you're paying the equivalent of a 20 percent front-end load. Why pay this annual charge when you can buy a fund for a maximum 8.5 percent front-end load or 6 percent back-end load?

Bargain-Basement Funds

Do it yourself, and you can save a bundle. There are more than 2,000 no-load funds that charge no commissions. You simply buy them directly from the mutual fund company rather than a broker. This way, you have 100 percent of your money invested from day one! Be advised, however, that even no-load funds have fees.

Remember, investing in no-load funds doesn't mean you won't get *any* help. Fund groups have service representatives that explain how the funds work, what they invest in, and whether they are the right type of investment for you. Some fund groups, such as Neuberger & Berman (800-877-9700), have in-house financial planners who provide help free of charge. Others, such as the SteinRoe Group of Funds (800-338-2550) and Fidelity Investments (800-544-8888), give you free ongoing professional advice if you have $50,000 to $100,000 to invest. In addition, all fund groups have easy-to-understand self-help booklets to help you get started.

No-load funds can save you money. If you invest $1,000 and pay a 5 percent commission, you've actually slashed your investment to $950. Suppose your mutual fund grows at a 10 percent annual return for 15 years. Your $1,000 investment will grow to $3,968.

Hot Tip
Watch for hidden charges in mutual funds. Regardless of whether you pay a commission or load, your fund may still have an annual 12b-1 fee that runs about one-half of one percent to one-quarter of one percent. Annual 12b-1 fees cover a fund's marketing and selling expenses.

Invest in a no-load fund at the same 10 percent annual return and your $1,000 grows to $4,177. You make an extra $209 for every grand you invest.

Not all no-load funds are alike. The 100 percent pure no-loads do not charge commissions or 12b-1 fees. By contrast, some no-load funds still sock it to you with a 12b-1 fee ranging from .25 percent to .75 percent. There also are low-load funds, which charge 3 percent commissions and 12b-1 fees. The 12b-1 fee doesn't sound like much, but paying a .5 percent 12 b-1 fee every year for 10 years is the same as paying a 5 percent front-end load.

Investment Value

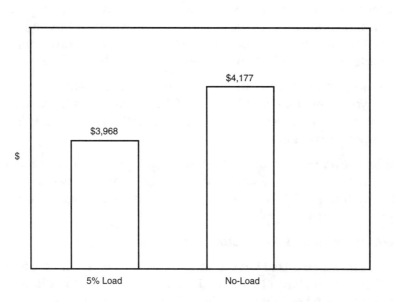

Earn more with no-load mutual funds. This chart compares the growth of $1,000 invested in funds with a 5% load and no load. The bars represent the value of each investment after 15 years if each returned 10% annually.

Sidelines

The 100% No-Load Mutual Fund Council publishes a directory of pure no-load mutual funds. Call 212-768-2477 for more information. The Mutual Fund Education Alliance also publishes a directory and self-help information on no-load and low-load mutual funds. For more information, call 816-471-1454. *The Handbook for No-Load Investors Fund* is another handy guide. Call 914-693-7420 for more information.

Save Through a Discount Broker

Another way you can buy no-load mutual funds is through a discount broker-age firm's *no-transaction fee (NTF) account*. You can invest in more than 300 no-load mutual funds by opening a brokerage account with companies such as Charles Schwab, Fidelity Brokerage, and Jack White & Company.

If you do it yourself, you can open a mutual fund account with a discount broker. You now can invest in over 300 funds from over 25 fund families with no transaction fees, or you can buy several hundred funds for as little as $28 per transaction.

Charles Schwab started the first one-stop shopping program a few years ago. Now Fidelity Brokerage and Jack White & Company are major players. There are 10 additional discount brokers who offer similar programs with a limited number of funds.

There are advantages to one-stop mutual fund shopping:

➤ It offers centralized buying and selling. This makes it easy to invest because you buy all your funds at one place. You don't have to call several fund groups to conduct business.

➤ Consolidated statements are made of all transactions and account balances. You get one statement with all account information on all your funds. You don't have to deal with sorting through several differ-ent statements each month. It makes it easy to keep records.

➤ You get a consolidated 1099 form at the end of the year that summarizes all capital gains and dividend income from all mutual fund investments in your account. (You get different statements for an IRA, SEP, UTMA, and so forth.) You have just one set of forms that cover the taxes due on your investments. You get one report on IRA or SEP retirement savings payouts, as well as other specialized accounts.

On the downside:

➤ You have to call your mutual fund group directly to get specific infor-mation about the fund holdings and portfolio positions.

➤ You get your financial reports more quickly when dealing directly with the mutual fund group.

➤ You do not receive the free educational material from the fund family if you do business through the discount broker.

➤ There's a limit to how many strong-performing funds you can buy with no transaction fee.

➤ There may be limits on trading funds. If you go over the limit, you can end up paying a transaction fee.

Here are some specifics on one-stop mutual fund shopping:

Charles Schwab OneSource (800-526-8600). Schwab currently offers more than 900 funds in its mutual fund marketplace. Three hundred of the funds are NTF. Schwab has flexible trading rules. You are allowed 15 free short-term trades per year. A short-term trade is considered under 90 days. If you do more than 15 short-term trades, you will pay transaction fees on your NTF funds. (On these 15 trades, there are no fees when you buy shares, but you still must pay the fees associated with selling the shares.) You can purchase a number of no-load funds if you pay a transaction fee. Depending on how much you invest, you pay a tiered commission rate.

Fidelity FundsNetwork (800-544-9697). Fidelity currently offers over 350 funds from more than 10 fund families on an NTF basis. There's a big advantage to this program: You can invest in Fidelity funds (except Magellan, New Millennium, and Select funds) at no load in tax-qualified accounts such as IRAs, 401(k)s, and profit-sharing plans. Outside the FundsNetwork, you may have to pay a small sales charge for certain Fidelity funds. Fidelity also has trading rules for NTF funds. You are not allowed to make more than five short-term trades per 12-month period. A short-term trade is considered a buy or a sell within six months of purchase. If you violate these rules, you will be charged a transaction fee. On non-NTF funds, Fidelity charges a commission based on the dollar amount of your investment.

Jack White & Company (800-323-3263). Jack White offers 500 funds from 52 fund families on an NTF basis and another 400 on a transaction-fee basis. The firm allows you five short-term trades within a rolling 12-month period. White defines a short-term trade as a buy and sell (round-trip) of the same fund within six months. Once you go over that limit you pay a fee.

Everyone Pays Certain Fees

Although you have control over whether you pay commissions, there are other charges for owning mutual funds that you're not likely to escape. You don't get a bill for these expenses and you don't have to write a check to pay for the charges. As mentioned earlier in the book, the fund deducts the expenses from the assets of the fund before it distributes dividends and interest income to shareholders. Everyone who has a mutual fund pays the following:

➤ **Fund management fees.** On average, you pay an annual charge of one-half of one percent in management fees. This covers the cost of hiring people, research, and investing your cash. Management fees may vary. Some funds charge more than one-half of one percent.

➤ **Administrative operational expenses.** This is a small charge for maintaining your account.

It's important to look at the fund's expense ratio, which shows total charges deducted each year from the fund assets. The expense ratio tells how much the fund deducts annually as a percentage of the fund's average net assets. These annual expenses represent the fund management fee and administrative operational expenses, including legal, accounting, and 12b-1 fees (usually stated separately from other operating fees). Excluded from the expense ratio are fund loads or redemption charges and brokerage costs.

Hot Tip
To make sure you're not missing any fees, ask your broker or fund representative to give you the fund's expense ratio. This tells you the total amount of your fund's earnings from dividends and interest income that is taken out to cover expenses, excluding front- or back-end commissions.

Stock funds typically have higher expense ratios than bond funds; international funds have higher expense ratios than U.S. funds because of the added cost of doing business overseas.

The average stock fund sports an expense ratio of 1.2 percent, and the average bond fund's expense ratio is .75 percent. By contrast, the average international stock and bond funds have expense ratios of 1.5 percent and 1.13 percent, respectively. Chapter 9 and the Chapters in Part III of this book present more on the subject of expense ratios and how to use them to help pick the right funds.

Compare Costs Before You Invest

Use this handy checklist to zero in on the cost of potential funds.

Compare Fund Fees

Fund Name	Load Percentage (if any)	Management Fee Percentage	Expense Ratio

Compare the fees for different funds before you choose which one to buy.

Load or No Load? That Is the Question

Ask yourself how much professional help is worth. If you invest $5,000, is it worth paying a broker or financial planner $250? What will that person do for you? Will your pro help you evaluate your goals and risk tolerance and find the best fund? Will he or she look at a number of different funds before recommending one? Will you get an explanation of the fund's investment objectives? A professional also should look at your tax situation if you are in a high tax bracket. If you answer positively on all these questions, the professional advice may be worth the price of admission, but if a broker or planner tries to talk you into a hot-performing fund that charges fat commissions, don't do it.

If you feel comfortable going it alone, the no-load funds are right for you. You make all your money work for you, not your stockbroker. Studies by Morningstar, Inc., a Chicago-based mutual fund service, show that you're not necessarily getting better performance from mutual funds that charge loads. For every well-performing load fund, there is a comparable no-load fund. Why not save and forgo paying someone?

Of course, you'll have to do some careful homework and read up on the funds if you shun the pros. Chapter 10 discusses some valuable resources you can tap.

The Least You Need to Know

➤ Load funds charge an average commission of 5 percent.

➤ All your money goes to work for you when you invest in no-load mutual funds.

➤ You should compare fund price tags before you invest. Check the load and expense ratio.

➤ Everyone pays a fund management fee of about one-half of one percent. It can be more or less depending on the size of the fund and the type of investments it owns.

Chapter 9

Secrets of Mutual Fund Shopping

In This Chapter

➤ How many mutual funds should you own?

➤ Deciphering important facts about how a fund invests

➤ Interpreting quarterly and annual fund reports

➤ Reading mutual fund tables in the newspapers

Do you routinely check the Sunday newspaper for sales on clothes and electronic gizmos? Smart shoppers do the same with mutual funds. Before you go to the shoe store for that year-end clearance sale, you first figure out how many pairs of shoes you need. Then you compare prices.

Picking a mutual fund works almost the same way. Before you shop, you figure out how many mutual funds you want to own. You also compare sales charges. Just as you don't want to overpay for that CD player, you don't want to overpay for a mutual fund either.

This chapter is a shopper's guide for mutual funds. You'll learn about the important documents you need to review before you invest in one or several mutual funds. Then, you'll discover a few quick ways to match what a fund costs and who the fund is for with your own personal needs.

How Many Funds Should You Own?

How many mutual funds should you own altogether? Just one? Or five or six?

One fund may not be enough. If you put all your money in one stock fund and the market tumbles, you could take a licking. That's why it's best to split the investment among at least two or three different kinds of funds.

Buy a baker's dozen and you have probably bought too many. Then you run the risk that the funds may own all or some of the same stocks. Not only that, but some of the stock fund managers could be buying the same stocks that your other mutual funds are selling. In fact, you actually could end up with the same investments that you started with, not to mention being overwhelmed with paperwork.

If you never have invested in anything other than bank accounts, it might be best to get your feet wet by first investing in a money fund. After you've accumulated a few thousand dollars, you can take a big step toward building your wealth by investing in a growth and income fund. Once you've gotten comfortable with your growth and income fund, you can begin splitting up the investment pie among a few types of funds.

The Magic Number

Five or six funds is a good number to have, but as you learned in Chapter 7, it's critical that you spread the investments among different types of funds. Your choices, depending on your investment comfort level and how long you intend to invest, probably should include the following:

➤ Aggressive growth or small company stock fund

➤ Growth fund

➤ Growth and income or balanced fund

➤ International stock fund

➤ Bond fund or income fund

➤ Short-term bond or money fund

When you own a wide variety of funds, it's easy to change your investment mix as financial conditions shift. Recall that younger investors can start building their nest eggs with stock funds. As they get older and build up a hefty stash, they may want to preserve what they have by reducing their risk.

Then they can put more into bond and money funds, and when they retire, they'll start looking for funds to give them income and low risk.

You also can split up your stock fund investments according to investment style. Chapter 4 discussed the difference between stock funds that invest for growth and funds that invest for value. It isn't a bad idea to own at least one fund that buys growth stocks and one fund that invests in undervalued stocks. These types of funds take turns outperforming each other, so if you own both of them, you have a better chance of having a winner.

Sidelines

Don't want to go through the hassle of owning several funds? Yes, Virginia, it is possible to own just one fund that does all the work for you. *Asset-allocation funds,* which are a hybrid type of balanced fund, invest both in U.S. and overseas stocks and bonds. Some also invest in large or small company stocks. With asset-allocation funds, you invest in a wide variety of securities under one roof. Asset-allocation fund managers usually make slight adjustments in their funds' mix of investments, based on their professional evaluation of how the stock and bond markets will perform.

Yuck! Read the Prospectus Before You Invest

Before you take one iota of your money and put it in a mutual fund, we sentence you to one of life's unpleasant little tasks—reading the fund's prospectus. Recall that this is the legal document that explains important information you need to know about the fund *before* you fork over your money. As a matter of fact, it is so important that a mutual fund company will not sell you a fund until it sends you this thing.

Don't worry. It's not quite as bad as it used to be—and we're here to help you along.

In the past, these things used to be in pure legalese. But now, along with the prospectus, funds typically send you a brochure that summarizes in plain English what's *in* the prospectus. Many mutual fund companies in mid-year 1995 were working on adding bar charts, making it much easier for you to see at a glance how a fund has performed over time. Some were issuing warnings on the risks right up front. But keep in mind that these summaries may be written, in part, by mutual fund companies' marketing departments, whose job is to get your business.

To get the full picture, you need to cover all bases.

PROFILE

New Horizons Fund

Investment Objective
- Long-term capital growth

Investment Strategy
- Invests primarily in the common stocks of small, fast-growing companies

Risk Profile
- Greater risk than a fund investing in established companies

Investor Profile
- Investors who seek aggressive growth of capital over the long term and who are willing to accept a high level of risk to achieve that goal

Fees and Charges
- No sales or redemption charges of any kind
- No 12b-1 marketing fees

Minimum Investment
- To open an account: $2,500
  To add to it: $100
- To open an IRA account: $1,000
  To add to it: $50
- To invest through Automatic Asset Builder*: $50 per month

*This periodic investment program cannot protect against loss in declining markets, nor assure a profit.

Source: T. Rowe Price Associates, Inc.

The profile section of a simplified prospectus.

TWENTY-FIVE LARGEST HOLDINGS

New Horizons Fund

March 31, 1995

Company	Percent of Net Assets
CUC International	3.6%
Paychex	3.3
Viacom	3.3
Xilinx	1.8
Foundation Health	1.6
Maxim Integrated Products	1.6
Synopsys	1.5
Oracle Systems	1.5
Sybase	1.5
SunGard Data Systems	1.4
Adobe Systems	1.2
Office Depot	1.2
Vishay Intertechnology	1.1
ADVO	1.1
Sbarro	1.0
Linear Technology	1.0
Catalina Marketing	0.9
Paging Network	0.9
United HealthCare	0.9
First Financial Management	0.9
General Nutrition	0.9
Sanifill	0.9
Franklin Quest	0.9
Broderbund Software	0.8
FIserv	0.8
Total	35.6%

This must be preceded or accompanied by a prospectus.

Source: T. Rowe Price Associates, Inc.

Twenty-five largest holdings.

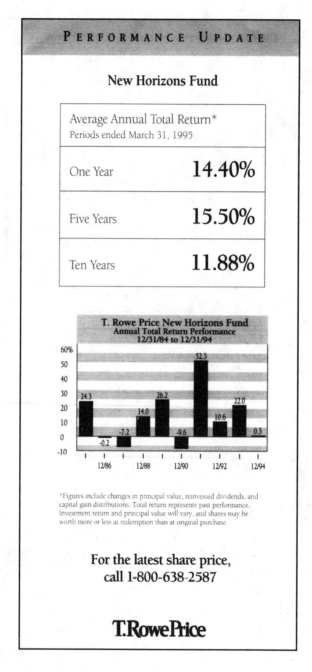

Source: *T. Rowe Price Associates, Inc.*

Performance update.

Mutual funds are making prospectuses user-friendly—easier to read and understand. In mid-1995, several mutual fund groups were testing a new profile prospectus intended to provide a clear and concise summary of key information that investors need to know about mutual funds, presented in a standarized format.

All prospectuses are required to present the same information to investors. Each prospectus has a table of contents to make your life a little easier (an example appears as an illustration). However, from one prospectus to another, the table of contents may have different labels for each section of the document.

It's a good idea to get a yellow marker or highlighter to underline the most important information. Read the entire prospectus and pay close attention to the following sections:

> **WHAT?**
>
> **Technobabble**
> The prospectus is a legal document that tells important information about the fund, such as investment objectives, risks, fees, and who runs the fund. The *annual* and *quarterly reports* are fund updates that tell you what the fund did and how it performed for the period.

TABLE OF CONTENTS

Source: Markman Capital Management.

An example prospectus Table of Contents.

➤ Look at the section covering the investment objectives of the fund. In the illustration, it is labeled "Investment Objectives." This tells how the fund intends to make money. It has a statement about the investment objectives and investment policy of the fund that you can match with your own investment objectives (*see Chapter 7*). Right off the bat you can tell the type of fund you are looking at. When you see words such as "maximum capital appreciation" or "capital growth," it's a sign that what you have in your hands is a prospectus for an aggressive growth fund. When you see "long-term growth," that's a sure sign the fund is a growth fund. "Growth with income as a secondary consideration" tells you it's a growth and income fund.

➤ Exactly how the fund invests is discussed in the section titled, "General Description," or something similar. In the illustration, it is labeled, "How We Invest."

If you read on a little further in this section, you likely will learn about how the fund invests in stocks or bonds. For stock funds, you may read that the fund invests in large company stocks that should raise their dividends. You might see something like, "The fund invests in companies that show a catalyst for change and should dominate their competitors." With bond funds, you may read something like, "The fund will invest 65 percent of its assets in U.S. government securities, but the fund may also invest in high-quality corporate bonds."

➤ The fund expenses section explains the fees charged by the fund. In the illustration, it is labeled, "Expense Information." You'll learn whether the fund has a load, or commission, or whether it's no-load, with no commission. You'll discover the fund's management fee, which is what the fund pays the investment advisor to manage the portfolio. You'll also learn whether the fund has a 12b-1 fee, covering sales and marketing expenses. Exchange fees, wire redemption processing fees, and other fees are disclosed in this section. If the mutual fund has a front-end load, a table shows the load based on the amount invested (see Table 9.1 for an example of this and other tables). Often, the fees are reduced if you invest a substantial amount, such as $50,000 to $100,000.

Another table shows the fees you pay, excluding any load, on a $1,000 investment, assuming that the fund earns 5 percent and you cash in the fund after 1 to 10 years.

With this information, you can compare the cost of different funds. For example, one stock fund may sock it to you with a total of $50 in fees after 10 years for every $1,000 you invest. Another may hit you up for $65. All other things being equal, cheaper is better.

Table 9.1 Example of a Fund Expense Information Table

Shareholder Transaction Expenses

Sales load imposed on purchases	None
Sales load imposed on reinvested dividends	None
Deferred (back-end load)	None
Exchange fee	None
Wire redemption processing fee	$15
Other redemption fees	None

Annual Fund Operation Expenses (as a percentage of average net assets)

Management fee*	0.95%
12b-1 fees	None
Other expenses	0.00%
Total fund operating expenses	0.95%

*The fund will voluntarily waive each of the fund's fees and expenses to the extent necessary to keep the total fund operating expenses no greater than 0.95%. Management fees paid by the fund do not include brokerage commissions, taxes, interest, or extraordinary expenses.

Example: You would pay the following expenses on a $1,000 investment, assuming a 5% annual return and redemption at the end of each time period:

1 Year	3 Years
$10	$30

➤ The fund's important financial information is listed. In the illustration, it is labeled "The Funds." This section helps you determine how much income you may receive for the fund, what expenses are taken out, and how the fund performed annually. You'll see a table that lists up to 10 years of very important year-by-year information, including the following:

How much was paid per share in distributions from dividends, interest, and capital gains

The fund's total return, year by year

The fund's yield, year by year

The fund's year-by-year expense ratio, the total percent of charges taken out of the fund, excluding the load

Look Out!
Even though the fees are listed in the prospectus, it pays to look at the fee table's footnotes. Often a new fund will absorb expenses, so you might see a big fat zero for expenses after 5 and 10 years, but you could wind up paying more in the future. This situation may be detailed only in a footnote.

Hot Tip
Examine the prospectus to determine whether the fund manager receives a bonus for doing a good job. Many investment companies reward a fund's portfolio manager for outperforming the market averages on similar funds. On the other hand, such a bonus could prompt the manager to take greater risks to show a more impressive return.

➤ The sections about risks and investment restrictions tell how the fund could lose money and what investments the fund cannot make. In the illustration, it is listed as "Risk and Other Considerations."

It should explain whether it uses risky investment tactics or borrows to invest in speculative stocks. You'll learn whether the fund is exposed to foreign currency risk or whether it invests in bonds issued by companies with poor credit ratings. You'll also find federally imposed restrictions, some of which we discussed earlier. Among them: A fund can't own more than 5 percent of assets in any one company.

➤ There also is information about the fund manager, the board of directors, and officers of the fund. In the illustration, it is listed as "Management of the Trust." It's important to know how long the fund manager has been at the helm. This part of the prospectus should describe the portfolio manager's experience and how he or she gets paid.

➤ The prospectus should offer information about how to buy and sell shares. In the illustration, this is listed under two sections: "How To Purchase Shares" and "How To Redeem Shares." These sections tell how to set up an account with the fund and explain whether the fund allows you to buy and sell shares by telephone or whether you must send notarized instructions, guaranteeing your signature. There also will be information on automatic investment programs and wire transfers.

➤ A section on shareholder services explains how to reinvest a fund's income, as well as provides information on automatic investment and withdrawal programs. Also covered is information on retirement savings plans such as IRAs, Keoghs, SEPs, and pension plans. In the illustration, it is listed as Shareholder Services.

➤ The distributions and tax information section tells you that the fund is required to distribute 98 percent of the income earned by the fund to its shareholders. There is other information about taxes in this section, as well as important information stating the dates and frequency that distributions are paid to shareholders. In the illustration, it is listed as Dividends, Distribution and Taxes.

There also are several other sections of the prospectus that present an auditor's report on the fund's financial condition and legal information regarding any lawsuits.

Read the Updates

Periodically, but at least once a year, you get progress reports on your fund, known respectively as quarterly and annual reports. You'll find out how the fund is doing and what stocks or bonds it owns. There are several important sections to the report:

➤ First, you get a message from the president of the fund recapping how the fund did in the past, including why the fund did or did not perform well, and the outlook for the future. For example, a stock fund's share value might have increased because interest rates are low and corporate profits are high and expected to increase in the future. A bond fund's share value might have declined a few bucks because interest rates rose and the value of the fund's long-term bonds dropped. The last part of the section tells shareholders what the fund expects in the future. Sometimes the news is good and sometimes it's bad. A fund's president may say that the near-term prospect for stocks isn't rosy due to the prolonged recession. Over the longer term, however, as business conditions improve, the outlook for the fund's investments might improve.

➤ A comparison of how the fund performed versus its peer group's average and the market averages is also provided. Aha! There is usually a bar chart that shows you how the fund did versus the stock or bond market average over several time periods. You may also learn how the fund performed against an average of similar types of funds. A stock fund's financial report will list the percentage of the fund's assets invested in different industries, such as financial services, natural resources, leisure, and technology. That way you can see in which type of business your hard-earned money is invested.

➤ You also get a list of all the fund's investments and how much is in each security. Usually, there is a list of the top 10 holdings. You might write down the names of the stocks or bonds and look them up in other reports. You can look up reports on the companies and learn about their revenues, expenses, profits, and business plans for the future. That way, you can get a feel for the types of investments a fund makes. If you see a refund that invests in AT&T, Coke, Walt Disney, Pepsi, IBM, Merck, and Exxon, you know you are investing in blue-chip stocks. By contrast, if you see a list of names such as Broderbund Software, LSI Logic, and Orbital Sciences, you are investing in small company stocks.

Look Out!
Make certain the fund sends the "Statement of Additional Information" along with the prospectus. This document might have some important details about risk and investment strategies that aren't in the prospectus. Check the "litigation" section of the prospectus to determine whether there are any current or pending legal actions against the fund.

➤ If you invest in a growth and income fund, income fund, or bond fund, there is information on how much dividend or interest income you received. If you invest in a small company stock fund or aggressive growth and growth funds, however, you may not see this information. The illustration of a quarterly report in this chapter, for example, shows just the fund's total return.

Check a Fund Every Day

You can learn even more frequently how a fund is doing. Merely check the mutual fund prices in your local newspaper's business section.

Every newspaper is a little different, but here's the way most work:

➤ To the far left, you'll see the name of the fund group or family. Underneath is the name of the fund—Pal Fund, in our example.

➤ Some tables do not list the investment objective of the fund; others do.

➤ Next is the "Buy" price of the fund, the sales price. If you are buying a no-load fund, the buy price equals the NAV. If you are buying a load fund, this is also known as the offering price you have to pay for the fund, including the load.

➤ Next is the "Sell" price, or the price of the fund minus the commission. Some tables list this as the fund's NAV.

To find out whether an investor pays a load, subtract the sell price from the buy price and divide by the buy price. For example, suppose the fund has a buy price of $21 and a sell price of $20. That means you pay a 1-buck commission on each share of the fund. One dollar divided by $20 means that you are paying a 5 percent front-end commission. Invest $1,000 in this fund, and the broker takes $50. You actually have $950 invested.

How can you tell whether the fund charges a 12b-1 fee? You will see footnotes after the fund's name, which refer to information that tells you about the fees and charges.

➤ Change means the number of cents the price of the fund went up or down, based on its buy price (the NAV) the previous day.

➤ Return is the total return of the fund. Some tables list the total return year-to-date, for one year, or as an annual average total return for three to five years.

Table 9.2 offers an example. You can buy Investors Friends' Pal Fund for $10 a share and there is no load. The fund went up 25 cents in value yesterday and this year-to-date the total return is 8 percent.

Table 9.2 Mutual Fund Newspaper Quotations

Fund	Buy	Sell	Change $	Return Year-to-Date %
Happy Growth Group's	$21	20	–.05	5.5
Giggle Fund				
Investors Friends'				
Pal Fund	$10	10	.25	8

5 Important Questions You Need to Answer

Now that you know what to look for in the prospectus and the mutual fund tables in your newspaper, make certain you've nailed down answers to these questions about a particular fund and are satisfied with those answers before you buy shares:

1. Is this a fund that invests only in stocks? Or is it a lower-risk fund that invests in both stocks and bonds? Does it invest both in this country and abroad?

2. What's this going to cost me? Is there a load? If so, how much?

3. Do I want income from this fund? If so, what's the yield over the past several years?

4. Do I want to see my money grow over the years? If so, what's the fund's total return over at least the last five or 10 years?

5. How many years has the portfolio manager been at the helm of the funds? What's his or her background?

The Least You Need to Know

➤ Read the fund's prospectus to learn the objective and risks of the fund before you invest.

➤ The prospectus' fee table shows how much the fund costs.

➤ It's generally best to own at least five or six funds, but no more than a dozen.

Chapter 10

SECOND OPINION? FINE. YOUR INVESTMENT STINKS AND YOU'RE UGLY...

Seeking a Second Opinion

In This Chapter

➤ Where to get a second opinion

➤ The best sources of information on funds

➤ The best newsletters for ongoing advice

You already have picked up many of the tools you need to select a mutual fund on your own, but let's face it, you're no idiot. Why venture into totally unknown territory when the experts already have been there? It pays to see what the pros have to say about the mutual fund strategy you're considering.

There are several excellent mutual fund newsletters you can read before you take the plunge. Sure, the subscriptions can be expensive. Maybe you can get some friends to chip in, or find them in the library. A financial newsletter can be like a good friend when it comes to making an investment decision.

This chapter takes a look at some important sources of mutual fund information. You'll learn what reports can help you pick funds and keep you up to date.

Check with the Experts

Wow... You're close to being a mutual fund expert by now. It's always a good idea to get a second opinion, though—particularly if it's free.

At the library, you can find several excellent sources of information on mutual funds.

The mutual fund reports, which we list in this chapter, all provide you with sufficient information to make a knowledgeable investment decision.

Second Opinion Mutual Fund Reporting Services

Most reports give you all the important ingredients you need to pick a fund. No matter what report you look at, you get the following information:

Look Out!
Not all mutual fund reporting services say the same things about the same funds. They all measure things a little differently. Look for a consensus of opinion from the reports or just stick with one report over the long haul rather than following one report for a month or so and then switching to another.

➤ Past performance. This covers both total return and yield.

➤ Investment objectives.

➤ How funds rank in rate of return over fixed periods of time relative to other funds. Funds are ranked against all funds, as well as against funds with the same investment objective.

➤ Risk ratings.

➤ How much funds have made in total return when the market has gone up and how much they have lost when the market has gone down.

➤ Funds' fees, expenses, amounts needed to invest, addresses, and toll-free phone numbers.

SShhh...Go to the Library

Take a friend to the library. It's always good to have some help until you get the hang of looking up things.

You'll know when you're near the mutual fund section. You'll see a long table with a group of binders filed neatly in rows. The following reports, which can help with your investment decisions, also provide the funds' toll-free numbers, addresses, and investment minimums.

➤ **Morningstar Mutual Funds.** These reports are published every other week and cover over 1,200 stock and bond funds. You get a comprehensive one-page report on each fund, including ratings of each. Funds rated with four or five stars offer the best returns with the least amount of risk for funds in their category. In addition, there's a list of each fund's 25 largest stock or bond holdings. You get a written evaluation of each fund plus information on how the fund does in down markets in relation to similar funds.

➤ **The Value Line Mutual Fund Survey.** This report provides information on more than 2,000 funds by investment objective. Funds are rated by number. One is best, five is worst. In addition, Value Line shows how the fund did in both up and down markets and lists each fund's holdings. There also is a written evaluation on each fund that may help you invest.

➤ **The Standard & Poor's/Lipper Mutual Fund Profiles.** This report covers approximately 1,000 mutual funds. You get a half-page profile on each. There are ratings on how the fund did in up and down markets compared with similar funds, lists of each fund's five largest holdings, and year-by-year returns.

➤ **The CDA/Wiesenberger Mutual Funds Panorama**. This annual directory covers the 10-year performance of more than 3,400 funds. There are no write-ups on the funds, but the beginning of the directory offers information on how to invest in mutual funds.

Tips on Using Mutual Fund Reports

The best bet is to stick with one service. We like Morningstar and Value Line the best. They are more comprehensive than the other two. If you want quick information, the Standard & Poor's/Lipper report and the CDA/Wiesenbeger Panorama will do.

You should pay particular attention to the following key items when examining either the Morningstar or Value Line mutual fund services:

➤ The written commentary on the funds, which tells how the fund has been managed. You will learn where the fund manager is investing shareholders' hard-earned cash.

➤ Annual rates of return over 1, 3, 5, and 10 years. This makes it easy to compare funds.

103

➤ How the fund performed in good and bad markets.

➤ The beta value of a stock fund, which, as you learned in Chapter 5, tells how volatile the fund is compared with the overall stock market.

➤ An overall risk rating of the fund.

➤ The duration of the bond fund. This, as you'll recall from Chapter 5, tells how much the fund will change in value if interest rates rise or fall.

Check Out a Good Newsletter

You also might want to see what professional money managers say about your mutual funds. There are several top-notch mutual fund newsletters available. Mutual fund newsletters make recommendations and track how their picks do over the years. The newsletters cost from $50 to $125 annually. That's not exactly small potatoes. Get a couple of friends to chip in for a subscription and have the report sent to your home each month. Then again, there's always the library.

Find the Right Newsletter

There's another good reason to subscribe to a mutual fund newsletter. Those annual subscriptions, which average $100 annually, can be tax-deductible.

True, you might have a rough time picking from the dozens of mutual fund newsletters on the market. Some use market timing indicators to recommend moves between stock funds and money funds. When using one of these as a guide, keep in mind that you could be making several trades a year if you follow its advice. Others take a longer-term perspective. They recommend funds with long-term track records. These reports also give asset allocation advice on how to slice the investment pie. Some newsletters specialize in sector funds or funds that invest in specific industries; others track fund groups such as Fidelity, Vanguard, and T. Rowe Price.

Before you subscribe, it's important to find out what the newsletter is all about. Many libraries carry the *Hulbert Financial Digest*. This is a monthly report and directory that tracks the performance of several hundred newsletters so you can see how well the advisors' fund picks have panned out. If the library doesn't carry this important report, you can purchase a trial subscription to the *Hulbert Financial Digest* for $35 (703-683-5905). Get your friends to chip in with you.

Here are some tips on choosing a newsletter that's right for you:

➤ Request a free sample copy of the report before you subscribe.

➤ See whether the newsletter's investment philosophy is the same as yours. If you're a conservative investor, for example, you don't want to use a newsletter recommending a high-risk market timing strategy.

Hot Tip
You can call and get a free copy of most mutual fund newsletters. That way you can tell whether the report is right for you.

➤ Determine whether the report includes news and information about the financial markets and the mutual fund industry.

➤ Make sure the newsletter gives advice on how to diversify based on your tolerance for risk, age, and investment goals.

➤ Compare the newsletter's returns versus the stock and bond market averages rather than relying on the newsletter's hype about its record.

➤ Consider a newsletter that has tracked mutual funds through at least one bull market and one bear market over the past three to five years.

➤ Subscribe only to a newsletter you can understand. Some are very technical and written for sophisticated traders. Others are written for the average investor.

➤ Call the newsletter before you subscribe. Find out whether the editor or investment advisor will answer any question you may have during the year.

Our Favorite Newsletters

Don't expect to hit a home run when you follow mutual fund newsletter advice. The good ones help you set up a solid long-term investment program. They're not interested in picking hot funds for those who want to get rich quick. At best, a good newsletter recommends well-managed stock and bond funds. It fills you in on the latest news and suggests ways to diversify your investments.

There are several newsletters published by some of the most highly respected mutual fund financial advisors in the country. Our favorites include the following:

➤ **No-Load Fund Investor** (510-254-9017). Sheldon Jacobs puts together a great monthly report. He evaluates no-load funds and tells which funds are best for the short or long term. Jacobs also calls the reader's attention to any important changes. The newsletter has a section on useful news. One section tracks the performance of no-load funds, plus there are recommended investment mixes or *portfolios*. Jacobs also publishes *The Handbook For No-Load Investors*, a directory of no-load fund track records.

➤ **The Mutual Fund Letter** (800-326-6941). This newsletter, by Gerald Perritt, Ph.D., is good for those who want to learn more about the ins and outs of investing and how the financial markets work. The newsletter focuses on no-load mutual funds that you can buy and hold for your lifetime. Perritt also publishes *The Mutual Fund Encyclopedia*, a directory of no-load mutual funds.

➤ **Mutual Fund Forecaster** (800-327-6720). We can't help taking a peek at Norm Fosback's newsletter every month. This report publishes estimates of how more than 1,000 mutual funds will perform over the next one and five years. Fosback has an excellent track record in predicting the future performance of the stock markets, so his mutual fund recommendations will give you an idea of where a fund stands.

➤ **No-Load Fund Analyst** (415-989-8513). If you're looking for low-risk funds to invest in for the long haul, consider this report. Publisher Ken Gregory shows how to split up your investments and invest for the long term. The report tracks funds that buy undervalued stocks. Gregory interviews fund managers monthly. He also keeps close tabs on international funds.

➤ **Mutual Fund Monthly** (800-426-6502). Every month, this newsletter interviews a lead portfolio manager. You learn what the pros think about the outlook for the stock and bond markets. Mike Stolper, publisher, recommends both load and no-load mutual funds. He also tells how to split up your fund investments, based on your tolerance for risk.

There are some other well-read mutual fund newsletters that recommend specific funds and model portfolios. They include *IBC/Donoghue's Moneyletter* (508-881-2800), *Funds Net Insight* (617-369-2000), *The Independent Advisor for Vanguard Investors*, and *The Independent T. Rowe Price Advisor* (800-435-3372).

Newsletters for the Really Brave Investor

Aggressive mutual fund investors check out several newsletters for advice about when to buy and sell funds to profit from changing share prices. These newsletters use market timing techniques, which are computer-generated buy-and-sell signals based on economic information. Most of these newsletters have investor hotline phone numbers. You can call and get the latest recommendations toll-free. Some of the best include the following:

➤ **Stockmarket Cycles** (707-579-8444). This newsletter looks at market trends and cycles and tells you when to switch between stock funds and money funds.

➤ **InvesTech Mutual Fund Advisor** (406-862-7777). This report looks at a number of economic and fund performance trends and recommends how much you should invest in stock funds, bond funds, and other types of mutual funds.

➤ **Growth Fund Guide** (605-341-1971) tells when to move into money funds, conservative stock funds, or aggressive stock funds depending on the newsletter's forecast of the stock market.

➤ **NoLoad Fund X** (415-986-7979). This newsletter recommends that you always invest in the funds with the best current performance. The idea is that if a fund is doing well today, it will do well tomorrow.

➤ **Fabian's Investment Resource** (800-950-8765). This newsletter uses market timing indicators so that you can switch between money funds and stock funds.

➤ **Jay Schabacker's Mutual Fund Investing** (800-777-5005). This newsletter recommends when to change the mix of funds based on the newsletter's forecast of the stock and bond markets.

When you invest with these newsletters, be prepared to stay on top of your investments and do some fund switching. Each month, the reports will tell you what to do. You also have to keep good records of your transactions, because trading funds can have tax implications.

Make the Best Use of a Second Opinion

There are two ways to use an investment newsletter. You can see what the newsletters recommend, then do your own homework. Not all funds are for all investors, so a blanket newsletter recommendation isn't always the best advice. Look at how the funds invest, their portfolio holdings, and their performance. There may be other funds that best fit your needs.

The other way is to pick funds and look to the newsletters to validate your selections. If a newsletter doesn't report on a fund you like, you shouldn't necessarily avoid that fund. The newsletters often cover just a small group of funds. Meanwhile, if a fund also is picked by the newsletter, there's a good chance you're on the right track.

The Least You Need to Know

➤ It never hurts to see what the experts say about the mutual funds you're interested in.

➤ *Morningstar Mutual Funds* and *The Value Line Mutual Fund Survey* are two of the best resources. They're available at most public libraries.

➤ Get your friends to chip in with you for a subscription to a mutual fund newsletter. You can use a newsletter as a source of information on the best funds to invest in, or you can use the newsletter to confirm your opinion of a fund you've already checked out.

Opening Your Mutual Fund Account

In This Chapter

➤ Filling out the forms

➤ Different ways to send money to the fund

➤ Avoiding the most common errors

➤ Adding on new services

It may *seem* like a simple case of fill-in-the-blanks, but fill out incorrect information on a mutual fund application, and you could find yourself in a mess and waste your time straightening out records. The way you fill out the application form also can make a difference in taxes you or your loved ones pay, as well as who inherits this impressive mix of investments you're so diligently working to develop.

It's easy to tell that lawyers had a major hand in developing mutual fund forms. They don't always ask the most easy-to-understand questions.

That's why this chapter is here. It will help put those questions on your mutual fund forms into simple language.

You'll learn about the types of forms you need to transfer an account or move an IRA to a new mutual fund family. You'll also find out where people get into the most trouble on their mutual fund forms—and what steps you can take to avoid it. If you get the basic forms filled out right, you're on your way!

Stuff to Fill Out

It may not be the sexiest part of investing in mutual funds, but it sure is important. You can't get started in a mutual fund until you obtain and fill out all the right forms.

You'll need the following:

➤ The prospectus and application form for the fund or funds you're interested in. You need to read the prospectus before you invest to determine whether the fund is right for you.

➤ An IRA application form, if you're starting an IRA (a retirement savings account).

➤ An IRA transfer form—if you're moving your IRA from one fund group or family to another.

With a broker or discount broker, often you just can walk into the nearest office and get all this. Are you buying funds directly from your mutual fund company? Just call the mutual fund group's toll-free number and ask for what you need.

The Fund's Application Form

Do not use this Application for IRA or Keogh Plans.
For special forms or if you need assistance completing this
Application, please call us at 1-800-782-6620.

Please print all items except signatures.

Please use blue or black ink only.

1 Account registration   *Please choose one.*

☐ **Individual or Joint* account**

_____
Owner's name (first, middle initial, last)

and _____
Joint owner's name (first, middle initial, last)

* *Joint tenancy with right of survivorship presumed, unless otherwise indicated.*

OR
☐ **Uniform Gifts/Transfers to Minors (UGMA/UTMA)**

_____ as custodian for
Custodian's name (one custodian only)

_____ under the
Minor's name (first, middle initial, last/one minor only)

_____ Uniform Gifts/Transfers to Minors Act
State

OR
☐ **Trust***

_____ as trustee(s) of
Trustee(s) name

_____ for the benefit of
Name of trust agreement

_____ dated _____
Beneficiary's name (if applicable)   Date of trust agreement

* *For Trust Accounts, a multipurpose certification form may be required to authorize redemptions and add privileges. Please call 1-800-782-6620 to determine if a multipurpose certification form is required.*

OR
☐ **Corporation, Partnership, Estate or Other Entity***

_____
Name of Corporation, Partnership, Estate or Other Entity

_____
Type of Entity

* *For Corporations, Partnerships, Estates or Other Entities, a multipurpose certification form is required to authorize redemptions and add privileges. If you have any questions please call Business Advisors at 1-800-842-3829.*

2 Social Security number or Taxpayer Identification number

This section must be completed to open your account.

☐☐☐ ☐☐ ☐☐☐☐☐

* **Individual accounts** specify the Social Security number of the owner.
* **Joint accounts** specify the Social Security number of the first named owner.
* **Uniform Gifts/Transfers to Minors accounts** specify minor's Social Security number.
* **Corporations, Partnerships, Estates, Other Entities or Trust Accounts** specify the Taxpayer Identification number or Social Security number of the legal entity or organization that will report income and/or gains resulting from your investments in the Fund.

3 Address

_____
Street or P.O. Box   Apt. No.

_____
City   State   Zip Code

(___) _____   (___) _____
Daytime phone number   Evening phone number

☐ If you are not a U.S. citizen, please check box and specify country of legal residence.

_____
Country of legal residence

4 Investment method   *Minimum investment: $2,500*

☐ **Check**
Enclosed is a check payable to   **Family of Funds.**
Neither initial nor subsequent investments should be made by third party check.

for $ _____
Amount

OR
☐ **Wire**
You may request your bank to wire your investment to
The Bank of New York, DDA #8900051906,

* your account is in a commercial bank that is a member of the Federal Reserve System, or
* your account is in any bank that has a correspondent bank in New York City.
The wire must include your account registration, address and Social Security number or Taxpayer Identification number. It should also indicate that you are opening a new account.

_____
Funds were wired on   Date

for $ _____ into account _____
Amount   Account number

5 Dividend and capital gains distribution options

Unless you choose an option below, all dividends and capital gains will be reinvested.

☐ Pay all dividends and capital gains by check.

☐ Pay all dividends by check and reinvest all capital gains.

Please turn over to complete this application.

The first page of an example mutual fund application form.

The following is a list of things you're likely to encounter on a mutual fund application form and a step-by-step guide on how to respond:

1. The Account Registration, or who owns the account, is no Mickey Mouse subject.

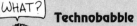

Technobabble

Joint tenancy with right of survivorship is a method of ownership that permits two people to own a fund equally. With *tenancy in common,* ownership of a fund is divided between two or more people.

Technobabble

The Uniform Gift To Minors or *Uniform Transfer To Minors (UTMA)* permits you to invest in your child's name and save on taxes.

The most common way to own a mutual fund is to put it in your name or to own it jointly with another person, such as your spouse. Officially known as joint tenancy with right of survivorship, this method of ownership permits you both to own the fund equally. If one person dies, your partner automatically gets your share of the whole investment.

Don't get joint tenancy with right of survivorship, confused with tenancy in common. With tenancy in common, ownership is divided between two or more people. If one person dies, that person's portion of the investment goes to his or her heirs based on the deceased's will. By contrast, with joint tenancy with right of survivorship, the property automatically goes to the joint owner.

You certainly don't *want* to pay any more taxes to Uncle Sam—particularly if you're already in a high tax bracket. Meanwhile, if you're taking the wise step of investing in a mutual fund for a minor child, there could be a way for you to cut your IRS bill. Just pay particular attention to the application line, Uniform Gift To Minors or Uniform Transfer To Minors account.

This portion of the application allows you to pay taxes based on your child's tax bracket once the child is over 14. If a child is under age 14, the first $650 of income is not taxed. The next $650 is taxed at the child's tax rate of 15 percent. Investment income over $1,300 is taxed at the parents' rate. However, if the child is 14 years or older, all the investment income is taxed at his or her rate, which usually is 15 percent.

Assuming your child is in a lower tax bracket than you are, this could be to your advantage tax-wise. However, you might want to consult with your tax advisor to be certain.

These accounts always are established under the child's name and under the child's social security number. If you decide to complete this portion of the application, list yourself as the custodian. This means you're in charge of the account until the child becomes an adult, generally age 21. Then it's transferred automatically.

You also can register the account so that a trust owns the mutual fund.

A business may also own the mutual fund. If this is the case, you have to fill out the business name and explain the nature of work it does.

Hot Tip
When you invest in a money fund or a bond fund, you may get check writing privileges. You just have to check the right box on the application form, then sign your name, much like you do when you open a bank checking account. Be advised, however, that when you write a check from your bond fund, it is a taxable event. Bond fund shares are sold in your account to cover the dollar amount of the check.

2. You have to write down your social security number or taxpayer identification number. That's, unfortunately, so the IRS can keep track of the income you earn from the fund.

3. Next fill in your name and address. If you're not a U.S. citizen, you have to check the box and list the country in which you are a legal citizen.

4. Send the fund a check for the amount of your investment along with your application. You also can have your bank send the money to the fund electronically by what is called a *wire transfer* by checking the Wire box or a similarly named box. You'll probably pay a fee for this, but because fund prices change daily, it could make a difference. Why? When you pay electronically, you can invest the same day. Pay by check, and it can take three to five business days before the money is invested.

5. Next, check the box indicating whether you'd rather have any income reinvested in new shares of the fund or sent to you by check.

6   Automatic Asset

Permits you to purchase shares automatically, on a regular basis by electronically transferring a specified dollar amount from your bank account to your   mutual fund account. Your bank must be a member of the Automated Clearing House (ACH).

☐ Yes, you want   Automatic Asset

You must attach a voided check to this Application in the area designated next to section 7. Money will be transferred only from the bank account indicated on the voided check.

Check the day of the month most convenient for you to have your bank account debited. You can invest once or twice a month.

☐ 1st   ☐ 15th   ☐ Both Dates

Amount you would like to invest each time: $ _____
                                              Minimum $100

This service is governed by Prospectus provisions as well as by Automated Clearing House rules and is established solely for your convenience. This service may be terminated or modified at any time without notice by Dreyfus or the Transfer Agent.

7   Teleservice privileges

TeleTransfer
Permits electronic transfer of money between your designated bank account and your   mutual fund account by telephone.

Wire redemption
Permits proceeds of redemption requests initiated by wire, telephone or letter to be transmitted by Fed wire to your designated Federal Reserve Member Bank.

☐ Yes, you want *TeleTransfer* and wire redemption privileges.

You must attach a voided check to this Application. Money will be wired or transferred only to the bank account indicated on the voided check.

☐ No, you do not want *TeleTransfer* and wire redemption privileges.

Fund exchanges
Permits exchanges by telephone among certain   fund accounts with the same registration.

☐ Yes, you want fund exchanges by telephone.

☐ No, you do not want fund exchanges by telephone.

The Fund will require its Transfer Agent to employ reasonable procedures, such as requiring a form of personal identification, to confirm that instructions relayed by telephone are genuine and, if it does not follow procedures, it may be liable for any losses due to unauthorized or fraudulent instructions.

(vertical text along left margin: PLEASE ATTACH VOIDED CHECK HERE.)

8   Optional information   We are required by the National Association of Securities Dealers, Inc. to request this information.

Owner's occupation _____   Owner's date of birth _____

Employer's name _____

Employer's address _____

Joint owner's occupation _____   Joint owner's date of birth _____

Joint owner's employer's name _____

Joint owner's employer's address _____

9   Signature and Taxpayer Identification number certification

By signing below, you certify and agree that:

- You have full authority and are of legal age to buy and redeem shares (custodians certify they are duly authorized to act on behalf of the investors).
- You have received a current Fund Prospectus and agree to its terms.
- Any representations accompanying this application are in conformity with state regulatory requirements.
- TSSG (the "Transfer Agent"),   any subsidiary and/or any of their directors, trustees, employees and agents will not be liable for any claims, losses or expenses (including legal fees) for acting on any instructions or inquiries believed genuine.
- You appoint the Transfer Agent, and any successor named at a later time in the Prospectus of the Fund(s) in which you have invested, as the Transfer Agent for receipt of all dividends and distributions.
- **You understand that mutual fund shares are not deposits or obligations of, or guaranteed or endorsed by, any bank or the U.S. Government, and are not federally insured by the Federal Deposit Insurance Corporation, the Federal Reserve Board or any other agency. The net asset value of funds of this type will fluctuate from time to time.**

Taxpayer Identification Number Certification

The IRS requires all taxpayers to write their Social Security number or Taxpayer Identification number in Section 2 of this Application, and sign this Certification. Failure by a non-exempt taxpayer to give us the correct Social Security number or Taxpayer Identification number will result in withholding of 31% of all taxable dividends paid to your account and/or withholding of certain other payments to you (referred to as "backup withholding").

Under penalties of perjury, you certify that:

1. The Social Security or Taxpayer Identification number on this Application is correct; and
2. You are not subject to backup withholding because a) you are exempt from backup withholding; b) you have not been notified by the Internal Revenue Service that you are subject to backup withholding; or c) the IRS has notified you that you are no longer subject to backup withholding.

Cross out item 2 above if you have been notified by the IRS that you are currently subject to backup withholding because of underreporting dividends on your tax return.

PLEASE SIGN HERE:

X _____
Owner or Custodian

X _____
Joint owner (if any). Corporate officer, Partner, Trustee, etc.

_____   _____
Date   Title

Mailing instructions

Please mail the Application to:

You will receive a confirmation showing your Fund account number, dollar amount received, shares purchased and price paid per share.

This Application must be filed with the Transfer Agent before any redemption request can be honored.

The second page of an example mutual fund application form.

6. In the Automatic Asset section, you can set up an automatic investment plan by checking the "yes" box in this section. Check this if you want to invest a regular amount each month to be deducted from a designated bank account. If you select this option, attach a canceled or voided check to your application. Your check has a series of numbers at the bottom that the fund uses to instruct the bank to send money automatically to your mutual fund. Be sure to note the time of the month you want the money automatically invested.

7. There are two parts to the Teleservice Privileges section, requiring you to indicate whether you want the convenience of phoning a fund group and telling it to move, buy, or sell shares of your fund. You must check "yes" or "no" to two separate questions.

   The first part queries whether you'd like your fund group to transfer or wire money between the fund and your bank account. Check "yes" and you must attach a voided or canceled check. Funds automatically will be directed to the bank account number on your check. The second, which refers to *fund exchanges,* asks whether you'd like the capability of phoning in orders to transfer money between funds in the family.

8. It's not necessary to fill in the Optimal Information section. This part just seeks voluntary information that fund groups use to get an idea of what kind of people invest in their funds.

9. Finally, put your John Hancock on the bottom line—the Signature and Taxpayer Identification Certification section. Your signature verifies that you're legally able to invest in the fund and you're the lucky person who gets to pay taxes on the fund's earnings.

Send the application in along with your check. It can take five business days or more before the account is opened, due to the U.S. mail.

Sidelines

Application forms can be for one specific fund or for a number of funds. That's why some application forms have a section for you to check off the specific funds you want and the amount you want to invest in each.

IRA Applications

When you open an IRA account with a fund, you have to fill out another form similar to the fund application, that is, the IRA application. In filling out this form:

1. First, list your name, social security number, and birthdate in the proper boxes and blanks.

2. Next, write your address and check whether you're a U.S. citizen, resident alien (foreigner), or nonresident alien (foreigner). You must include both day and evening telephone numbers where you can be reached.

3. Check whether this is your regular IRA contribution, and for which year, or a *rollover IRA*. If it's a rollover from an employer-sponsored plan, you also need to indicate whether your check is enclosed or your employer is sending it.

Look Out!

IRS rules for transferring IRAs are technical. Be certain to check with your accountant or a retirement account specialist at the IRS (800-829-1040) before you make a move. Keep good records of whom you spoke with and when.

4. If you are transferring funds from another institution, check the box that tells how you're making the IRA transfer. Is it a custodial transfer, in which you are authorizing the fund group to obtain your funds from another company or financial institution? Are you taking advantage of a once-a-year 60-day window Uncle Sam gives you to take your IRA funds and physically redeposit them elsewhere without incurring a federal penalty?

5. Next, designate how much of your IRA you want in each fund.

6. You also must state who will inherit your IRA as the *main beneficiary*. Yes, you can have more than one beneficiary. Just list the names of the person or persons who should receive the money, what proportion you want each to have, and how each person is related to you (son, daughter, friend, relative). These are your *primary beneficiaries*. You also should select someone to receive the IRA if the primary beneficiaries pass away. These are known as *contingent beneficiaries*.

Look Out!

Be sure to call your fund group and notify them if you change your address. Otherwise, money will be sent to the wrong place and it could take a few extra days for the U.S. mail to forward the check.

IRA Transfers

Suppose you want to move your IRA from your bank (or another kind of account such as another fund account or a stock investment account) to a mutual fund. You must fill out the IRA transfer form that you get with your new IRA application. This application asks you to identify the name, address, and telephone number of the institution that has your IRA, your old IRA account number, and which investments you want to transfer.

Signing Up for New Services

Each month, a growing number of investors faithfully send a check to their mutual funds. They suddenly realize that they could save time and a few dollars in postage by signing up for the *automatic investment plan*. Others who like to squirrel away money in a bank account until they have a large chunk to invest may suddenly decide to have the money wired electronically to their funds. Still others occasionally might want to have money wired out of their mutual funds into their checking accounts to pay large bills.

Oops! All these people already opened their accounts.

With most investment companies, though, it's never too late to change the details of the account. You just call the fund and ask for a *shareholder services form* (see the example in this chapter) to complete. This form covers several services you might not have signed up for when you initially opened your account.

Use the shareholder services form to make changes to certain options for your fund:

1. The first section of this form asks for your social security number or employer identification number, name, address, and telephone number. (Be sure to check the box at the end of this section if this is a new address. Otherwise, important investment information and records may not get forwarded to your new digs.)

2. The next section asks how you prefer to do business with the fund family. Do you want the fund to accept telephone instructions from you or other registered account owners? Do you want the option of mailing written instructions without having to get your signature guaranteed by a notary public? If not, check the box that says "In Writing Only" or something similar. This establishes that all written instructions must have a signature guarantee.

1 Shareholder Information.

Taxpayer Identification Number or Employer Identification Number:

or

Social Security Number   ID Number

Name

Address

City   State   Zip Code

Is this a new address? ☐ yes ☐ no

2 How do you want to do business? *Please check the service you want.*

☐ **By Telephone and In Writing.**
I want the fund to accept telephone instructions from me or any other registered owner by telephone or in writing without a signature guarantee to redeem or convert shares

OR

☐ **In Writing Only.**
I want the fund to accept only written instructions signed by me and all registered owners to redeem or convert shares and to require that signatures be guaranteed on redemption requests.

If no box is checked, the fund assumes you want to do business with the fund in writing only.

3 Optional Services. *Please check the service you want.*

☐ **Wire and Electronic Funds Transfer of Redemption Proceeds.**
Check this if you want to have redemption proceeds sent to your bank by wire or electronic funds transfer. Be sure to check the section "By Telephone and In Writing" in Section 2 above.

☐ **Telephone Investments.**
If you want to be able to make telephone investments, check this box to authorize us to draw from your bank account. The minimum is $50.
Please attach a preprinted voided check below.

☐ **Automatic Monthly Investments.**
When do you want your automatic monthly investments to begin?

Month   Day   Year

_____ $ _____
Fund name and account number if known   Minimum $50.

_____ $ _____
Fund name and account number if known   Minimum $50.

Please note: If the date selected falls on a weekend or holiday, investments will be made the next business day. Be sure to attach a voided check below.

☐ **Telephone Access Code.**
Please check if you want to apply for your personal and confidential access code.

Attach Voided Check Here.

4 Signatures

* I authorize the fund to act upon my instructions for the services I have checked on this form.

* I certify under penalties of perjury, that the tax identification number shown on this form is correct and that I am not currently under IRS notification that part of my dividend and interest income is to be withheld as a result of my failure to report all dividend and interest income on my tax return.

* If signing for a personal trust, all trustees must sign with the word trustee following each signature. This form must be accompanied by a copy of the portion of the trust document that names the trustees only if you haven't previously provided this document to the investment company.

* If signing on behalf of a bank (or bank acting as a trustee/custodian), please provide the signature of the office at the level of senior vice president or above.

All registered owners of the accounts listed under the taxpayer identification number shown on this form must sign below.

X_____   _____
Signature of owner, custodian, or trustee   Date

X_____   _____

X_____   _____

Note: In electing to do business by telephone or in writing without a signature guarantee, you have indemnified the fund and affiliated companies from liability for any loss you may sustain. The fund will employ reasonable procedures to confirm that instructions communicated by telephone are genuine. These procedures include personal identification, recording of telephone conversations, and providing written confirmation of each transaction. A failure on the fund's part to employ such procedures may subject us to liability for any loss due to unauthorized or fraudulent instructions.

Example of shareholder services form.

3. The third section asks whether you want to add "wire and electronic funds transfer of redemption proceeds" to your account. Choose this option if you want to sell shares of your fund and have the money wired electronically to your bank account.

Most funds also enable you to specify whether to authorize the fund to withdraw money automatically from your checking account and invest it based on your telephone instructions. Always attach a voided check when you choose either this box or the Automatic Monthly Investment box, which instructs the fund to withdraw funds electronically from your checking account and invest them in your fund.

Hot Tip
If you plan to use your mutual fund investments to pay for your child's college education, or if you think you might pay off the mortgage one day, sign up for the fund's "wire and electronic funds transfer of redemption proceeds." You can have money transferred to your bank account the same day you need the money.

4. If you want a telephone access code number to track your account status 24 hours a day, check the box for this option. You may not see this option on all mutual fund services forms.

5. The last part of the form asks for your signature. It's necessary to enable the fund to carry out your instructions.

If Things Can Go Wrong, They Will

Before you send in the forms along with your check, double-check your paperwork. It's easy to write down the wrong number, check the wrong box, or overlook certain questions entirely. It's a good idea to fill out the form and let it sit for a day. Then go back to it. Make photocopies of all the completed forms.

In addition to writing in the wrong numbers or transposing them, here are a number of common errors to avoid:

➤ **Registering the fund incorrectly.** Registration determines who pays taxes on your mutual fund and who eventually inherits your fortune when you go to the above and beyond. For example, if you plan to open a joint account, make certain you remember to include the name of the joint owner!

➤ **Forgetting the zip code in the section that includes your address.** Do this and your mail could wind up back at your fund group.

➤ **Forgetting to check the box asking whether you want income to be mailed to you in the form of a check.** If you don't check this, your income automatically gets reinvested in your mutual fund!

➤ **Checking the wrong funds when the application applies to several different funds.** Use a ruler when you go over this section. Sometimes the fund names are in small type. There are so many funds nowadays that many have similar names!

The Least You Need to Know

➤ Your application is a record of how you want your money invested.

➤ You can register your fund in your name or share ownership in a joint account or an account set up as tenants in common.

➤ You must fill out a special IRA form to open a retirement savings account for your mutual fund investment.

➤ If you want to move your IRA, you must fill out a transfer form.

➤ Double-check your paperwork. It's easy to write in a wrong number, check a wrong box, or overlook an important section of your application.

Part 3
Zoning In on the Picks

This section of the book puts the different types of mutual funds under a microscope. You'll see exactly how money market mutual funds, bond mutual funds, and stock mutual funds stack up against each other and against similar investments. You'll learn how risky each type of fund is and get some idea of which funds are among the most well-managed. You'll also learn which funds to avoid like the plague.

Earlier chapters introduced you to the basics of mutual fund investing. The next chapters get into the nitty-gritty.

Chapter 12

Money Market Funds Versus Insured Bank Accounts

In This Chapter

➤ How do money funds work?

➤ You can have a high-yielding checking account

➤ Other advantages of money funds

Money market mutual funds are the closest thing to a bank account that you'll find in the mutual fund world. They are *not* FDIC-insured bank accounts, however. You'll discover the differences in this chapter.

On the plus side, a money market mutual fund, money market fund, or money fund, as this animal frequently is called, generally allows you to write checks against the balance in the account. Money market funds also often pay higher yields than similar bank accounts.

This chapter takes a close look at money market mutual funds. It examines exactly how risky money funds are, whether they are for you, and the best ways to use them in your investment game plan.

Money Funds: The Least Risky

Whether you're starting out in the investment world, looking for a temporary parking place for some cash, or seeking to diversify your investment mix, money funds are a low-risk starting place.

How can money funds be so low-risk if they are not FDIC-insured?

As you learned in Chapter 3, money funds invest in very short-term debt instruments. These debt obligations include short-term government notes and bills with maturities of up to 90 days, jumbo certificates of deposit of financially strong banks, and commercial paper issued by corporations. When you loan money for such a short time to financially strong organizations, there's little chance your money fund won't be paid back.

Even more importantly, money market mutual funds have one unique low-risk advantage over all other mutual funds. Whatever money you put into a fund, you should get back. Each share you buy is kept at $1. Remember, no mutual funds are risk-free! There have been several instances of a money market fund's share price having dropped below $1. However, in most cases, though not all, the funds have dipped into their own coffers to bring the price back to $1 a share.

In effect, this means that exactly what you invest in a money market fund is exactly what you should get back. On top of that, a money fund pays you interest income. You can take this interest in cash or plow it back into the fund and buy more shares.

Sidelines

Money funds actually are the babies of the mutual fund industry. They only began in the early 1970s as investors looked for low-risk ways to take advantage of high rates. Bank rates, at the time, were restricted by federal law. By the early 1980s, when short-term interest rates hit double digits, even the most conservative investors began withdrawing money from CDs and putting it into money funds, which dangled check-writing privileges and lower minimum required opening investments than many bank CDs. By year-end 1994, money market funds represented $611 billion of the more than $2 trillion in mutual fund assets, according to the Investment Company Institute, Washington, D.C.

Money market funds are subject to several SEC investment rules aimed at preventing the portfolio managers from making risky investments, including the following:

➤ Recall from our discussion in Chapter 3 that long-term bonds can lose money when interest rates rise. You're unlikely to encounter this problem with money market funds. The average maturity of a money market fund is limited to 90 days.

➤ As with other mutual funds, a money fund may invest no more than 5 percent of its assets in any one company or government agency that raises money by issuing bonds. In fact, the maximum most funds invest in any one issuer is about 2 to 3 percent. This way, if one investment does happen to perform poorly, it should not dramatically affect the value of the entire fund.

➤ If a money fund invests in corporate I.O.U.s, also known as *commercial paper,* it's required that 95 percent of those corporate I.O.U.s have the highest ratings by Standard and Poor's and Moody's. Top-rated commercial paper carries an A1 rating by Standard and Poor's and a P1 rating by Moody's.

➤ The SEC also has ordered money market mutual funds to limit their investments in derivatives.

> **WHAT?**
>
> **Technobabble**
> *Derivatives* are securities used by sophisticated traders whose performance is "derived," at least in part, from the underlying security. These newfangled investments, which often are used to manage risk, tend to be variable-rate instruments manufactured by brokerage houses. Derivatives, which can be particularly sensitive to interest rate swings, took a beating in 1994, when interest rates headed up and bond prices dropped.

Different Strokes for Different Folks

Assuming you can live without FDIC insurance, there are four types of money market mutual funds that you can buy either from a broker or directly from an investment company. The one you choose depends on your investment comfort level and tax situation:

➤ **U.S. Treasury-only money funds.** These funds invest only in good old Treasury bills or T-bills, which are short-term I.O.U.s of the U.S.

Treasury. The funds typically pay the lowest yields, but are considered the least risky investments. Treasury securities are backed against default by the "full faith and credit" of Uncle Sam. U.S. Treasury-only money funds have one added advantage. In most states, their income is exempt from state and local taxes.

➤ **Government-only money funds.** These funds typically limit their investments to T-bills and U.S. government securities, and are considered among the least risky money funds. They're backed by the U.S. government. The government agency bonds that these funds invest in include those of the Federal Home Loan Mortgage Corporation, the Small Business Administration, the Student Loan Marketing Association, the Farm Credit Program, and the Federal Home Loan Bank. Government-only funds typically pay higher yields than U.S. Treasury-only funds. Funds investing in U.S. Treasury obligations carry the added advantage of paying no state taxes on income earned from these investments.

➤ **General-purpose money funds.** These funds invest in government and corporate loans as well as bank CDs. They generally pay the highest yields. Money market fund yields tend to be highest when investments are concentrated in short-term corporate loans, called commercial paper, and Eurodollar deposits in foreign branches of U.S. banks.

➤ **Tax-free money funds.** Look for the words "tax-free" in the name or investment objective. With these funds, which invest in short-term loans to state governments, cities, and towns, your income is sheltered from federal taxes. Recall that there also are single-state money funds that shelter income from federal *and* state income taxes.

Watch Those Money Fund Critters

Even though money market mutual funds are considered the least risky mutual fund investments, one of our cardinal rules is always to read the investment objective section of the prospectus. That tells what kind of money market investments the fund owns.

The investments also are listed in the fund's financial statements. There are several different kinds of money market investments, and it's important to understand what each is. Here are the types you're likely to see in a general-purpose money fund:

➤ **Certificates of Deposit (CDs).** These are CDs issued by the largest banks in the country. The money fund manager and his or her research staff looks at the credit ratings of the banks to invest in only the financially strongest institutions.

➤ **Yankee Dollar CDs.** These CDs are issued by some of the largest foreign banks in the world that have offices in the United States. They often yield a little more than U.S. bank CDs.

➤ **Eurodollar CDs.** These are CDs issued by U.S. banks that have branches in other countries. The CDs are in U.S. dollars and tend to have higher yields than domestic CDs.

➤ **Bankers Acceptances (BAs).** These are short-term loans to companies that export worldwide. Bankers Acceptances actually are secured by the goods that are to be sold.

➤ **Commercial Paper (CP).** These are short-term loans to large corporations.

➤ **Repurchase Agreements.** These generally are overnight loans to banks secured by U.S. Treasury securities.

➤ **Treasury-bills.** These are short-term debt obligations issued by what most consider the most solid creditor of all: the United States Treasury.

Technobabble
Yankee Dollar CDs are certificates of deposit issued by U.S.-based branches of foreign banks. *Eurodollar CDs* represent deposits in U.S. bank branches overseas. *Bankers Acceptances* are short-term loans used to finance exports. *Repurchase agreements* are collateralized overnight loans to banks.

WHAT?

A Checking Account to Boot

You don't need much cash to invest in a money fund. Generally $500 to $1,000 is enough to start. After that you can invest as little as $50 at a time.

With a money fund, you receive checks, which frequently must be written in denominations of at least $500. Your money earns interest income until the check clears. So, for example, if you write a check on a Monday and it doesn't clear your account until Thursday, your money accumulates interest Monday through Wednesday.

If you plan on using your money fund checking account, it's best to limit your purchases to large-ticket items. It can take as much as a week for the money fund check to clear through the banking system. You earn extra interest until that happens, but the checks that come with money funds typically are not written directly on funds deposited in a bank and might take longer to clear than a traditional bank check.

We Repeat: Money Funds Are Not Bank Accounts!

Yes, money market funds are relatively low-risk, but they're not FDIC-insured! Nor are they guaranteed by banks. It's easy to get confused about this because of all the "money market" talk you hear in the media.

Bertha Biddle sure had her mind muddled. Bertha invested in a money fund when she opened an account with a mutual fund family at a branch of Bank Onus. She got a checkbook in the mail along with some investment slips and put it next to her bank checkbook on her dresser. When she got statements from both her money fund and the bank, she noticed she earned more interest in her money fund, so she quickly canceled her bank checking account.

After all, the money fund sales rep said her money fund was invested in CDs. She needn't worry.

Bertha, who has invested only in banks her whole life, didn't realize that her money market mutual fund was not FDIC-insured.

Even though the investments in Bertha's money market mutual fund might have been in CDs, those CD investments are in larger amounts than the FDIC might insure—plus, the fund had some other investments that were not CDs.

Look Out!
Unlike with a bank deposit, the federal government does not guarantee money that's invested in a money fund to $100,000!

Bertha was a little upset by the fact that the money fund was not insured. But she didn't cash it out. Fortunately, her neighbor Jack, a retired stockbroker, sat down with her and together they went over her money fund holdings. Bertha learned that the money fund invested in Treasury bills and CDs from some of the largest and least risky banks in the country. So, she decided to keep the fund—it was a low-risk investment. However, she realizes that there is always a possibility that the money fund can drop below $1 per share.

A Word About Bank Accounts...

In 1982, a federal law was passed that permitted banks to offer a *money market deposit account (MMDA)* or *money market account.* This FDIC-insured savings account at a bank actually was designed to compete directly with money market funds.

Bank MMDA yields are lower than those of money market funds because of banks' higher operating costs. Part of that cost is for the FDIC insurance, which bank accounts offer and money market funds do not.

If you opt for FDIC insurance at a bank, remember that you are protected to only $100,000 per person.

Sidelines

Although money market mutual funds average higher yields than bank money market accounts, you can get a relatively high rate of return on an FDIC-insured money market account if you shop around. 100 Highest Yields, North Palm Beach, Florida (800-327-7717) tracks the highest yields on money market accounts and CDs nationwide. Some banks may also pay higher yields for larger balances or if you have another account at the institution.

Picking a Money Fund

➤ **Read the fund's prospectus and annual reports before you invest.** Get the facts!

➤ **Look at the type of investments the fund makes.** The safest funds invest only in U.S. Treasury securities, but these funds may pay lower yields. The highest yielding funds frequently invest in commercial paper, Yankee CDs, and Eurodollar CDs.

➤ **Check the fund's expenses, listed in the prospectus as the expense ratio.** The average money fund has an expense ratio of .5 percent, but there are many lower than that.

➤ **Check the quality of the securities held by the fund.** If you're a conservative investor, stick with funds that hold issues that receive the highest quality ratings by Standard and Poor's or Moody's.

MONEY MARKET PERFORMANCE
TOP 100 PREFERRED MONEY MARKET FUNDS

As of July 26, 1995

TOP 40 TAXABLE RETAIL MONEY FUNDS

Fund	7-Day	30-Day	Avg. Mat.	Phone Number
Strong Money Market Fund	6.29%	6.33%	50	(800) 368-3863
OLDE Premium Plus MM Series	6.17	6.24	35	(800) 872-6533
Dreyfus BASIC MMF	6.11	6.18	77	(800) 548-2412
Dreyfus BASIC US Govt MMF	6.05	6.14	49	(800) 548-2412
Aetna Money Market Fund/Cl A	6.04	6.12	46	(800) 367-7732
Fremont Money Market Fund	5.93	5.97	57	(800) 548-4539
Westcore Money Market Fund	5.90	5.97	23	(800) 392-2673
Capitol Treas Reserves/Class A	5.84	5.96	56	(800) 321-7854
Vanguard MMR/Prime Port	5.83	5.92	50	(800) 662-7447
Schwab Value Advantage MF	5.81	5.84	64	(800) 435-4000
Fidelity Spartan MMF	5.80	5.84	51	(800) 544-8888
Marshall MMF/Class A	5.79	5.86	68	(800) 245-0242
Seven Seas Series MMF/Cl A	5.79	5.85	57	(800) 548-2868
USAA Money Market Fund	5.77	5.83	61	(800) 382-8722
Dean Witter/Active Assets MT	5.76	5.79	61	(800) 869-3863
United Services Govt Secs Svgs	5.76	5.81	71	(800) 873-8637
Vanguard MMR/Federal Port	5.76	5.82	43	(800) 662-7447
Evergreen Money Mkt Trust/Cl Y	5.71	5.76	62	(800) 235-0064
Fidelity Daily Income Trust	5.71	5.75	51	(800) 544-8888
RBB MMP/Sansom Street Class	5.71	5.82	44	(800) 888-9723
Westcore Treasury MMF	5.71	5.78	15	(800) 392-2673
Fidelity Cash Reserves	5.70	5.75	56	(800) 544-8888
Fidelity Spartan US Govt MMF	5.70	5.77	30	(800) 544-8888
Kemper MMF/Govt Secs Port	5.70	5.75	44	(800) 621-1148
Kemper MMF/Money Market Prt	5.69	5.75	35	(800) 621-1148
T Rowe Price Summit Cash Res	5.69	5.77	68	(800) 638-5660
Dean Witter/Liquid Asset Fund	5.67	5.72	65	(800) 869-3863
Northern Money Market Fund	5.65	5.72	51	(800) 338-1579
RIMCO Monument Prime MMF	5.65	5.72	76	(800) 245-0242
Woodward Money Market Fund	5.64	5.74	55	(800) 272-4742
The Rodney Square Fund/MMP	5.63	5.68	42	(800) 336-9970
Warburg,Pincus Cash Reserve	5.63	5.68	43	(800) 888-9723
Prudential/Command Money Fund	5.62	5.66	58	(800) 225-1852
Benham Prime Money Market	5.61	5.69	68	(800) 472-3389
Inventor Prime Obligs MMF/A	5.61	5.65	45	(800) 342-5734
Compass Capital Cash Res Fund	5.60	5.66	77	(800) 342-5734
Nations Prime Fund/Investor A	5.60	5.66	59	(800) 321-7854
Scout Money Market Fund Prime	5.60	5.66	26	(800) 422-2766
Woodward Government Fund	5.60	5.69	75	(800) 272-4742
Northern US Govt MMF	5.59	5.69	49	(800) 338-1579

TOP 10 TREASURY-ONLY RETAIL MONEY FUNDS

Fund	7-Day	30-Day	Avg. Mat.	Phone Number
Gabelli US Treasury MMF	5.55%	5.57%	39	(800) 422-3554
Vanguard MMR/US Treasury Port	5.46	5.55	44	(800) 662-7447
Fidelity Spartan US Treas MMF	5.41	5.47	64	(800) 544-8888
Capital Preservation Fund	5.35	5.37	46	(800) 472-3389
CMA Treasury Fund	5.31	5.33	83	(800) 262-4636
T Rowe Price US Treasury MF	5.30	5.31	58	(800) 638-5660
Neuberger & Berman Govt MF	5.29	5.29	62	(800) 877-9700
Schwab US Treasury Money Fund	5.29	5.32	70	(800) 435-4000
Dreyfus 100% US Treas MMF	5.27	5.29	60	(800) 548-2412
Alex Brown Cash Res/Treas Ser	5.23	5.25	48	(800) 553-8080

TOP 25 TAX-FREE GENERAL PURPOSE MONEY FUNDS

Fund	7-Day	30-Day	Avg. Mat.	Phone Number
Dreyfus BASIC Muni MM Portf	4.00%	3.82%	67	(800) 548-2412
Strong Municipal MMF	3.91	3.93	59	(800) 368-3863
Calvert T-F Reserves/MMP	3.77	3.71	43	(800) 368-2748
1784 Tax Free MMF	3.72	3.70	86	(800) 342-5734
Kemper MMF/Tax-Exempt Port	3.71	3.66	37	(800) 621-1148
Evergreen Tax-Exempt MMF/Cl Y	3.69	3.62	25	(800) 235-0064
Vanguard Muni Bond/MMP	3.58	3.59	60	(800) 662-7447
USAA Tax Exempt MMF	3.57	3.56	70	(800) 382-8722
Fidelity Spartan Municipal MF	3.53	3.54	66	(800) 544-8888
Centennial Tax-Exempt Trust	3.50	3.42	58	(800) 525-7048
Northern Municipal MMF	3.46	3.44	58	(800) 338-1579
General Municipal MMF	3.45	3.27	75	(800) 548-2412
Daily T-F Income Fund/Class A	3.42	3.30	37	(800) 676-6779
UST Master S-T Tax-Exempt	3.42	3.47	43	(800) 367-6075
Evergreen Tax-Exempt MMF/Cl A	3.37	3.35	25	(800) 235-0064
The Rodney Square T-E Fund	3.37	3.36	32	(800) 336-9970
Fidelity Tax-Exempt MM Trust	3.35	3.38	66	(800) 544-8888
Victory Tax-Free MMF	3.35	3.32	55	(614) 899-4600
Cash Equivalent Fund/T-E Port	3.33	3.27	36	(800) 621-1148
Lehman Bros/Muni Income Fund	3.33	3.29	74	(800) 851-313
Woodward Tax-Exempt MMF	3.32	3.23	49	(800) 272-4742
CMA Tax-Exempt Money Fund	3.28	3.21	40	(800) 262-4636
Federated/T-F Instr Tr/Invmt Cl	3.28	3.30	63	(800) 245-0242
Smith Barney Municipal MMF	3.28	3.24	64	(800) 451-2010
Dean Witter/Active Assets T-F Tr	3.27	3.19	49	(800) 869-3863

TOP 25 TAX-FREE STATE SPECIFIC MONEY FUNDS

Fund	7-Day	30-Day	Avg. Mat.	Phone Number
Salomon Bros NY Municipal MMF	3.55%	3.50%	44	(800) 725-6666
Vanguard PA Tax-Free/MMP	3.54	3.45	34	(800) 662-7447
Fidelity Spartan NJ Muni MMP	3.50	3.51	71	(800) 544-8888
USAA Tax Exempt CA MMF	3.50	3.51	75	(800) 382-8722
Fidelity Spartan CA Muni MMP	3.48	3.46	70	(800) 544-8888
Vanguard NJ Tax-Free/MMP	3.48	3.43	51	(800) 662-7447
Vanguard CA Tax-Free/MMP	3.45	3.41	54	(800) 662-7447
Fidelity OH Municipal MMP	3.38	3.32	61	(800) 544-8888
Fidelity Spartan FL Muni MMP	3.38	3.40	47	(800) 544-8888
Fidelity Spartan PA Muni MMP	3.37	3.38	64	(800) 544-8888
Calvert T-F Reserves/CA MMP	3.36	3.34	14	(800) 368-2748
Fidelity Spartan NY Muni MMP	3.34	3.32	59	(800) 544-8888
Benham CA Municipal MMF	3.30	3.23	42	(800) 472-3389
Pacific Horizon Shrs CA T-E MM	3.27	3.18	46	(800) 367-6075
Midwest OH Tax-Free Money	3.26	3.25	67	(800) 543-8721
Landmark NY Tax-Free Reserves	3.23	3.20	74	(800) 331-1792
Fidelity CT Municipal MMP	3.21	3.20	60	(800) 544-8888
Fidelity MI Municipal MMP	3.21	3.26	52	(800) 544-8888
Stagecoach CA Tax-Free MMF	3.20	3.09	40	(800) 552-9612
Benham CA Tax-Free MMF	3.19	3.16	43	(800) 472-3389
Fidelity NJ Tax-Free/MMP	3.18	3.19	73	(800) 544-8888
Fidelity NY Tax-Free/MMP	3.18	3.17	58	(800) 544-8888
CMA NC Municipal Money Fund	3.15	3.15	38	(800) 262-4636
Dreyfus CT Municipal MMF	3.14	3.15	60	(800) 548-2412
Dreyfus NY Tax-Exempt MMF	3.14	3.03	61	(800) 548-2412

Note: *Funds are ranked by 7-day compound yield. Fund yields are 7-day and 30-day compounded. Restricted funds, funds with greater than $25,000 minimum initial investments, and funds with assets of less than $200 million are excluded. All funds have been contacted with respect to "risky" derivatives. All funds have indicated they do not hold such securities. However, this is still no guarantee that the fund is immune from problems due to market conditions.*

Source: IBC's Investing for Income

The best deals in money funds.

➤ **Check the average maturity of the fund.** The lower the average maturity, the greater chance you have to earn higher yields when interest rates rise. The fund manager will be rolling over the money into higher-yielding securities.

➤ **Watch out for hidden charges.** There may be charges for check writing privileges, exchanges, or even to withdraw money.

➤ **Look for the check minimums.** These can range from $100 to $500.

➤ **Seek funds with wire transfer capabilities.** This enables you to move money electronically to and from your bank account and money fund.

The Least You Need to Know

➤ Money market funds are the least risky mutual funds.

➤ Money market funds generally allow check writing, but check the minimum check amount.

➤ You can park money in a money market fund, then switch into other funds with just a toll-free call to your fund group.

➤ Money market funds are not FDIC-insured.

➤ Money market funds typically pay higher yields than bank money market accounts or interest checking accounts.

Chapter 13

Investing for Income: Bond Funds

In This Chapter

➤ Who should invest in a bond fund?

➤ How do bond funds differ from bonds?

➤ The unique risks of bond funds and how to reduce 'em

➤ Managing your bond funds when interest rates rise and bond prices fall

Why would anybody want or need a bond mutual fund? After all, you already learned about bond critters in Chapter 3 and about the least risky mutual funds, money market mutual funds, in Chapter 12.

What more could bond mutual funds possibly bring to the table? You'd be surprised. Nearly two-thirds of all mutual fund assets are in bond mutual funds or money market funds. Stock mutual funds carry more risk than money market or bond funds and don't generate interest income. Investors in bond funds get regular income with less risk than with stock funds.

In this chapter you'll learn whether you're better off buying a bond mutual fund or the bond critter itself. Although these guys both are in the same family, they are completely different animals. There are different risks and rewards to each. Read on, and you'll also learn some low-risk ways to make money from a bond mutual fund.

Who Should Have One?

Now we're getting into the investment big-time. Invest in a bond fund, and you're investing in a riskier investment than a money market fund, in exchange for the longer-term potential of greater income and earnings. Before you even consider investing in a bond mutual fund—or any of the other mutual funds we're going to talk about in this chapter and beyond, for that matter—you must pull out some of the earlier pencil work you did. You need to re-examine the game plan you worked out in Chapter 2, listing your time horizons. Then, peek at the results of your risk tolerance quiz in Chapter 6. Remember, you want money in a bond fund only if you can stomach seeing your original investment or principal fluctuate. Your bond mutual fund investment also should be just one facet of your long-range plan.

There are good reasons to invest in a bond mutual fund that could pay off handsomely down the road. First, you need to nail down whether these reasons fit your own personal needs and game plan. Then you need to figure out specifically how bond mutual funds fit the plan.

How do you determine whether a bond mutual fund is a good candidate for your mix of investments?

Retirees Make Good Candidates

Bond mutual funds are particularly attractive for retirees or those who need regular income for living expenses. They typically pay regular income, generally monthly. In fact, our very own Mom Lavine has a U.S. Treasury securities bond fund. She gets about $400 monthly from the fund—more than she ever would get from a CD.

Mom Lavine loves this investment because it combines advantages of both the bond critter and mutual funds, all of which we discussed in Chapter 3. Remember? With a mutual fund you can do the following:

➤ **Invest as little as $500 to $1,000 to get started.** Standalone bond critters can require minimum investments as high as $25,000! Most require a $1,000 to $5,000 initial investment.

➤ **Get professional management.** Our Mom sure would hate to have to pick out each individual bond investment on her own.

➤ **Become an owner of many investments.** Mom Lavine, for example, is well-diversified with her bond fund. It won't be the end of the world if one bond in her fund does poorly. In addition, she doesn't have to worry about the U.S. government going out of business.

➤ **Switch funds or get cash with just a toll-free phone call to your fund group.** Mom Lavine knows that if she needs the cash, she can get it quickly.

Do You Want to Diversify Your Investment Mix?

Bond funds are great for diversifying your investments. You don't want to put 100 percent of your money in the stock market, because you can't tolerate the idea of losing a large chunk of your precious money. At least, that's the way we look at it! Because bond funds don't always move in the same direction as stock funds, a bond fund might perform well if a stock fund loses.

Are You in a High-Income Tax Bracket?

Tax-free bond funds are great for wealthier taxpayers in the 28 to 39.6 percent tax brackets. Because you avoid paying taxes, you can sometimes profit more in tax-free bond fund investments than in higher-risk taxable investments. Chapter 14 explores tax-free bond funds in more depth and discusses who should own them.

Bond Funds Versus Bonds

Although bond mutual funds add a number of advantages to bond critters themselves, there also are some major differences between these two investments. In fact, these differences are so significant it pays to think twice before determining which you really want.

You might be pretty surprised to hear this, but an investment actually is *less risky* if it is invested directly in a U.S. Treasury bond and held to maturity than it is in a bond mutual fund. With a bond, the U.S. Treasury promises to pay your interest and to repay your principal at the end of the term. That's a guarantee from the nation's top creditor!

Yes, it's true that a bond mutual fund might include U.S. Treasury bonds. Nevertheless, you get no such principal guarantee with a mutual fund. Unlike Treasury bond critters themselves, Treasury bond mutual funds have no specific terms to maturity. Rather, these funds have an average maturity based on the maturity values of the bonds held (more on this in Chapter 14). The fund manager always is buying new bonds to replenish those that mature. As a result, the bond fund never matures.

We've been comparing Treasury bonds with Treasury bond funds. It works the same way with corporate bonds, however, as you will learn later in the chapter. Corporate bonds have an extra layer of risk compared to Treasury bonds. Because you invest in a corporation, not the U.S. government, you run the risk that the corporation's business can sour and the company can have a tough time repaying the principal and/or paying interest on its bonds.

Recall from Chapter 3 that bond prices move in opposite directions of interest rates. When interest rates rise, bonds prices fall. A bond mutual fund investor who sells at the wrong time can take a licking.

Sidelines

Unlike a bond fund, a bond has a specific term to maturity and guarantees you'll get your principal back at the end of the term or when the bond is called. A bond fund carries no such guarantee because the fund manager always is buying and selling bonds. On the other hand, bond funds pay interest monthly, but most bonds pay interest every six months.

Like other mutual funds, bond funds often come with checks, giving you instant access to your cash. It's generally best to avoid using them, however. Once you cash a check on your bond fund, you're selling shares and could be required to pay taxes on your profits!

There's one more reason for selecting bonds over bond funds. There are no expenses when you buy a Treasury bond. You can buy a bond at no charge from the nearest Federal Reserve Bank or by calling the Bureau of Public Debt (202-874-4000). With a bond fund, you're paying an ongoing management fee. There also might be a load, or commission. In addition, you could shell out a 12b-1 fee for sales and marketing expenses.

Of course, not all bonds are free and clear of fees either. Although Uncle Sam cuts you a break on that score, you do get zapped if you buy a corporate or municipal bond from a broker. Then, you pay a commission that already is taken out of the price you pay for the bond.

Bond Funds for Reliable Income

The great thing about bond mutual funds is they pay investors periodic interest income from the bonds in which they invest. To refresh your memory, bonds are loans to governments or corporations. The bond issuer, who is the borrower, agrees to pay the bondholder, or lender, interest on the loan and to repay the lender on a specific date.

Many bond issuers guarantee the loan with collateral. Bond fund portfolio managers look for this collateral when they invest in bonds. This way, if the company issuing the bond goes under, a mutual fund likely gets at least something to resell and make back some of the losses.

Chapter 14 discusses the different kinds of bond funds and their investments in more detail.

Hot Tip
Bond funds generally pay higher yields than long-term federally insured bank CDs. Why? With a bank CD, you're guaranteed to get your original investment back at maturity. With a bond fund, you're not. So, the bond fund pays you more interest for taking on more risk.

Bonds Versus Bond Funds—More to Consider

There are other issues to look at when considering to invest in individual bonds or bond funds:

➤ Municipal and corporate bonds can be called after a period of years (typically ten). You can invest thinking you will earn high stated rates of interest for 20 years only to learn the bond issuer is redeeming the bonds after ten years when interest rates have declined. You get your principal back, but you're forced to reinvest the money at lower rates. This is referred to as call risk.

➤ If you buy corporate or municipal bonds, you should own at least 10 to 20 securities in case one or two bonds decline in price as a result of bad news about the bond issuer. This means you probably need at least $50,000 to invest in individual corporate or municipal bond funds to diversify properly.

➤ Individual bonds pay higher rates of interest than bond funds. Why? There are no annual expenses deducted from individual bonds. By contrast, you pay an annual management fee, possibly a 12b-1 fee, and operational expenses for corporate or municipal bond funds.

Low-Risk Ways to Pad Your Pocket

Here are three strategies that potentially could boost your total return, while limiting some of the risk associated with bond funds:

1. If you are a low-risk-minded investor who is used to investing in CDs and money funds, you may be able to earn 1 percent more income by investing in *short-term bond funds*, which you learned a little about in Chapter 4, but will explore further in Chapter 14. These funds have longer average maturities than money funds—typically up to 3 years, compared with a money market fund average maturity of 90 days. You can earn 6.5 percent in a short-term bond fund, compared with 5.5 percent in a money fund or one-year CD during the beginning of 1995. Don't forget, though, by extending your maturity, you are taking in a bit more risk.

2. Bond fund investors can make more money with little more risk by investing in U.S. government GNMA bond funds, rather than funds that invest directly in U.S. Treasury bonds. GNMA bonds, which you'll learn more about in the next chapter, are backed by the "full faith and credit" of Uncle Sam against default.

3. Invest in corporate bond funds that invest in highly secure bonds rated single A to triple A by Standard & Poor's and Moody's. In mid-year 1995, corporate bond funds investing in highly secure bonds, based on SEC yields, earned 7.5 to 8 percent interest income. Of course, your total return can vary based on interest rates and business conditions.

Unique Risks and How to Reduce 'Em!

Unfortunately, there's no free lunch when you invest in bond funds.

Before you invest in a bond mutual fund, it is important to do your homework so that you don't get burned by this investment. Here's what to watch for:

➤ A company that issues a bond to your mutual fund could default on its interest and principal payments.

Solution: Stick with bond funds that invest only in the strongest companies and governments. Fortunately, two major companies, Standard and Poor's and Moody's, rate bond issuers' strength.

Bonds rated single A to triple A are lowest in risk, as illustrated in Table 13.1. Anything below that, and you could run into trouble. Bond funds that invest in below A-rated securities pay higher yields because there is a greater risk that the companies could default on their interest and/or principal payments.

Look Out!
As a general rule of thumb, the higher the yield on a bond fund, the greater the risk that you could lose money. You don't get something for nothing! Invest in a bond fund that yields more than 10 percent today and you might pay for it later. The fund manager could be gambling on risky bonds.

➤ As you learned in Chapter 3, when interest rates rise, bond prices fall. Unfortunately, many investors learned this the hard way in 1994. The longer the maturity of the bond, the greater the risk of a price decline. (Chapter 14 shows how much the price of your bond fund changes when interest rates change.)

Solution: Limit your losses by investing in short- or intermediate-term bond funds. The longer the term, the greater the risk.

➤ The steady income from your bond fund may not be enough down the road to cover the rising prices of groceries, gas, utilities, and clothes. This is known as inflation.

Solution: Invest regularly in your bond fund. You buy more shares when bond rates are higher, so you get more income over the years.

Table 13.1 Bond Credit Ratings

Standard & Poor's	Moody's	Meaning
AAA	Aaa	Highest quality bonds. Unquestioned credit quality.
AA	Aa	High quality, but slightly more risk than triple A bond issuers.

continues

Table 13.1 Continued

Standard & Poor's	Moody's	Meaning
A	A	Strong, but issuers don't have the financial strength of triple or double A rated issuers.
BBB	Baa	Medium-grade bonds. Short-term financial strength of issuer is good, but there could be long-term risks.
BB to B	Ba to B	Speculative bonds. Risk that debts may not be repaid.
CCC to C	Caa to C	Danger of default is high.
D		Highest degree of uncertainty with respect to payments of interest and repayment of principal.

What to Do when Interest Rates Rise

It was rapidly rising interest rates that caused many bond fund investors to lose 5 to 8 percent in 1994. Does that mean that the next time interest rates shoot up, you should sell?

Nope, with a capital N. There are several ways to cut losses on your bond fund. You may have to do some fund switching to protect yourself, but it's not all that complicated. Here are just a few ideas:

1. **Just calmly sit tight and reinvest bond fund distributions.** Interest rates go up and down all the time. Even if interest rates rise over the shorter term and a long-term bond's price has dropped, investors should profit over time.

2. **Invest in a money market fund to play it safe.** Then every month, take money out of the money market fund and put it into an intermediate- or long-term bond fund. You'll earn higher yields, but you don't have to worry about losing a bundle if you invest a big chunk of money in a bond fund.

3. **Diversify your fixed-income investments.** We've already warned you about this. Don't put all your eggs in one basket. Invest in federally insured CDs, Treasury bills, and bonds, as well as bond and money market funds.

4. **Ladder your bond funds.** Don't invest in just one bond fund. Put money in bond funds that have different average maturities. Invest in a money market fund, short-term bond fund, intermediate-term bond fund, and a long-term bond fund. You'll earn high yields, but with less risk than putting all your money in one long-term bond fund. Chapter 14 discusses the average maturity of bonds owned by short-term, intermediate-term, and long-term bond funds.

> **Hot Tip**
> If the bonds in your bond fund are issued by the U.S. Treasury or U.S. government, don't worry too much about those agencies going under. You still could lose big, though, if interest rates rise or inflation escalates.

The Least You Need to Know

➤ Invest in bond funds for regular income.

➤ You get monthly income from bond funds; individual bonds typically pay interest income every six months.

➤ Reduce your risk of losing money by putting money in shorter-term bond funds that invest in either U.S. government securities or highly secure corporate bonds rated single A to triple A.

➤ Make regular investments in a bond fund to combat inflation. When inflation heats up, interest rates rise. By investing regularly, you can earn higher yields to keep pace with inflation.

THE GAME'S A FOOT...

Finding the Right Kind of Bond Funds

In This Chapter

➤ Picking a bond fund that's right for you

➤ Can you save taxes with bond funds?

➤ Avoiding the biggest mistakes with bond funds

You now know that bond mutual funds are great for providing regular monthly income. They're convenient. They're also less risky than many stock mutual funds, so it may be a good idea to have one in your hip pocket.

In this chapter, you'll learn how to tell a good bond mutual fund from a bad one and exactly how to stay clear of the high-risk bond funds. You'll see how much of an impact rising rates can have on the value of your investment, and you'll find out what to ask to make sure you're getting the best deal you possibly can.

How Long Is Your Bond Fund?

Here's the long and short of investing in bond funds, so to speak. As you learned in Chapter 4, there are bond funds that invest for the short, intermediate, and long term in U.S. government bonds or notes, corporate bonds, foreign securities, and tax-free municipal bonds. In general, the higher-yielding bond funds in each category—in other words, the funds that pay the most—typically invest a larger percentage of their assets in corporate and/or foreign bonds and notes. The lower-yielding funds in each category generally invest more heavily in U.S. Treasury or government agency bonds or notes. You learn more about these different categories of bond funds later in this chapter.

It's important to understand how the average maturity of your bond fund can affect your total return.

Short-Term Funds

Short-term bond funds generally own a portfolio of bonds with an average maturity of one to five years. This doesn't mean they invest *only* in bonds with those terms. They can own some bonds that mature in 5, 10, or 20 years or they can invest in cash or money market instruments that mature in 90 days or less and notes that mature in just a few years. Add everything up, though, and the average maturity of a short-term bond fund is 1 to 5 years.

Short-term bond funds generally provide a less risky bond fund investment—one that will not show large increases or declines in total return. Although they generally pay higher yields than CDs or money funds, the total return of short-term bond funds is less vulnerable to changes in interest rates than funds that invest in longer-term bonds. That makes them a good short-term parking place for your money. If interest rates rise or fall 1 percent, a $1,000 investment in a short-term bond fund drops 3 to 4 percent.

Intermediate-Term Funds

The average bond owned by an intermediate-term bond fund matures in 5 to 10 years. The total return, however, is more volatile on intermediate-term bond funds than it is on short-term bond funds. If interest rates rise or fall 1 percent, the total return of an intermediate-term bond fund rises or falls about 6 percent.

Sidelines

Surprisingly, Ibbotson Associates research shows that intermediate-term bonds have provided about the same total returns as long-term bonds with significantly less risk. It might seem as though long-term bonds provide a greater total return because they pay higher interest rates than short- or intermediate-term bonds. However, from 1946 through 1994, long-term bonds grew at a average annual total return of 5.2 percent.

What's more, the number of down years when the total return declined into negative territory was 16. The average total return was –3 percent. The worst one-year return was –9.2 percent.

By contrast, intermediate-term bonds grew at a slightly higher average annual total return of 5.9 percent. The number of down years was just 5. The average decline in total return was 1 percent. The worst one-year total return was –1.3 percent.

Intermediate-term bond funds are ideal investments for individuals with a moderate tolerance for risk. Typically, you receive about 85 percent of the interest income that you would receive from long-term bond funds; however, intermediate-term bond funds have less volatile total returns. That makes intermediate-term bond funds a good long-term investment for those who want income or modest growth in the value of their investment over the longer term. They can be used as a lower-risk way to save for a child's college education, a downpayment on a house, or retirement.

Long-Term Funds

Long-term bond funds invest in bonds with an average maturity of 10 to 20 years. Long-term bond funds tend to pay the highest interest rates, but their total returns are more volatile. The total return on long-term bond funds can be +12 or -12 percent when interest rates rise or fall 1 percent. As a result, long-term bond funds are best suited for investors with a high tolerance for risk. The bond funds can be used as a source of retirement income, for a long-term saving plan, or to help you diversify your investments.

Narrowing the Field

Don't worry, troops. Choosing a bond fund is not an impossible task. In fact, it's kind of like buying detergent, which we all manage to do on a regular basis, right? There are detergents for cold water and detergents for hot water. You use some for towels and sheets, and others are for delicate fabrics. Wash your underwear with the wrong kind of detergent, and you wind up scratching yourself all day.

Fortunately, we've already given you the basics to avoid scratching yourself with bond funds. You already know these facts:

> ➤ Bond funds issued by the U.S. Treasury or government agencies are the least risky. You have the backing of the U.S. government against default.

> ➤ For low risk, any bonds in your corporate bond fund should be rated single A to triple A by Standard & Poor's and Moody's. These funds own bonds issued by the most creditworthy companies.

> ➤ The longer the average maturity of the bonds in your fund, the greater the risk. For lower risk, invest in short-term or intermediate-term bond funds.

> ➤ Invest regularly in your bond fund to combat inflation. Then when inflation heats up and bond rates rise, you can invest to take advantage of the situation.

Your Safest Bets

It's time to nail down your choices even further. If low risk is as much of an issue for you as it is for us, we suggest that you look at your fund's investment objective. Then, limit your bond fund selection to the types described in the next sections.

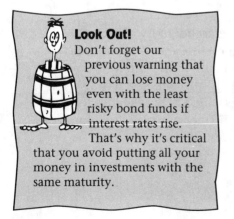

Look Out!
Don't forget our previous warning that you can lose money even with the least risky bond funds if interest rates rise.
That's why it's critical that you avoid putting all your money in investments with the same maturity.

U.S. Treasury Bond Funds

Treasury bond funds, like the one Mom Lavine has, invest in U.S. Treasury bonds and notes. They come in three sizes. Short-term Treasury bond funds invest in T-bonds that mature in three to five years. Intermediate-term funds invest in Treasury bonds maturing in six to 10 years, and long-term funds invest in 20- and 30-year T-bonds.

Zero Coupon Treasury Bond Funds

Treasury bond funds also have a distant cousin, known as *zero coupon Treasury-bond funds*. The difference is that instead of getting monthly income from these mutual funds, the investor collects accumulated income and principal at the bond's maturity. However, if these funds are outside a retirement plan, federal income taxes still must be paid on the interest annually, even though it has not been received. With these funds, often used in financial planning, investors can determine exactly how much they'll earn by a certain date. The Benham Group of Funds and the Scudder Group of Funds both have zero coupon bond funds.

Look Out!
Zero coupon bonds and bond funds are more volatile than other types of bonds and bond funds. Brokerage firms actually manufacture these bonds by splitting Treasury bonds and selling the interest and principal as separate securities.

U.S. Government/Mortgage Bond Funds

U.S. government/mortgage bond funds are ranked next lowest on the risk list, but investors in these bonds have one extra-special risk to deal with that they don't have with U.S. Treasury bond funds.

Recall from Chapter 4 that U.S. government/mortgage bond funds invest in longer-term U.S. government agency bonds, primarily used to finance home mortgages. They pay about 1 to 1.5 percent more than pure Treasury-bond funds because virtually any creditor, even a government agency, is riskier than the U.S. Treasury.

These mortgage bond funds are particularly attractive to those living on fixed incomes because the federal guarantee makes them low-risk.

They're tricky little devils, though, because they're different from traditional bond funds that pay you monthly income, based on their yield. If you've ever paid off a mortgage, you know that monthly payments on mortgages include more than just interest payments, right? They also include principal.

As a result, the mutual fund, which owns the mortgage bonds, distributes the interest income to shareholders. It takes the principal portion of the payments and reinvests it.

That *sounds* great on the surface. After all, the mutual fund is relieving its shareholders of the need to reinvest the principal themselves. It can be a killer when interest rates fall and homeowners refinance, paying off their entire mortgages! Then the mortgage bond fund gets more principal returned faster than expected. The fund manager is forced to reinvest the principal at lower rates.

Guess who's the final recipient of those lower rates? That's right—you, the shareholder.

High-Quality Corporate Bond Funds

High-quality corporate bond funds buy bonds issued by the nation's financially strongest companies. There are a variety of high-quality corporate bond funds to pick. There are short-term, intermediate-term, and long-term bond funds available from most mutual fund families. Typically, these funds yield about 2 percent more than comparable U.S. Treasury bond funds.

Technobabble

Swap means to switch, as in what bond fund managers do to obtain higher-yielding bonds that have credit ratings equal to their existing bonds. *Junk bond funds* or *high-yield bond funds* invest in bonds issued by companies or governments with an average credit rating below A by Standard & Poor's or Moody's.

High-quality corporate bond funds must invest 65 to 75 percent of their assets in investment-grade bonds—rated A to triple A by Standard & Poor's and Moody's. The other 25 to 35 percent can be invested in cash, U.S. government securities, lower credit-rated bonds (usually rated BBB to BB), and overseas bonds.

Corporate bond fund managers have a number of ways they can earn higher returns or reduce risk. Depending on their outlook for interest rates, they can invest in short-, intermediate-, and long-term bonds. They often look for mispriced bonds from issuers expected to get an upgrade in their credit ratings—from A to AA, for example. Often, they will swap bonds or switch to higher-yielding bonds that have the same credit ratings as their existing bonds.

Insured Municipal Bond Funds

Municipal bond funds invest in bonds whose interest is paid by cities, towns, states, toll roads, schools, water projects, and hospitals. The interest income from municipal bonds is tax-free and the bonds are insured against default by large private insurance companies, such as American Municipal Bond Assurance Corp. (AMBAC) and Municipal Bond Insurance Association (MBIA).

These insurance companies, incidentally, don't insure just *any* municipal bond. The state or city has to be economically strong and have a lot of tax revenue.

Typically, insured municipal bond funds yield between one-quarter to one-half of one percent less than uninsured municipal bond funds. Why? The bond issuers have to pay for the insurance coverage, so they pay less interest.

However, insured municipal bond funds often outperform uninsured bond funds based on total return—price gains plus the yield. The reason for such performance is the strong demand for these bonds, which results in higher prices. Protection against defaults makes insured municipal bonds more attractive to investors.

How good is the bond insurance? The insurance companies conduct a worst-case scenario before they insure any issuer. According to Standard & Poor's and brokerage firms' evaluations, the default rate on insured municipal bonds has been less than one-half of one percent over the past 20 years. Insurance companies have made good on the losses.

Uninsured High-Quality Municipal Bond Funds

Uninsured high-quality municipal bond funds also invest in the least risky municipal bonds, rated single A to triple A. They're just not insured. In addition, there are municipal bond funds that limit investments to a single state if you want to escape state taxes.

Sidelines

Invest in municipal bond funds only if you're in a high tax bracket (28% or greater). You can tell whether these funds are worth it by doing a little math:

Subtract your tax bracket from 1. Then divide that number into the municipal bond fund's yield. That gives you the taxable equivalent yield on your municipal bond funds.

If the taxable equivalent yield is higher on the municipal bond fund than on the taxable bond fund, you've got a good deal.

For example, suppose you're in the 31 percent tax bracket and the municipal bond fund yields 6 percent:

1 - .31 = .69

6 ÷ by .69 = 8.7 taxable equivalent yield

Comparable taxable bond funds yield 7.5 percent, so the municipal bond fund is a better deal.

Avoiding High-Risk Funds

High yields might be your objective, but they also can spell big trouble, particularly in an economic downturn. The following types of bond funds should be tackled by only the most sophisticated investors!

Junk Bond Funds

Junk bond funds in mid-year 1995 were yielding 10 percent. It's no wonder. Junk bond funds, also known as high-yield bond funds, invest in companies with poorer credit ratings. The bonds are rated below A by Standard & Poor's and Moody's. With these funds, there's a greater chance you may not get back your principal and interest.

Convertible Bond Funds

Convertible bond funds invest in bonds that can be converted into stock. You increase your risk when you invest in these funds because you lose if either the bond or stock markets do lousy.

Uninsured High-Yield Municipal Bond Funds

You earn the highest tax-free yields from uninsured high-yield municipal bond funds. The funds invest in states or municipalities with lower credit ratings. You may run into trouble with these funds. In 1994, when Orange County, California, defaulted on some of its tax-free bonds, some funds were stuck with uninsured Orange County bonds that were maturing at the end of the year. Fortunately, the bond funds that owned insured Orange County bonds did not have to worry.

International Bond Funds for Diversification

There are all types of international bond funds, with varying degrees of risk. Once you get into international bond funds, however, you are adding one extra element of risk to the whole mutual fund bond proposition. Fund managers must convert U.S. dollars into foreign currency to buy the bonds. Therefore, if the value of the dollar rises against foreign currencies, the value of your investment can drop. True, you can earn higher yields and make bigger profits in funds that invest in some of these critters, but they're not for beginners. Nor do you want to sock all your money in them.

Given that caveat, the international bond funds considered least risky invest in bonds issued by foreign governments worldwide. Others invest in governments and large multinational corporate bonds. Global or world funds may also own U.S. bonds. All these types of mutual funds are among the least risky of the international bond funds. The fund managers diversify not only by country but by corporate bond issuers and the industries of the companies.

There also are bond funds that invest in Latin American bonds and other emerging markets. These are high-risk investments because these countries may be politically or economically unstable.

As in this country, you can tell a well-managed international bond fund by focusing on total return as well as yield. You don't want to invest in a high-yielding international fund only to find the market value of your investment declining. Investors want to see that the fund is managing its investments properly. That means international bond fund managers try to limit losses when interest rates rise and bond prices fall. If they believe interest rates are rising in one country, they may invest in another, where rates are expected to decline. They may reduce the average maturity of the fund to cushion the blow of rising interest rates in some countries.

The world's economies don't move the same way our bond markets do. There's a good chance that when rates are low in the U.S., they are higher elsewhere. That's why a well-diversified international bond fund that invests in government and/or high-quality corporate bonds can be a good deal. You might consider keeping a small part of your bond fund holdings in a well-managed bond fund that invests worldwide. Three of the best-rated world bond funds over the past five years, according to Morningstar, Inc., include the T. Rowe Price International Bond Fund (800-638-5660), the IDS Global Bond Fund (800-328-8300), and the MFS World Governments Fund (800-343-2829). Remember, though—when you invest in international bonds, you face

151

an extra layer of risk. That's why it's a good idea to keep only a small part of your bond fund holdings in these types of funds.

The Long and Short of It

See? That wasn't so bad, was it? You've figured out which type of bond fund you want to invest in based on the amount of risk you can tolerate. The next step is to determine the average maturity of the bonds you want in your fund. Should you invest in a short-, intermediate-, or long-term bond fund?

As we told you in earlier chapters, you earn higher yields with longer-term bond funds. Of course, there's a trade-off. When interest rates rise, longer-term bond funds drop more in value.

Here is how the value of a $1,000 investment changes if interest rates change 1 percent. As you can see, if interest rates rise 1 percent, the value of your $1,000 investment in a short-term fund drops only $38—but a long-term bond fund drops 94 smack-a-roos:

Type Rates	Rise 1%	Rates Fall 1%
Short-term	$962	$1,040
Intermediate-term	938	1,067
Long-term	906	1,112

As a rule of thumb, short-term bond funds are less risky than longer-term bond funds. Follow these rules:

➤ Invest in a short-term bond fund if you are investing for two years or less.

➤ Invest intermediate-term if you are investing for 10 years or less, or if you want to play it safe with your principal and still get decent income from your fund over your lifetime.

➤ Invest in long-term bond funds if you want higher income and you can tolerate seeing the value of your principal drop 10 percent or more in any given year.

Avoid These Mistakes

There's a lot of material to digest when considering a bond mutual fund. If you decide to go that route, try not to make the following costly errors. You'll save a lot of heartache—*and* money:

➤ Chasing after high-yield funds without understanding the risks.

➤ Investing in long-term bond funds when you only want to park your money for less than a year.

➤ Investing in a tax-free municipal bond fund if you're not in a high-tax bracket.

➤ Paying more than 1 percent annually in expenses for your bond fund. The average bond fund expenses run just under 1 percent a year. Be sure to check the prospectus.

➤ Investing in municipal bond funds in an IRA or other retirement account. Your IRA is already in a tax-deferred retirement savings account. It makes no sense to put something that is tax-free into a tax-deferred investment.

➤ Using your bond fund as a checking account. Most bond funds come with checkbooks, but each time you write a check, you are selling shares and could be paying taxes on your profits.

How to Pick a Bond Fund

You have to do your homework when you invest in bond funds:

➤ Read the bond fund's prospectus before you invest to be sure the fund's investment objectives match your own.

➤ Ask yourself why you want to invest in this fund:

Do you need the interest income to live on?

Do you want to diversify your investments—hedge your stock fund investments by owning a bond fund?

Do you want to use a bond fund as a temporary place to park your money until a better investment comes along?

How long do you expect to invest?

➤ Decide whether you want to invest in short-, intermediate- or long-term bond funds.

➤ Compare similar bond funds' charges. Use the Bond Fund Picking Worksheet to help out:

What's the load or commission (%)?

What is the management fee (%)?

Is there a 12b-1 fee (%)?

What's the expense ratio, or percentage of assets taken out to cover expenses?

➤ What does the fund yield compared with other funds (%)? You can check various bond fund reports like the one illustrated next to compare.

➤ Look at the fund's *total return* over at least three years. You don't want to own a high-yielding fund only to discover the total value of your investment is declining. You want consistent returns, not wild price swings.

➤ Check the credit ratings of the fund's holdings, which are listed in the fund's prospectus and quarterly reports.

Bond Fund Picking Worksheet

Fund	Yield	Load	12b-1 Fees	Management Fee	Expense Ratio	Term--S,I,L

Use this worksheet to compare different bond funds.

TOP YIELDING FUNDS

As of June 27, 1995

	SEC 30-Day (%)	YTD Returns	Assets ($mil)
Government General Short-Term (0 - 2.99 Yrs)			
MFS Govt Limited Maturity Fund	6.45	5.16	247.9
PIMCO Advisors Short-Intmd/Class C	6.34	6.88	65.0
Kemper Short-Intmd Govt/Cl B	6.32	6.54	214.2
Government General Intmd-Term (3 - 10 Yrs)			
PaineWebber Strategic Incm/B	10.74	8.92	40.9
Piper Jaffray Instit Govt Income	7.72	15.49	375.0
111 Corcoran Bond Fund	7.13	13.30	87.4
Government General Long-Term (+10 Yrs)			
Nations Diversified Income/Trust A	7.32	13.17	24.9
Putnam American Government Income	7.09	11.33	2,255.7
Sierra US Government Fund/Cl A	6.85	10.12	460.2
GNMA			
Federated GNMA Trust/Inst Shares	7.32	13.17	24.9
Benham GNMA Income Fund	7.09	11.33	2,255.7
Vanguard Fixed Income Secs/GNMA	6.85	10.12	460.2
Government Mortgages			
Fidelity Mortgage Securities Port	7.27	10.94	423.6
Oppenheimer Mortgage Income/Cl A	7.27	10.66	79.0
Van Kampen Merritt US Govt Fund/A	7.26	11.80	3,025.2
Corporate General Short-Term (0 - 2.99 Yrs)			
Bayfunds S-T Yield Port/Instit	6.80	3.35	46.6
Nations Short-Term Income Fund/Tr A	6.67	6.70	170.5
Bayfunds S-T Yield Port/Investor	6.55	1.74	25.1
Corporate General Intmd-Term (3 - 10 Yrs)			
Oppenheimer Mortgage Income/Cl A	8.52	6.90	3,154.2
John Hancock Strgc Incm Fund/A	8.22	9.38	330.9
Oppenheimer Strategic Income/Cl B	8.21	6.55	1,828.7
Corporate General Long-Term (+10 Yrs)			
Fortress Bond Fund	8.37	12.11	174.9
Janus Flexible Income Fund	8.09	11.60	502.4
Phoenix Multi-Sector Fxd Income/A	7.73	11.05	164.6
Corporate High Quality Short-Term (0 - 2.99 Yrs)			
PIMCO Short-Term Fund	8.15	3.69	78.5
PIMCO Low Duration	7.38	5.91	2,493.2
PIMCO Low Duration II	6.77	6.60	192.0
Corporate High Quality Short-Term (0 - 2.99 Yrs)			
PIMCO Total Return III	7.28	11.11	110.3
PIMCO Total Return	7.08	10.63	8,232.5
First Union Mgd Bond Port/Cl Y	6.96	11.88	74.8
Corporate High Quality Long-Term (+10 Yrs)			
Scudder Income Fund	7.27	11.53	525.1
Federated Intmd Income Fund/Inst	7.22	13.37	34.4
PaineWebber Invmt Grade Income/A	7.04	12.52	267.6
Corporate High Yield - Junk			
Fortis Advantage High-Yield	12.45	8.39	126.2
PaineWebber Fxd Incm–High Incm/A	11.14	8.10	263.3
PaineWebber High Income/D	11.09	7.85	110.4
Global & International Short-Term			
Alliance Multi-Mkt Strategy Tr/Cl A	10.06	-1.62	84.6
Alliance Multi-Mkt Strategy Tr/Cl B	9.33	-.2.13	132.8
Alliance S-T Multi-Market/Cl A	8.33	-1.22	357.0
Global & International Long-Term			
Scudder Emerging Markets Fund	10.06	-1.62	84.6
Merrill Lynch Americas Income/Cl B	9.33	-.2.13	132.8
Alliance N American Govt Incm/Cl A	8.33	-1.22	357.0
Municipal Short-Term (0 - 2.99 Yrs)			
Strong Short-Term Muni Bond Fund	4.49	1.42	142.7
USAA Tax-Exempt Short-Term Fund	4.34	4.17	785.2
Calvert T-F Reserves Ltd-Term/Cl A	4.32	3.05	491.2
Municipal Intmd-Term (3 - 10 Yrs)			
Calvert National Muni Intmd/Cl A	5.83	8.65	37.2
Morgan Grenfell Municipal Bond	5.51	7.54	197.0
Nations FL Intmd Municipal/Trust A	5.45	8.87	43.4
Municipal Long-Term (+10 Yrs)			
Strong High-Yield Municipal Fund	7.55	7.52	182.2
Putnam Tax-Free High-Yield/ A	6.87	9.71	464.7
MFS Municipal High-Incm Fund/Cl A	6.71	10.60	1,004.3

Source: IBC's Bond Fund Report

Source: IBC's Bond Fund Report

Top-yielding bond funds.

The Least You Need to Know

➤ For safety, invest in U.S. Treasury bond funds, U.S. government securities bond funds, and high-grade corporate and municipal bond funds. Avoid junk bond funds, convertible bond funds, and international bond funds.

➤ Short-term bond funds lose less money when interest rates rise than longer-term bond funds.

➤ Longer-term bond funds pay higher yields.

➤ Invest in the least risky and highest-yielding bond fund that charges the least amount of expenses.

Building Your Wealth with Stock Funds

In This Chapter

➤ Why do stock funds grow in value?

➤ The different types of stock funds

➤ The best-rated stock funds

➤ Building your wealth for the long term

With this chapter, you're headed into the big stakes. Of all the major types of mutual fund investments, stock mutual funds can make you the most money fastest. They also can lose the most equally as fast.

This chapter discusses how stock mutual funds work. You'll learn about each category of stock fund and how it is best used. You'll also get a dose of the best long-term performers in each category—plus, you'll find out what to stay away from in considering stock mutual funds.

Stock mutual funds, we admit, are not for the faint-hearted. When used as part of a long-term diversified plan, however, they can provide a significant hedge against inflation and play a key role in building your wealth.

Stock Funds Are Long-Term Affairs

Buy a stock mutual fund for as little as $1,000, and you are starting to take a completely active role in the American dream. You're actually an owner of not one, but many businesses.

Of course, you need a certain mentality to own a business, and it's a good idea to refer to your risk tolerance quiz in Chapter 6 to see exactly how much of that stuff you have. With a stock mutual fund, you need to be prepared to take the lumps as well as the good times that come not only with your fund's stocks themselves, but with the economy and the stock market. Fortunately, the fact that you own not one, but several, businesses in a mutual fund, and for such a potentially small up-front investment, helps make the whole idea of stock mutual funds palatable for many investors.

To get an idea of how a stock mutual fund can quietly build wealth, let's peek in on Comfortably Retired Ralph. When Ralph was in his early 30s in 1959, he started investing in a stock mutual fund. In those days, there were few no-load mutual funds around. A mutual fund salesman went from door to door to pitch funds.

The salesman knocking on Ralph's door, coincidentally, was Vinny, a distant cousin of Ralph's. Vinny talked Ralph into investing $100 a month in a blue-chip common stock fund. Ralph had been dabbling in stocks for several years at the time, so he knew how stocks worked. This time, Ralph was looking for something he could buy and hold and forget about until he retired. He settled on the Rainbow Growth Fund, suggested by his cousin, Vinny.

Everything went well until 1961. The Rainbow Growth Fund was up almost 30 percent over the first two years. Then wham! The economy turned sour.

Look Out!
Stock mutual funds are the riskiest type of mutual fund. To minimize losses, anyone considering stock mutual funds should be prepared to keep the investment a rock-bottom minimum of five years, and closer to 10 or 20 years.

The economy went into a recession and the Rainbow Growth Fund lost 14 percent. Ralph's wife, Eleanore, wanted him to sell, but Ralph refused. He was stubborn.

Fortunately, the Rainbow Growth Fund had some smooth sailing after that. The fund made back its losses and more. The total return on the fund was 19% in the fourth year. The Rainbow Growth Fund lost money in only those two original years. Then boom! In 1973 and 1974, the value of Ralph's stash plummeted 45 percent. Those were bad years for the economy and the stock market.

Did Ralph sell? No. He hung in there, although it was an incredibly tough decision. Eleanore even threatened to get a divorce at one point. Ralph just kept pumping $100 a month into his stock fund. The move turned out to be a good one. By the time Ralph retired at age 66 in 1994, his $100-a-month mutual fund investment was worth $481,000. His investment grew at an annual average total return of 11.8 percent.

Now, Comfortably Retired Ralph always has a smile on his face. He and Eleanore retired to Boca Raton, Florida, several years ago. They have their Social Security, other income, and a nice mutual fund nest egg. The mutual fund's stash pays them more than $2,400 a month. The investment continues to grow.

Ralph did pretty darned good.

The Rainbow Growth Fund that Ralph invested in actually is a fictitious fund, but its performance is based on the historical return on the average diversified stock fund, according to Lipper Analytical Services, Summit, NJ.

Of course, past performance is no indication of future results. Nevertheless, this gives you a strong idea of how a stock fund can do if you invest for the long term. Invest in a stock fund for the short haul, however, and you can lose big-time.

Is the Risk of Losing Money Worth the Return?

Ralph kept his Rainbow Growth Fund through the rough periods. Whenever the stock market loses more than 10 percent, it's usually called a bear market. There have been a number of bear markets over the years, but so far, the stock market has bounced back after about a year. Then bull markets occur when the stock market moves higher for a couple of years running.

Ralph could have bailed out in 1973 or 1974 during the worst bear market since the Great Depression. Many of his friends did. They sold and took their losses. In fact, some swore off mutual funds forever. However, those with the courage to stay put made their losses back and more. Over the past 20 years since the bear market of 1973-74, the average stock fund gained 15 percent annually.

Technobabble
When the stock market loses more than 10 percent, it's a *bear market*. When the stock market moves higher for a couple of years straight, it's a *bull market*.

WHAT?

It Ain't Hay!

Stock funds tend to outperform other investments long-term largely because ownership in corporations is one of the best ways to make money. During periods of economic prosperity, business profits. As a result, owners of the companies profit.

The ABC Pen Company, for example, is having a great year. It can sell its pens for $2 each instead of the $1.59 it charged last year. Meanwhile, it costs no more to produce and sell the pen. The owners of the company are happy because the stock they bought at $10 a share now sells for $14 a share. That's how both stocks and stock mutual funds grow in value.

Over the long term, stocks have outperformed all other types of investments, such as bonds and CDs. Of course, just as Comfortably Retired Ralph experienced, there have been dips along the way. That happens during an economic recession. Businesses start to lose money and people get laid off.

How Stocks Grow

Let's get back to Comfortably Retired Ralph. He gave up short-term losses in return for long-term gains when he socked away money in the Rainbow Growth Fund. Ralph started putting it away in 1959. The average stock fund gained 11 percent annually over the past 36 years. Wow! A $1,000 investment grew to a whopping $481,000.

You never can predict the future when it comes to mutual fund investing. History *does* give you at least some idea of what you can expect from a well-managed stock fund over the long term.

Now don't think when you invest in a stock fund, you will earn 11 percent a year. The highest you would have made from the average stock fund over the past three decades was +37.3 percent in any one year. The worst was -24.3 percent according to Lipper Analytical Services. Year after year, it will be a bumpy ride. Remember Ralph, however. He traded a string of good years for just a few bad ones.

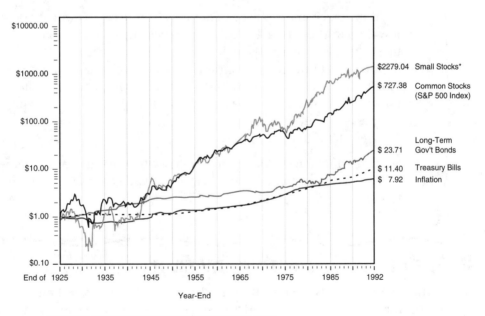

Sidelines

Stock funds are one of the best ways to protect your money from the ravages of inflation. The price of goods and services rose at about 3.5 percent a year since 1959. Stock funds, on average, grew at an annual average total return of 11 percent. Therefore, less 3.5 percent inflation a year, stock funds grew at an annual average total return of 7.5 percent. You were protected from rising prices.

Is the risk worth the return? It sure is if you have a game plan, know why you are investing, and do it for a long time. Chapters 6 and 7 helped you zero in on your tolerance for risk, then helped you match up your investment comfort level with the right funds. There are different kinds of stock funds—some more risky than others. If you are not prepared to invest for an absolute minimum of 5 years—and to lower the risk, 10 to 20 years—you should stick with less risky money funds and short-term bond funds.

Source: © *Stocks, Bonds, Bills, and Inflation 1993 Yearbook*,™ Ibbotson Associates, Chicago (annually updates work by Roger G. Ibbotson and Rex A. Sinquefield). All rights reserved.

Value of $1 invested at the end of 1925.

Sidelines

What do stock fund portfolio managers look for in a company be-fore they invest? No two fund managers think alike. However, they make their decisions based on a number of factors:

➤ Most professional portfolio managers visit or talk to a company's management to discuss the firm's business plans and goals. The manager wants to know what the company has up its sleeve in regard to research, development, and marketing, as well as how financial problems are being solved.

➤ Fund managers look at a company's financial statement for gems of information about financial strength and profitability. They may want to own companies whose profits have been rising over the past couple of years, or may spot stocks selling at very low prices in relation to their future earnings potential.

➤ Fund managers may look at a company's industry to evaluate how it will do in the future. For example, when the economy is picking up steam, employment is high and people spend money. Then, leisure, entertainment, and airline stocks do well. People tend to buy houses when interest rates decline. Then, homebuilding stocks do well. By contrast, when a recession is looming on the horizon, businesses serving basic necessities, such as utilities and food manu-facturers, tend to do well.

➤ Some fund managers look at trends. They buy stocks that are show-ing strong upward price trends. They sell based on downward price trends.

If You're an Aggressive Investor...

Although stock funds in general are riskier than bond funds and money funds, there are different categories of stock funds, and some are riskier than others. You can curb your risk a bit based on the type of stock fund you se-lect. Keep in mind that the more conservative your fund, the fewer price swings you'll have—and those price swings can be up as well as down. The next sections present the most aggressive categories of stock funds, which can bring you the greatest returns as well as the greatest losses.

Aggressive Stock Funds

Recall from Chapter 4 that aggressive stock funds invest in both small, medium, and large companies. The typical aggressive stock fund buys and sells stocks for quick, and hopefully, big profits. The fund managers may use speculative tactics to boost returns. Most aggressive stock funds own stocks for less than a year and trade them frequently. Why? The managers look for opportunities to buy low and sell high.

The typical aggressive stock fund owns companies whose sales and profits are growing more than 20 percent a year. You will see familiar names such as Home Depot, Toyota, and Microsoft, as well as smaller technology companies in the portfolios of many of these funds.

Aggressive stock funds are characterized by high portfolio turnover and low yields. The average aggressive stock fund owns stocks for about six months. The portfolio manager likes to trade stocks for rapid profits or to cut losses. When you look at the fund's portfolio holdings in the financial reports, keep in mind that the fund may no longer own some of these securities. Aggressive growth funds invest in smaller companies that are pumping their profits back into their businesses instead of paying shareholders dividends. The funds focus on growth in the share price of the stocks they hold. What little dividends the shareholders of the funds would receive are paid out quarterly. However, any capital gains for the profits on the sale of stocks are paid to shareholders at the end of the year.

The best-rated aggressive stock funds frequently have the capability of buying hot stocks early and getting out with a tidy profit. The manager invests in small companies before they show strong sales. Some funds like to buy out-of-favor companies that can bounce back with a vengeance.

Table 15.1 Top Performing Aggressive Growth Funds, Average Annual Total Return, 10 Years Ending in June 30, 1995

Fund	Average Total Return %
AIM Constellation	20.32
PIMCO Advisors Opportunity C	19.15
Twentieth Century Ultra	19.02

continues

Table 15.1   Continued

Fund	Average Total Return %
State Street Research Capital C	18.18
Putnam Voyager A	17.15
AIM Aggressive Growth	16.94
Smith Barney Aggressive Growth A	15.98
Delaware Trend A	15.64
Founders Special	15.47
Keytone America Omega A	15.31

Source: Morningstar Mutual Fund Performance Report, July 1995

Small Company Stock Funds

Small company stock funds own little acorns that can grow into oak trees. The funds buy new companies or smaller companies that plow all their profits back into their businesses. These companies may have annual revenues of several hundred million dollars a year. By contrast, blue-chip companies pull in several billion dollars in revenue per year. Most small stock fund portfolio managers use the growth stock investment style. They invest in rapidly growing companies whose earnings are growing at a rapid clip, such as Maximum Integrated Products, LSI Logic, and HealthSource. Many of these companies, but not all, are in the technology business.

There also are small company funds that look for undervalued stocks—overlooked companies that should register strong profits in the future. The fund managers buy and hold stocks such as Long Drug Stores, Anthony Industries, and Caesars World for the longer term. These fund managers look for gems. They buy early and wait for the companies to do well. Then they profit when others invest.

Most small company stock funds tend to buy and hold stocks for a few years. Funds such as the Acorn Fund, which has grown at a 19 percent annual rate over the past 20 years, buy and hold attractive new companies for three to five years. The fund managers need time to see the companies prosper.

The typical small company stock fund owns its securities longer than aggressive stock funds. Why? Sometimes it takes a while for a small company to show growing business profits, which stimulates the demand for the firm's stock. Just like aggressive growth funds, however, small company funds pay little if any dividends to the fund's shareholders. You are more likely to see annual distributions of capital gains from small company stock funds.

You also can go for a wild ride when you invest in a small company stock fund. Small company stocks perform in streaks. They may do well for three or four years running. Then they die before things pick up again. That's why you have to invest in them for the longer term. The average small company stock fund gained 50 percent in 1991, but lost 10 percent the year before, according to Morningstar.

There's a fine line between aggressive growth stock funds and small company stock funds. Small company stock funds tend to be less volatile than aggressive stock funds because the fund managers want to own small companies, watch them grow, and sell them at a profit when they are bigger outfits.

Table 15.2   Top Performing Small Company Stock Funds, Average Annual Total Return, 10 Years Ending in June 30, 1995

Fund	Average Total Return %
Twentieth Century Gift Trust	24.36
FPA Capital	19.33
Janus Venture	16.93
Putnam OTC Emerging Growth A	16.91
Seligman Frontier A	16.18
Twentieth Century Vista	16.10
Keystone American Hartwell Emerging Growth	16.07
John Hancock Special Equities A	16.07
Heartland Value	15.69
Acorn	15.68

Source: Morningstar Mutual Fund Performance Report, July 1995

> **Sidelines**
>
> How do you pick a stock fund? When shopping for a stock fund, look for the following:
>
> ➤ Compare a fund's year-by-year performance. Avoid funds with wide swings in annual returns. Invest in funds with the most consistent year-by-year returns.
>
> ➤ Compare a fund's annual average returns over at least a three-to-five-year period.
>
> ➤ Compare how the fund did in bad years such as 1981, 1984, 1987, 1990, and 1994. You want the fund that loses the least amount of money.
>
> ➤ Check the fund's prospectus and annual report to be sure the investment objective of the fund is in line with the type of stocks it owns.
>
> ➤ Check the fund's prospectus for the fund's expense ratio and loads. You want the fund with the lowest expenses and the best track record so that you will earn more money.

Growth Funds

Growth stock funds are typically a little different than aggressive growth and small company stock funds. Growth funds stick with proven companies that have a solid track record of sales and profits. These funds invest in larger well-established, well-managed companies—brand-name companies such as Sears, Disney, General Motors, and General Electric. These companies like to plow their profits back into the company so that they can improve and produce more popular products. In addition to investing in brand-name companies that are expected to profit for years to come, many growth funds may own a small stake in small companies and overseas stocks.

Some growth funds like to buy and hold undervalued stock for a few years. These funds are characterized by low portfolio turnover, so you are likely to see some of the same stocks in your growth fund's portfolio for a couple of years running. By contrast, other growth funds turn over the stocks they own more than once a year. These funds look for rapid profits from the sale of securities.

Because growth funds invest in larger, more established companies, you're likely to receive some quarterly dividend income from the funds. You are more likely to receive annual capital gains distributions from growth funds, if they sold stocks at a profit during the year.

Fidelity Magellan Fund is one of the best growth funds in recent history—up at an annual average total return of 22.8 percent over the past 15 years, according to Lipper Analytical Services. Nevertheless, growth funds still are aggressive investments. In 1991, the typical growth fund gained 37 percent. The year before, when we had an economic recession, it lost 5 percent.

Table 15.3 Top Performing Growth Funds, Average Annual Total Return, 10 Years Ending in June 30, 1995

Fund	Average Total Return %
Fidelity Advisor Inst'l Equity Growth	19.89
Fidelity Contrafund	19.36
CGM Capital Development	18.43
Fidelity Destiny I	18.29
Berger 100	18.28
Fidelity Magellan	18.28
AIM Value A	17.60
Fidelity Growth Company	17.24
New York Venture A	17.09
IDS New Dimensions A	16.83

Source: Morningstar Mutual Fund Performance Report, July 1995

More Conservative Wealth-Building Funds

Some funds are designed for more conservative investors. They are willing to risk their principal a little in exchange for greater long-term profits, but can't bear the thought of large losses in their portfolios. The next sections discuss these funds.

Growth and Income Funds

All those sexy stories you hear at parties about the hot stock fund that doubled its money in two years are lies. If they're not lies, they're likely to be lies by the time you plunk down your hard-earned money. We're willing to wager the fund promptly will lose 20 percent! Face it. When the little guys get wind of a sizzling mutual fund, it's generally too late.

If you own just one fund, it should be a growth and income fund. It's a great investment for moderate investors. (Refer to your risk tolerance quiz in Chapter 6.) The objective of this type of fund is long-term growth of your money, plus income. Growth and income funds can achieve this goal because they invest in blue-chip stocks. When you have blue-chip stocks, you are an owner of American companies that have stood the test of time. Sure, they may lose some money when there's a recession, but their profits keep rising almost every year. They pass on 50 to 60 percent of it to their shareholders through stock dividends.

The secret of growth and income investing is reinvesting the income your fund gets from these blue-chip companies such as Gillette, Pepsi, Coca Cola, Colgate-Palmolive, Anheuser Bush, Kellogg, and Wal-Mart. If these business continue to grow and profit, so will your investment in them through your growth and income fund.

You don't get as big a bang for your buck from growth and income funds as you would from more aggressive stock funds, but you get a steadier investment. The income from the fund cushions some of the losses when the value of the fund declines. For example, in 1991, the average growth and income funds gained 27 percent. Aggressive stock funds gained almost twice as much. In 1990, growth and income funds lost 4 percent, and aggressive growth funds lost more than 8 percent, according to Morningstar.

Table 15.4 Top Performing Growth and Income Funds, Average Annual Total Return, 10 Years Ending in June 30, 1995

Fund	Average Annual Return %
Mutual Beacon	15.93
Fidelity Congress Street	15.64
Safeco Equity	15.56
Dodge & Cox Stock	15.52

Fund	Average Annual Return %
IDS Managed Retirement	15.50
Mutual Qualified	15.34
Fundamental Investors	15.33
MAS Value	15.27
Neuberger & Berman Guardian	14.93
Lexington Corporate Leaders	14.91

Source: Morningstar Mutual Fund Performance Report, July 1995

Sidelines

Some of the best-performing mutual funds over the past 50 years have been growth and income funds, such as Investment Company of America (800-421-9900), Affiliated Fund (800-426-1130), Seligman Common Stock Fund (800-221-2450), Fidelity Fund (800-544-8888), Mass Investors Trust (800-343-2829), State Street Investment Fund (800-882-0052), Putnam Investors (800-225-1581), United Income (800-366-5465), and Safeco Equity Fund (800-426-6730). As you will see in Appendix C, you earn solid returns for years to come with these funds.

Equity Income Funds

Equity Income Funds are second cousins to growth and income funds. The difference is that equity income funds emphasize more income than growth. The fund managers invest in large companies that typically pay out more of their profits to their shareholders compared with other companies. You will see a lot of telephone and oil company stocks in the portfolios of equity income funds. You'll also see some of the same stocks that growth and income funds own.

Table 15.5 Top Performing Equity Income Funds, Average Annual Total Return, 10 Years Ending in June June 30, 1995

Fund	Annual Return %
United Income A	15.62
Invesco Industrial Income	14.92
Fidelity Advisor Inst'l Equity Income	13.29
Managers Equity Income	12.72
Fidelity Equity Income	12.64
American Capital Equity Income	11.77
Oppenheimer Equity Income A	11.67
Delaware Decature Income A	11.63
American National Income	11.44
Safeco Income	10.88

Source: Morningstar Mutual Fund Performance Report, July 1995

Stock Funds for Very Conservative Investors

Are you worried you will lose a lot of money in a stock fund? You might consider low-risk alternatives such as balanced funds and income funds.

Balanced funds typically own just 50 to 60 percent of the fund in blue-chip stocks. The rest is invested in government and high-grade corporate bonds. Historically, balanced funds earn about 80 percent of what a stock fund makes, but balanced funds lose half as much money when things turn sour. If your stock fund is down 8 percent, chances are your balanced fund is down just 4 percent. Fair trade-off!

Asset allocation funds are balanced funds that invest in a greater variety of stocks and bonds than the typical balanced fund. An asset allocation fund may split its stock investments among U.S. and foreign, large, and small company stocks. On the bond side, it might own U.S. government, corporate, and foreign government bonds. Unlike a typical balanced fund, which generally splits investments relatively equally between stocks and bonds, asset allocation fund managers act according to their own analyses of the markets.

Income funds are funds tilted toward income and low risk. They yield almost as much as bonds because they usually invest in a combination of government and corporate bonds, preferred stock, and utility and blue-chip stocks. These funds are ideal for those who live on a fixed income or who want a slightly riskier alternative to bank CDs. The funds pay higher yields than all other kinds of stock funds.

Sidelines

Two of the most tried-and-true balanced funds are Fidelity Puritan Fund (800-544-8888) and Vanguard's Wellington Fund (800-662-7447). A more aggressive balanced fund to consider is the CGM Mutual Fund (800-345-4048). All three funds carry top ratings by Morningstar. Best-rated asset allocation funds include SoGen International (800-334-2143) and USAA Investment Cornerstone (800-382-8722).

Boosting Your Returns Overseas

The U.S. stock market isn't the only game in town. There are stock markets throughout the world. Many foreign corporations are as profitable as their U.S. counterparts. In addition, economies in Asia, the Pacific Basin, and Latin America are growing faster than ours. There are a lot of investment opportunities abroad. That's why it's a good idea to consider investing in a well-managed mutual fund that invests overseas.

There's no free lunch, however, when you invest in mutual funds that invest overseas. About one-third of the increase or decrease in the total return of international stock funds can be attributed to the changing value of the dollar. (You learn more about foreign currency risk later in the chapter.) In addition, you have other risks when you invest overseas, such as the impact of a political or economic crisis on the country's stock market.

Despite the pitfalls, it could pay to invest in a well-managed fund that invests overseas if you want to diversify your portfolio.

How You Gonna Keep 'Em Down on the Farm After They See Paris?

In Chapter 14, you learned about international bond funds, which are good for diversification. It's even more important to have some kind of international stock fund. Why? Two-thirds of the world's companies exist outside

171

the good old USA. Over the past 10 years ending in 1994, international funds grew at a 14.7 percent annual average total return. By contrast, the average U.S. stock fund gained 12.5 percent annually, according to Morningstar.

As with international bond funds, international stock funds come in all shapes and sizes. Some funds invest in blue-chip stocks around the world. Nestlé, Canon, Hitachi, and Heineken are common holdings in such funds. Others invest in small company stocks worldwide. Funds that invest world-wide are often called global funds. Global funds invest overseas as well as in the U.S. There are funds that invest only in foreign countries, not the U.S. Some funds invest only in European, Latin American, or Asian companies. Others invest in single countries such as Japan.

Table 15.6 Top Performing International-Foreign Stock Funds, Average Annual Total Return, 10 Years ending in June 30, 1995

Fund	Annual Return %
GAM International	22.16
Templeton Foreign I	17.43
T. Rowe Price Interntional Stock	17.38
EuroPacific Growth	17.37
Fidelity Overseas	16.75
Vanguard International Growth	16.74
Pilot Kleinwort Benson International Equity	16.00
Vanguard Trustees' Equity International	15.74
Scudder International	15.40
Kemper International A	14.87

Source: Morningstar Mutual Fund Performance Report, July 1995

A Yen for Investing

You learned about some of the foreign currency risk involved in investing internationally in Chapter 14. Fund managers have to change all their U.S. dollars into foreign money, such as the Japanese yen or German mark, before they can buy overseas stocks. Sometimes, U.S. money is exchanged at a rate worse than it was when you put up your dollars to buy it. Even *after* the fund buys overseas stocks, the exchange rate between U.S. dollars and foreign dollars can fluctuate, affecting the value of your fund.

Fortunately, fund managers take steps to protect themselves from foreign currency risk. Nevertheless, here's a taste of how this foreign currency risk can affect an international fund:

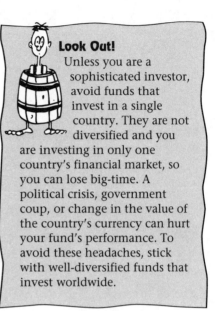

Look Out!
Unless you are a sophisticated investor, avoid funds that invest in a single country. They are not diversified and you are investing in only one country's financial market, so you can lose big-time. A political crisis, government coup, or change in the value of the country's currency can hurt your fund's performance. To avoid these headaches, stick with well-diversified funds that invest worldwide.

➤ The value of your fund may drop if the foreign currency declines in value against the U.S. dollar.

➤ The value of your fund can rise if the foreign currency increases in value against the U.S. dollar.

The Least You Need to Know

➤ You invest in stock mutual funds for long-term growth.

➤ Aggressive growth funds buy and sell all types of stocks for profits.

➤ Small company stock funds invest in companies that the portfolio manager expects will grow into profitable larger corporations.

➤ Growth and income funds invest in blue-chip stocks.

➤ Minimize the risk with balanced funds. They own both stocks and bonds.

Chapter 16

Mutual Funds for Special Situations

In This Chapter

➤ Risks and rewards of funds that sell at bargain prices

➤ The funds that invest in specific businesses

➤ Hedging your investments against inflation

➤ Investing with a conscience

Got a hankering for something a bit different from the run-of-the-mill stock or bond fund? This chapter delves into even more mutual funds options that are available to those looking for even greater challenges.

For example, there are funds that you can buy for 80 or 90 cents on the dollar. There also are high-risk funds that promise unbelievable profits because they invest in one type of industry. Do you have strong moral and ethical feelings about how companies do business? You have still other funds to pick! This chapter examines some specialized kinds of mutual funds.

Closed-End Funds

Know how you can't pass up those President's Day sales? You can buy all those clothes and shoes with Italian names cheaply. Last year, for example, one of us (guess who?) picked up a pair of $200 Ferragamo shoes for $80. One of us, although not necessarily the other, was mighty proud of that find.

Sometimes, you also can buy certain types of investments on sale. They don't have sexy European names, nor are they big box office draws. They go by names such as Baker Fentress, Tri-Continental, Gabelli Equity Trust, and Royce Value—these funds may be good, but overlooked, investments.

A Different Breed of Mutual Fund Lookalike

Up to this point, you've learned about open-end funds, generally classified as mutual funds. They have no limit as to the number of shares that investors can buy and sell.

There are some other animals known as closed-end funds, which, although frequently grouped with them, are not technically mutual funds. These are also called closed-end investment companies and publicly traded funds. So that you don't get them mixed up with open-end mutual funds, we will refer to closed-end funds as closed-end investment companies. Sometimes you can buy some well-managed, closed-end investment companies for 80 to 90 cents on the dollar.

Closed-end funds, although similar to mutual funds, are not mutual funds. Mutual funds are open-ended because they continually offer new shares for sale to the investment public. By contrast, closed-end investment companies issue a limited number of shares and do not redeem them. Instead, closed-end shares are traded in the securities markets, with supply and demand determining the price. The closed-end investment company's shares of stock traded on the securities exchange just like the stock of a corporation. The closed-end investment company's business is managing a portfolio of securities. Some may invest in stocks, bonds, overseas securities, or a combination of securities. There are broadly diversified closed-end investment companies, as well as ones that concentrate on a specific industry or group of industries. Some invest in single countries of the world such as

Technobabble

Closed-end funds are investment companies that sell a fixed number of shares that are traded on the stock exchange. Mutual funds are *open-end funds*, which means that there is no limit to the number of shares that investors can buy and sell.

Japan, and others invest in regions of the world such as Europe. There are closed-end investment companies that invest in Treasury, corporate, and foreign bonds. High-tax-bracket investors can invest in closed-end investment companies that buy municipal bonds.

There also are dual-purpose, closed-end investment companies that issue two classes of shares. The first class of shares is for investors who want income, and the second class of shares is for those who want growth. You can't buy and sell shares of the closed-end investment company's portfolio. You can only buy or sell the closed-end investment company's stock, which is traded on a stock exchange. The shares of stock easily can be bought or sold through a stockbroker just like any other stock.

Closed-end funds work this way:

➤ You own stock in the closed-end investment company that manages a portfolio of securities. You have to buy or sell shares of a closed-end investment company from a stockbroker. Don't forget: You pay the broker a commission for that.

➤ Depending on investment objective, a closed-end investment company pays its shareholders distributions in the form of interest, dividends, and capital gains based on the earnings of its portfolio of securities.

➤ The investment company charges a management fee that ranges from one-half of one percent to 1.5 percent based on the amount of assets in the portfolio. Shareholders can take the distributions in cash or reinvest them and buy more shares of the closed-end investment company.

➤ Do you want to buy a closed-end fund? There are two prices to examine: the investment company's stock price and the net asset value or share price of the closed-end investment company's portfolio of securities.

➤ When a share of stock in the investment company sells for significantly less than the share price of the mutual fund, you might have found a good deal. Voilà!

Buy at 80 to 85 Cents on the Dollar

You can find some real bargains when you invest in closed-end investment companies. For example, suppose you talk to a stockbroker (you also can get the information from the stock tables in the newspaper) and find that the stock of the XYZ closed-end investment company sells for $8 per share. Then you check the net asset value of the portfolio of securities managed by the closed-end investment company. It's $10 per share. That means it costs you $8 per share of stock to become a shareholder of an investment company with a portfolio of securities that are priced at $10.

That's a real bargain!

The idea is to buy shares of stock in the closed-end investment company at a discount to the net asset value of the portfolio of securities it manages. You've invested for less than the assets of the investment company are worth. You can buy and hold a well-managed, closed-end investment company for the long haul. Or, you might sell your stock at a profit when it rises in price, and the discount between the share price of the closed-end investment company and net asset value of the portfolio narrows.

Focusing In on Sector Funds

Recall that sector funds or specialty funds, which you learned about in Chapter 4, are not for beginners either.

When you invest in a sector fund, you're betting on stocks in a specific industry sector, such as technology, banking, chemicals, oil and gas, durable goods, paper products, and so on. You've got to know what you're doing. You have to be able to understand business conditions and anticipate changes in the economy to make money in sector funds.

Several fund groups have a stable of sector funds. With these programs, you typically can switch in and out of different sector funds as investment conditions change. Most are low-load or no-load. Fund groups with such programs include Fidelity Investments (800-544-6666), The INVESCO Group of Funds (800-525-8085), and Vanguard Group of Funds (800-662-7447).

You've Got to Move like Greased Lightning!

Investing in sector funds can be like riding a roller coaster. For example, Fidelity Select Air Transportation fund's total return was 31 percent in 1993, but in 1994, the fund lost 22 percent in total return.

Those who make investment decisions at a turtle's pace should probably forget sector funds. To be successful, you have to use sophisticated investment tactics and buy or sell quickly. Otherwise, you can buy a fund only to find its price sink like the Titanic.

Investors in sector funds should understand business cycles and use trend indicators to make the right investment decisions. Here are some examples of key trends that influence sector funds:

➤ When the economy starts to churn, stocks of industries such as heavy metals, machinery, and chemicals tend to rise in anticipation of demand for manufactured goods.

➤ When the economy is strong but starting to slow down, foods, consumer products, and health care stocks do well because investors favor steadier businesses.

➤ In an economic recession, stocks in the auto and construction businesses tend to do well in anticipation of an economic recovery.

Hot Tip
Considering sector funds? It could pay to subscribe to a newsletter that tracks sector funds, such as The Sector Funds Newsletter, (619-748-0805).

Utility Stocks for Mom and Pop

As you learned in Chapter 4, utility stock funds are low-risk sector funds. No matter how bad it gets, everyone uses electricity, gas, water, and the like. Retirees like utility stock funds because they get monthly income. Individual utility stocks, by contrast, mail dividend checks quarterly. Most utility stock funds own a large number of electric utility companies, as well as telephone and other communication companies.

Utility stock funds invest in all kinds of utility companies, which are cash cow businesses. Over the past 10 years, the average utility stock fund gained more than 10 percent annually. Half the gain came from income and half from the price appreciation of the funds.

Look Out!
When interest rates rise, utility stock funds can lose money because investors flock to high-interest bonds. In 1994, when both short- and long-term interest rates rose, utility stocks lost 8 percent. Even with utility stocks, the type of sector fund with the least risk, you need to be prepared to ride out all sorts of weather.

Inflation Hedges

Precious metals funds, which invest in gold mining stocks, and real estate stock funds are also popular. These funds perform well when inflation heats up. In 1978, when inflation was unbearable and prices were rising at more than 12 percent annually, share prices of precious metals funds soared. There also have been bad times for these funds. The average precious metals fund lost 23 percent in 1990.

The best bets in precious metals funds, according to Morningstar, are U.S. World Gold Shares, Vanguard Specialized Gold, and IDS Precious Metals. All outperformed the average precious metals fund, which gained just 3 percent annually, over the past five years.

Real estate stock funds also perform well in times of inflation. Compared with precious metals funds, real estate stock funds don't give you as big a bang for your buck, but you also lose less when the economy sours. The best real estate stock fund over five years, according to Morningstar, is The Fidelity Real Estate Investment Fund. It grew 11.7 percent annually.

Sidelines

As a rule of thumb, you can keep about 5 percent of your mutual fund investments in a real estate or precious metals fund as a hedge against inflation. You can lose at least 20 percent in these funds in any given year, however. That's why it pays to invest only a small amount. Let it sit. Then, when inflation heats up, these funds should gain.

Funds for Pure Hearts

Do you have strong feelings about gun control and the arms industry, the environment, pollution, or how workers are treated?

Socially responsible funds do not invest in any old company. These funds have super-strict investment rules. Social funds specifically scout for companies in the alternative energy business or those committed to staying out of the arms or nuclear energy business. They want to invest in companies with great employee benefits. They like firms that don't discriminate against women, minorities, or other groups. They do not invest in tobacco companies, the gambling businesses, or alcohol.

In mid-1995, there were more than 20 socially responsible mutual funds with more than $2.5 billion in assets, but don't expect to hit a home run when you invest in socially responsible stock funds. These types of funds tend to track the market averages, although a few that invest in undervalued small company stocks have registered impressive returns over the past several years.

Technobabble

Socially responsible funds invest in companies that don't pollute the environment or sell arms. They will not own tobacco or alcohol stocks, nor will they invest in companies with poor employee relations.

Socially responsible investors tend to be conservative. We are told that a lot of churches and religious groups invest in these funds. There are some great brand-name companies, however, such as Wal-Mart, Coca-Cola, and Hewlett-Packard, on the buy list of many socially responsible stock funds.

Great Funds for the Ethical Investors

There are several socially responsible funds you can pick. Some invest in large companies, others go after cheap stocks or smaller firms in the alternative energy business. The following are some examples of socially responsible funds:

➤ **Domini Social Equity Fund** (800-762-6814). This fund invests in a basket of socially responsible companies that make up the Social Stock Index. The fund is designed for growth and income. Over the past three years, the fund has grown at an 11.2 percent average annual total return.

➤ **Dreyfus Third Century Fund** (800-645-6561). This fund invests for growth. Over the past 10 years, it has grown at a respectable 10.9 percent average annual total return.

➤ **Parnassus** (800-999-3505). This fund invests for growth and may own large, midsize, and small company stocks. Over the past 10 years, the fund has grown at an annual average total return of 14.8 percent.

➤ **Pax World** (800-767-1729). This is a balanced fund that invests in Treasury bonds and large company stocks. Over the past 10 years, the fund has grown at a 10 percent average annual total return.

➤ **New Alternatives** (800-423-8383). This is a small company stock fund that invests in companies involved in alternative energy businesses. Over the past 10 years, the fund has grown at a 10.8 percent average annual total return.

The Least You Need to Know

➤ A closed-end fund can be a real bargain when the share price is less than the NAV (net asset value).

➤ Most sector funds are risky investments. Investing in them can be like riding a roller coaster.

➤ Utility stock funds are low-risk sector funds considered attractive by those who need regular monthly income. Even utility stock funds can lose money when rates rise.

➤ Precious metals and real estate stock funds perform well during periods of high inflation.

Part 4
The One-Hour-a-Year Investment Plans

Picking a mutual fund to buy, unfortunately, is not the end of the line when it comes to investing. You need to keep on top of your fund's performance. Is it up or down as much as similar funds? Is it a dud?

Yet, if you're like most of us, you don't have time to manage your investments. It's no wonder! How can you possibly stay on top of all the wheeling and dealing on Wall Street when you have to work full time and raise a family?

Mutual funds help make it easy to invest. This part of The Complete Idiot's Guide to Making Money with Mutual Funds *makes it even easier. You'll learn easy ways to evaluate your mutual fund's performance, and you'll find out tried and true strategies you can use to get the best mileage out of your investments with the least amount of time and worry.*

Chapter 17

How 'Ya Doing?

Even though you've probably selected the right mutual funds for you by now, you're not quite finished with the exercise of setting up your investment portfolio. At least once a year—better yet every three to six months—you want to be sure your mutual funds are doing what they say they're supposed to do: make you money.

This chapter reviews ways to monitor your mutual fund performance. You'll learn how to evaluate how your fund is doing and whether you should sell your old fund and buy a new one.

Your Mutual Fund Check-Up

You've got a couple of funds. Now what?

With a car, you get an oil change about every four months. Once a year, you take it in for a tune-up. Mutual funds are no different. You probably should give your funds a financial check-up at least every three months.

Check on them daily and you'll drive yourself bonkers. On the other hand, you don't want to be an ostrich. If you bury your head in the sand and forget about your fund, much can change. A portfolio manager's hot hands can turn into ice cubes. Or, you suddenly could discover that your fund manager has retired from your fund to write a best-selling book!

If you've done your homework and invested in funds with good long-term track records, you probably can rest assured that your funds will grow in value over the years.

You might not own the number one fund for the year, but based on your investment comfort level, you want your funds to lose less in down markets and do well compared with similar funds over 3-year, 5-year, and 10-year periods.

There are more than 6,000 mutual funds. The odds of investing in next year's top-performing fund are equivalent to your chances of winning the Kentucky Derby.

Remember, though, with mutual funds, just because you didn't cash in a winning ticket, doesn't mean you forfeit bragging rights.

Every three months, when you do your check-up, it's best to compare your funds' returns with similar funds. Look at the average annual total return of the entire group of funds over the last three months, one year, three years, and five years.

The best place to look is in *The Wall Street Journal, Investor's Business Daily,* or *Barrons*. These publications list the return on the S&P 500, the Lehman Brothers Bond Index, and average return on mutual funds based on their investment objectives.

Here is another option: Most public libraries have either the Morningstar, Value Line Mutual Fund Survey, or CDA/Wiesenberger mutual fund performance reports.

These services are the most comprehensive sources of information on mutual funds. They list performance year-by-year and annual average total returns of return for one through 10 years. These reports also tell how the fund ranks when compared with similar funds.

Here's what to do once you've looked up the information:

1. Ask yourself, "What was my fund's total return this year-to-date compared with the total returns on similar funds and the fund group average?" Compare the average annual total returns on your fund to similar funds and the peer group average over the past one-year, three-year, or five-year periods.

2. You also can compare your fund or funds' total returns to the market averages this year-to-date and over one-, three-, or five-year periods. The S&P 500 is an index that shows the performance of a large group of stocks in the United States. If you have an international stock fund, you can compare it to the Europe, Australia, Far East Index (EAFE), which tracks stocks listed on major world stock exchanges.

   You can compare how your fund or funds performed based on total return to the Lehman Brothers Long-Term Bond and Treasury Bond Indexes. These indexes tell you how the bond market is performing so that you can see how your funds stack up against the performance of the bond market.

3. Subtract the total return on your fund from the average peer groups' return, often listed under a heading such as "Investment Objective Averages" in a separate area. You also can subtract the return from the market averages. If the difference is positive, your fund is doing better than other funds. If it's negative, you're doing worse. You can use the Fund Performance Worksheet to get started comparing funds.

Hot Tip
Have a computer? You can buy software that keeps track of your investments. Quicken (520-295-3220) and Kiplinger's Simply Money (800-225-5524) will keep tabs on how your mutual funds perform.

187

Fund Performance Worksheet			
Your Fund	Your Fund's Total Return %	Peer Group or Other Funds' Return % (Subtract from Your Fund's Return %)	Difference

Create a worksheet like this one to compare your fund's performance with the performance for similar funds.

Let's take the Janus Fund, a no-load growth fund. Assume you owned the fund for five years. Over the past five years ending in June 1995, the Janus Fund had an annual average total return of 12.33 percent, according to Morningstar. The S&P 500 had a 12.08 percent annual average total return, and the average growth fund a 11.54 percent annual average total return over the same period. So, over the past five years, the Janus Fund earned .25 percentage points annually more than the stock market average and .79 percent points annually more than the average growth stock fund.

Not too shabby. But what's Janus done more recently? Year-to-date, for the first six months of 1995, the fund's total return was 16.51 percent. By contrast, over this period, the average growth fund's total return was 17.36 percent, and the S&P 500's total return was 20.19 percent.

Does this mean you should sell the Janus Fund because it lagged behind these indexes over the first six months of the year? Nope. You know it's been a winner over the past five years, even though it's lagged behind over the past six months. In a half-year or year's time, even a good fund can trail others.

The same fund has also ranked in the top 40 percent of funds in its class—done better than 60 percent of all other growth stock funds over the past year. Good enough!

You know your stock or bond funds are doing particularly well when they beat their market averages. Don't forget—with your fund, you're paying management fees, and some of your fund's holdings are kept in cash. Indexes, such as the S&P 500, don't reflect these factors.

How Does the Fund Rank Against Others?

You also can check newspapers, magazines, or even the fund's financial reports for information on how your fund compares funds with the same investment objectives over several time periods. Chapter 9 discusses the annual, semi-annual, or quarterly financial reports shareholders receive from their fund. Look for how your fund stacks up against funds with the same investment objective—and market averages, such as the S&P 500.

Depending upon which publication you pick up, the fund's *ranking* may be expressed either as a number or coded percentile. A numerical ranking provides a number showing how the fund did relative to other funds or funds with the same investment objective. The percentile ranking explains in which percentile of funds your fund ranks. Listings may compare your fund with all mutual funds. They also can compare your fund to funds with the same investment objective. A fund with a percentile ranking of 5 means its performance ranks in the top 5 percent of its category.

You don't need to buy the paper everyday—just when you do your quarterly to annual review. The *Wall Street Journal,* for example, lists fund performance and ranks funds by investment objectives based on Lipper Analytical Services data. On Fridays, you'll see the total return and ranking for one year, three years, and five years, so you can get a clear picture of how a fund stacks up against its peers over different periods of time. See Table 17.1 for an example of the *Journal*'s rating system.

Table 17.1 Wall Street Journal's Fund Rankings: What They Mean

Rank	Group Ranking Based On Investment Objective
A	Top 20 percent
B	Next 20 percent
C	Middle 20 percent
D	Bottom 20 percent

Investor's Business Daily takes a different approach, which is equally useful (see Table 17.2). Funds are ranked based on total return against all other funds over the past three years. It's always a good idea to see how a particular fund stacks up against all other funds. This information may help you decide whether to invest in a fund that's doing better than other funds over the past

few years. If you're a bottom-fisher, the rankings may help you spot funds
that have lagged behind other funds, but could rebound and register higher
total returns in the future.

**Table 17.2 *Investor's Business Daily* Fund Rankings:
What They Mean**

Rank	Ranking Compared with All Funds
A+	Top 5 percent
A	Top 10 percent
A-	Top 15 percent
B+	Top 20 percent
B	Top 25 percent
B-	Top 30 percent
C+	Top 35 percent
C	Top 40 percent
C-	Top 45 percent
D+	Top 50 percent
D	Top 60 percent
D-	Top 70 percent
E	Below 70 percent

Sidelines

There are a couple of other items to check besides performance.
Look at your fund's latest financial report or call the fund group
and get information about the following:

➤ Are there major changes in the fund's holdings? Has the fund
manager put more of the fund in small company stocks? Has
he or she loaded up in one industry or diversified among
many industries? This information, along with current performance, gives you a feel for how the fund is being managed.

> ➤ If you own a bond fund, check to see whether there has been a major change, such as a change in the average bond ratings of the fund's holdings or a change in the average maturity of the fund. If a bond fund's average credit rating has dropped—for example, from AA to A—and the average maturity has lengthened, it means the fund manager is taking on more risk to earn higher returns. By contrast, if the average credit rating has increased and the average maturity has shortened, the bond fund manager may be playing it safe.

Why Do Funds Lose Steam?

Why would a fund with a good long-term track record suddenly fall behind? Its stock-picking style may be out of favor. Growth fund managers may lag behind because bargain-priced undervalued stocks are in favor. By contrast, a couple of years down the road, growth stocks, which tend to show 25 percent to 30 percent annual earnings growth, may be in and undervalued stocks out.

Funds that have too much money in cash instead of stocks may trail the overall stock market and stock funds that are fully invested in a bull market. The fund's manager may have misjudged the direction of the stock market and kept money in cash as a safe haven. As a result, the manager may have just 70 percent to 80 percent of the fund's holdings invested in stocks when the market moves higher.

Plain old lousy stock picks are another reason a fund may do poorly. The fund manager's evaluation of a company, an industry, or the economy could be off the mark.

Bad timing can also be a factor. The companies a fund owns could look good on paper, but the darned stock price doesn't move. For some unexplained reason, there could be more sellers than buyers of the stocks the fund happens to own.

Does this mean you should dump your fund? No. You must look at several factors before you decide when to sell.

When to Sell Your Funds

When should you sell your fund? Give it at least three years. Stock returns tend to move in cycles. It definitely could be time to make a change if your fund underperforms similar funds over at least a five-year period.

You should also consider changing funds under the following conditions:

➤ Your fund manager has a good track record and then leaves.

➤ The fund changes its investment objective.

➤ The fund merges with another fund that has a mediocre track record.

➤ Your own financial condition or tolerance for risk has changed.

Evaluating Your Fund Picks

What if you own several different types of funds?

You have to look at the total return on your investment and compare it to a similar type of benchmark. Suppose that you have 50 percent of the investment in a growth stock fund that registers a total return of 10 percent for the year and 50 percent in a bond fund that has a total return of 6 percent for the year. Figure your investment's total return for the year by following these steps:

1. Multiply .50 times 10 percent, the total return on your growth stock fund for the year. That equals 5 percent.

2. Multiply .50 times 6 percent, the total return of your bond fund for the year. That equals 3 percent.

3. Add the total returns that represent the growth fund and bond fund's share of your portfolio: 5 percent plus 3 percent equals 8 percent. This represents a weighted average total return on your entire portfolio.

Now you have to compare that to a couple of benchmarks, such as having 50 percent invested in the S&P 500 and 50 percent invested in the Lehman Brothers Aggregate Bond Index, to see how well you did versus the market averages. Suppose the S&P 500 total return for the year was 9.5 percent and the Lehman Brothers Bond Index total return was 5.8 percent. Fifty percent of 9.5 percent equals 4.75 percent. Fifty percent of 5.8 percent equals 2.9 percent for a combined total return of 7.65 percent.

To see how your investment mix did against the market averages, subtract 7.65 percent, the combined total return of the market averages, from 8 percent, the combined total return of your funds. The result is .35 percent.

Your mix of mutual funds gave you some extra return over the appropriate benchmarks, which reflect the market averages. If your mix of funds underperformed the benchmarks by a wide margin, it may be an indication that you might want to consider selling those funds and find funds that perform better. You also can use this method to compare the combined total return of your investment mix with similar funds or the fund's investment objective averages.

The Least You Need to Know

➤ Compare your fund's performance with similar funds, the average of funds with the same investment objective, and indexes, such as the S&P 500 index.

➤ If your fund is underperforming by a small margin, give it a chance— at least three years.

➤ Use the mutual fund tables available in the newspaper or through several reporting services to monitor your fund's performance every three months.

➤ Sell if your fund underperforms similar funds over three to five years.

Chapter 18

Getting Rich a Little Bit at a Time: Dollar Cost Averaging

In This Chapter

➤ Investing regularly

➤ Starting a savings program

➤ The best kinds of funds for dollar cost averaging

Well, people, you have a choice. You can read the paper daily, sweat out all the market's hiccups, and try to sell when you think your mutual fund's share price has peaked. Unfortunately, most of us don't know when that's actually going to happen, so there's a good chance you also can miss out on some big profits this way.

Your other option is to just sit tight and play it cool. This chapter focuses on one investment strategy that enables you to do the latter. You merely invest a certain amount of money regularly. This way, some of your cash is invested at high share prices, and some at lower share prices. Even though many of us have been doing this same type of thing for years with our plain old bank savings account, the gurus have a fancy name for this style of investing— *dollar cost averaging*.

With dollar cost averaging, you can build your wealth in a systematic level-headed manner. You don't have to watch every single move the market makes. You don't need an MBA or PhD either. This chapter goes into the pluses and minuses of dollar cost averaging, which is one of the simplest ways to invest. This is the kind of investment strategy you can use for at least five to ten years.

A Piggy Bank for Grown-Ups

One member of this writing team once enjoyed a free weekend in Disney World—and it wasn't by winning a contest. It was the result of periodically dumping the pennies, quarters, and dimes from a bulging purse into an empty one-gallon plastic water jug for a full year.

Then, on a quiet holiday weekend, this change was systematically wrapped and counted. It wound up being close to $100—enough for a hotel room for one night!

Dollar cost averaging works kind of like that, but in a slightly more disciplined way. The results, for those who keep it up for several years, are apt to be even more impressive.

With dollar cost averaging, you invest $50 or $100, for example, every month into the mutual fund of your choice. Whether you're saving for your child's future education, a vacation home, or your retirement, this is a low-risk way to invest.

> **WHAT?**
>
> **Technobabble**
> With *dollar cost averaging*, you make regular investments and have your earnings automatically reinvested. When the share price drops, you accumulate more shares at lower prices.

When you fill out your mutual fund application form, don't forget to check the box that indicates that you want your earnings to be reinvested automatically. When you do that, your earnings also buy more shares of your fund each month.

With dollar cost averaging, there's no need to worry if the fund's share price drops. When this happens, your regular monthly investment, plus any earnings, is purchasing new shares of the mutual fund at the lower prices. Look at the value of your fund a few years after doing this, once the price rises again, and you'll be in for a shock—a pleasant one!

Mutual fund families even help you dollar cost average through some of the services they provide. Most have automatic investment savings plans. You can have the money automatically taken out of your checking account and invested in the fund of your choice before you have a chance to miss it.

Sidelines

The stock market, as measured by the S&P 500 index, has grown at an average annual rate of 12.8 percent over the past 20 years.

Those who tried to move between cash and stocks at the right times didn't have much room for error. If they missed the five best investment months over the past 240 months, the return on their investments dropped to 9.3 percent.

Taking the Guesswork out of It

Dollar cost averaging takes the guesswork out of investing. When you dollar cost average, you don't have to worry about timing the markets. You are always buying shares. Because you always have money invested, you profit during periods in which a fund's price rises. Other times, the share price may decline. But like a squirrel accumulating nuts for the winter, you are accumulating shares. Then when the fund's share price rises, your investment is worth more.

How Dollar Cost Averaging Works

Suppose you invest $100 each month in a no-load stock fund that sells at $20 per share. You invest $100 and receive five shares. The market drops and the fund's share price drops to $10 per share. You again invest your $100. At $10 per share you receive 10 shares for your $100. Let's assume by the next month, the market has returned to where it was when you started and your fund is now selling at $20 per share. You now receive five shares for your $100 investment. Table 18.1 shows what your investment looks like.

Table 18.1 How Dollar Cost Averaging Works

Month	Regular Investment	Share Price	Shares Acquired
Month 1	$100	$20	5
Month 2	$100	$10	10
Month 3	$100	$20	5
Total	$300		20

Average Share Cost: $15.00 ($300 divided by 20 shares)

Average Share Price: $16.67

Hot Tip

For a free booklet on how dollar cost averaging works, write the Investment Company Institute, 1401 H Street, NW, Suite 1200, Washington, D.C. 20005.

You own 20 shares of the fund in which you invested $300. Your shares are worth more than what you paid. The average purchase price of your shares was $16.67. The average cost was $15.00 because you invested $300 and bought a total of 20 shares.

The idea behind dollar cost averaging is to invest for the longer term. You have to invest through thick and thin, sticking with a fund in down markets. If you bail out early, you can be forced to sell shares at a loss.

The Downside

Dollar cost averaging is simple and effective, but, like anything else, it's not perfect.

Our friend, Sheldon Jacobs, who publishes the *No-Load Investor Newsletter*, Irvington-on-Hudson, NY, encourages regular investing through dollar cost averaging, but he also issues some warnings.

He says that you should be aware of dollar cost averaging limitations. This type of investment strategy may not be for everyone. If you are an aggressive investor who can tolerate a big drop in total return in return for long-term growth, you may want to invest a lump sum.

Sheldon points out that dollar cost averaging loses its value over time. If the same amount is invested each month, the money you've accumulated may not go as far as you thought when you consider inflation or the increasing costs of necessities. As a result, he suggests increasing your monthly investment each year by $25 or $50, for example, to keep up with rising inflation.

Second, there are no rules to tell you when to sell after you've used dollar cost averaging for a number of years. There are no guarantees that the average cost of the fund shares you bought over the years will be less than the market price of the fund when you sell. To make dollar cost averaging work, you have to pick the right time to sell the fund.

Third, if you're just starting out with dollar cost averaging, you might find it hard to invest in a fund at bargain prices. Jacobs says that bull markets last twice as long as bear markets. Most of the time, you'll buy fund shares at higher prices. His solution is to invest twice as much in your fund during bear markets.

Fourth, if you invest a lump sum in a fund, you have more money working for you at the beginning, compared with stashing away a little bit every month. Over the long haul, the lump sum investment grows much more. Of course, if you don't have much money in the first place, dollar cost averaging is better than nothing at all.

Finding the Best Funds

Dollar cost averaging works well with all types of stock funds, ranging from aggressive growth and small company stocks to tried-and-true growth and income funds. It works best with more volatile funds—the ones that drop and then soar in value. In Chapter 3, you learned about the beta value, a mutual fund measure that tells whether a fund is volatile. The higher the beta, the more the fund's price can bounce up and down. If you invest in a fund with a good long-term track record that also sports a beta value of greater than one, you've found a great fund for dollar cost averaging. Even Nervous Nellies can cheer when the fund loses money. Why? You're buying more shares of the fund at a lower price. When it rebounds, you build up a tidy sum. Use this tactic over the years, and dollar cost averaging will serve you well.

Look Out!
Don't dollar cost average all your spare cash. Even with dollar cost averaging, there's never a guarantee that your fund will rebound from a few bad years. If you pick the wrong fund, the money you invest over the years may not grow to what you expected.

When shopping for a mutual fund to use in a dollar cost averaging investment plan, consider the following:

➤ The ideal dollar cost averaging candidate should have outperformed its peers over the longer term. You want a fund with a good long-term track record. Look at the fund's annual rate of return over at least a five-year period. Then look at the fund's return from year to year. You want to invest in funds that have performed as well or better than similar funds over the long term.

Hot Tip
The Value Line Mutual Fund Survey is the only rating service that shows dollar cost averaging performance on more than 3,000 stock and bond funds. The report is available in most public libraries.

➤ The fund should have shown a proven ability to bounce back from bad years such as 1973, 1979, 1981, 1987, 1990, and 1994.

➤ If the fund is part of a no-load mutual fund family, you don't pay brokerage commissions on your investments. You can save a lot.

➤ The fund group should have an automatic investment plan. That way you can have money automatically taken out of your checking account and invested in your mutual fund.

The Worst Funds

Some funds are better dollar cost averaging candidates than others. If you dollar cost average into money funds or shorter-term bond funds, you accumulate money that earns a lower rate of interest. With these kinds of funds, you're saving not investing. Dollar cost averaging also won't build your wealth as much in a balanced fund or income fund as it will in a growth fund. To make dollar cost averaging work best, you need to invest in more aggressive funds that have the ability to grow.

For those who are nervous about socking away money in an aggressive growth or growth fund, consult Chapter 21. You'll learn about some low-risk ways to dollar cost average into stock funds to build your retirement nest egg.

What about bond funds?

Dollar cost averaging can work with long-term bond funds. When interest rates rise or fall 1 percent, most long-term bond funds can move down or up in value about 10 to 12 percent. Over the past 10 years, long-term bond funds have grown at an annual rate of close to 9 percent. If you invested $12,000 through thick and thin in your bond fund over the past 10 years, your money grew to $18,232. Not bad!

Getting Started with DCA

Even before you start dollar cost averaging, as you learned in Chapter 2, you need to make sure that you have money socked away to meet emergencies such as medical bills, a leaky roof, or an unexpected financial crisis. This money should be put in a low-risk investment such as a savings account or money market fund. You need to establish your goals and determine your investment mix based on your tolerance for risk as shown in your answers to the quiz in Chapter 6.

Dollar cost averaging should begin only after you develop a financial cushion for emergencies and determine that you're willing to take on a little more risk in exchange for building your wealth, long term. Then you can pick a fund for dollar cost averaging.

The first step is to start saving regularly in a passbook savings account until you have $1,000 to make the initial investment required by most funds. After that, you can invest as little as $50 a month. But there is no upper limit on what you can sock away regularly. Once you decide how much you want to invest, there are several ways to go about it.

1. You can write a check and send it to the fund each month. That way you can increase or decrease your investments as time goes by. You also can skip a payment if you have a financial emergency. What's the drawback to this method? You need to make sure you have the discipline to invest every month.

2. You can sign up for the fund's automatic investment plan, as discussed in Chapter 11. That way you don't have to do anything. It's taken care of for you by the fund. If you need to make changes in the amount you want to invest, you can always call the fund. The drawback? You've got to be sure you keep a balance in your checking account large enough to cover your monthly investment. Otherwise, you might find yourself overdrawn and face extra charges for bounced checks. That's a no-no.

3. There also are special contractual plans available for dollar cost averaging when you invest in load funds with stockbrokers. Often, the broker will agree to waive the minimum initial investment as long as the investor agrees to certain terms. For example, the investor might agree to make monthly investments for 10 years. In return, the broker will take half of all commissions for 10 years in the first year of your investment. That may sound like a pretty stiff penalty, but investors who agree to

these programs are forcing themselves to save for the long term.

Contractual plans differ greatly from broker to broker, but many may come with special features. For example, the commissions may be lower if you make large investments. You might be able to withdraw money and later put it back into the fund without paying a commission, or you might reinvest distributions commission-free. Drawbacks? You're paying a lot in commissions up front and you're locked into the deal for a specific term.

The Least You Need to Know

➤ With dollar cost averaging, you invest every month for the long term.

➤ You can invest as little as $50 a month though a mutual fund's automatic investment program.

➤ Dollar cost averaging takes the guesswork out of investing.

➤ It takes a few years for dollar cost averaging to work. You have to accumulate enough shares to benefit from the growth of the fund.

Chapter 19

EZ Way to Buy and Sell: Constant Dollar Investing

In This Chapter

➤ Boosting the return on your investments

➤ Buying low and selling high

➤ Avoiding large losses in your stock funds

You're not convinced. "Buy low, sell high" was the advice your very first financial advisors, Mom and Dad, probably drummed into your head shortly after you outgrew your diapers.

Yet, we already told you the downside of this strategy. How many times have you talked to people who regretted not taking profits from their stock fund before its value went sinking like a ship in a bear market? When things are going great guns, most investors don't want to sell because they think the share price of their fund will go higher. What happens? Of course, the share price plunges. Then, when the fund is headed lower, they start selling shares because they fear it will drop more. Guess what happens? It goes higher, of course.

We keep telling 'ya. The stock market is a unique animal unto itself. You can't predict what it's going to do. However, by using a couple of easy rules, you might, at least, be able to buy *a little* lower and sell *a little* higher. This chapter tells you how.

Simple Rules to Buy And Sell

Constant dollar investing is an EZ way to take the guesswork out of when to buy and sell. Unlike with dollar cost averaging, which you learned about in Chapter 18, you can't exactly put this strategy on automatic pilot. You need to take a slightly more active role.

You might also find the constant dollar investment plan a little more conservative than dollar cost averaging. In other words, you might not make quite as much over the long haul with this program. With the constant dollar investment strategy, though, you preserve your stock fund profits while buying more shares at lower prices than you originally paid.

Look Out!
There's no way of predicting the stock market. Even with the constant dollar investment plan, it's still possible to lose. Be prepared—keep investing while your stock fund is dropping, in anticipation of higher returns down the road.

Assuming you have six months' worth of emergency cash in a bank or CD and you're able to tolerate some risk, all you need are a stock fund and a bond or money market fund to get started.

The objective of constant dollar investing is very simple. You merely keep the value of the stock fund the same as it was on the day you first bought it. You do this by evaluating your funds at least once a year and taking the following steps:

➤ If your stock fund's total value is worth more than when you first bought it, you take the excess cash and deposit it in the bond fund or money market fund.

➤ If your stock fund's total value is worth less than when you first bought it, you take money from the bond fund or money fund and deposit it in the stock fund to restore its original value.

By doing this, you always maintain the same amount in your stock fund each year. You don't need a lot of money to start the constant dollar investing plan. It's best to begin with $1,000 to $10,000.

The constant dollar investment method gives you an easy-to-use formula that tells you when to take profits and when to invest. It's a good idea to check the total value of your stock fund once a year. If it's up in value at the end of the year, take out your profits. If it's declined in value, kick in more money to bring the investment back to the constant dollar amount you designated when you started the investment plan.

Constant dollar investing works this way: Suppose you start out with $1,000 in your stock fund. At the end of every year, your stock fund should be worth $1,000. If you have more than $1,000, take the profits and invest them in your bond or money fund. If you have losses, take an amount equal to those losses from the bond or money fund and redeposit it into the stock fund to restore its value to $1,000.

Suppose your stock fund is up to $1,300 at the end of year one. You take $300 and sock it away in your money fund. Next year, the stock fund drops to a value of $875. You kick in $125 from your money fund and bring the value of the stock fund back to $1,000. In the following year, the fund is up to $1,300. You take the extra $300 and put it back in your money fund.

Technobabble
With *constant dollar investing,* you make sure that you have the same amount invested in your stock fund at the beginning of each year.

Hot Tip
Constant dollar investing, as well as other investment tactics, works best for tax-deferred retirement savings investments such as IRAs and 401(k) company pension plans. You don't pay taxes on your switches in a retirement plan. If you invest in taxable funds, you may pay 15 percent to 39.6 percent of your profits to Uncle Sam.

Should You Use Constant Dollar Investing?

Constant dollar investing is a viable plan for virtually any investor who feels more comfortable taking profits and hates to see the value of his or her investment decline in a bear market.

A constant dollar investor typically is focused on the nearer term than an investor who uses dollar cost averaging. Remember our discussion in the previous chapter? An investor using dollar cost averaging is socking money away for a lifetime through thick and thin.

Getting Started

With constant dollar investing, it's important to open an account either with a no-load mutual fund family or a load fund group that charges no commissions on trades between existing funds. Otherwise, you pay through the nose for switching money between funds. You have a greater choice of stock funds if you invest with a large fund family. Find out when your fund family sends out statements so that you can plan to adjust your investments around the statement dates. You need your statement information to make the adjustments. Otherwise, you have to keep tabs on the funds yourself.

Next, select the stock fund of your choice. Invest at least $1,000. You get the most for your money by investing in an aggressive stock fund or a small company fund, but growth and income funds also work well. Why? You get more growth in the share value of your fund if it invests in stocks rather than bond and money funds.

Remember to have the stock fund distributions reinvested into new shares. That way you build a larger number of shares to work with.

Select a bond fund or money fund as a place to stash your cash. Money funds are the less risky option because the fund's price, as you learned in Chapter 12, stays at $1 a share.

Look Out!
Avoid low-risk income stock funds and balanced funds for the constant dollar investment plan. You don't get enough of a return to make the tactic worth using.

However, if you want higher income and the possibility of some growth when interest rates fall and bond prices rise, select a bond fund rather than a money fund. Remember—you can lose money even with the least risky bond funds. Recall from Chapters 3 and 14 that bond prices and interest rates move in opposite directions. Also, if you select a mortgage bond fund, your mortgage-holders could refinance, forcing your fund manager to make new investments at lower rates.

Look Out!
Avoid stock funds that hold a lot of cash. You want your stock fund to be fully invested to reap the maximum profits.

The best combination is to invest in a stock fund with a good long-term track record and a high-yielding money fund.

Finally, once a year, at least, bring the balance in your stock fund back to its original balance. You either take profits from your stock fund and invest them in a money fund, or you kick in from the money fund to replenish your losses in the stock fund.

For the sake of simplicity, suppose you invest $1,000 as your constant dollar amount. Realistically, the investment program should be started with a constant dollar amount of at least $2,000 to $5,000, but for the example, suppose you invest $1,000 and the stock fund is worth $1,500 at year's end. Take $500 out and invest in a money fund. Now you're back to square one with an investment of one grand. Say, in the following year, your stock fund is down $100 to $900. You kick in $100 from your money fund to bring the stock fund's value back to a grand.

You can make adjustments every three or six months if you prefer, but one-year intervals provide more time for your money to grow. Over the long term, you take profits when the fund increases in value, and invest more when the price dips. On the other hand, if you make adjustments every three or six months, you're assured of taking profits before something serious happens. By taking profits every six months, an investor would have avoided big stock market losses in October 1987 and November 1990.

How It Works

We cranked up our computer and did a mini-study using Morningstar data, to see how constant dollar investing has worked over the years.

Table 19.1 gives an example of how a dollar cost investing strategy could have worked for you. It assumes $1,000 invested in a growth and income fund and $1,000 invested in a money fund that earns 4 percent.

Table 19.1 How Constant Dollar Investing Works

Year Invested	Constant Dollar Amount	End-of-Year Stock Fund Value	End-of-Year Money Fund Value	End-of-Year Total Value
1986	$1,000	$1,160	$1,040	$2,200
1987	1,000	1,020	1,248	2,268
1988	1,000	1,150	1,319	2,469
1989	1,000	1,240	1,470	2,710
1990	1,000	950	1,778	2,728
1991	1,000	1,290	1,798	3,088
1992	1,000	1,080	2,172	3,253

continues

Table 19.1 Continued

Year Invested	Constant Dollar Amount	End-of-Year Stock Fund Value	End-of-Year Money Fund Value	End-of-Year Total Value
1993	1,000	1,110	2,255	3,365
1994	1,000	980	2,369	3,349
1995*	1,000	1,150	2,416	3,566

* Worth of investments at mid-year 1995

The table shows how your money grew based on a hypothetical example, using the total returns of the average growth and income fund and a money fund that registered a hypothetical 4 percent annual average return.

Column 1 lists the year your investment started, 1986. Column 2 lists the constant dollar amount, which in Table 19.1 is the $1,000 that is invested in the stock fund. You want to have this anount in your stock fund at the beginning of each year. Column 3 lists the end-of-year value of your stock fund, and Column 4 lists the end-of-year value in the money fund. Column 5 lists the end-of-year value of the total investment. As you can see, for example, in 1986, the $1,000 constant dollar stock fund amount listed in Column 2 grew to $1,160. The money fund grew to $1,040 as listed in Column 4, and the total amount of the combined investment was $2,200 (Column 5). Because the stock fund grew to $1,160, you took $160 out of the fund and invested it in the money fund. So in 1987, as shown in Column 2, the constant dollar amount is back to $1,000.

To find out how much you have to take out of your stock fund or add to your stock fund to bring it back to the constant dollar amount, you have to do some figuring. Subtract column 3, the year-end value of the stock fund from column 2, the constant dollar amount. If the result is positive, that is the profit you take out of the stock fund and sock away in the money fund. If it's negative, you have to take money out of the money fund and put it in the stock fund.

In the years listed in the table, you would have taken profits in 8 of the 10 years. You would have kicked more money into your fund in 2 of the 10 years. In the years following your losses, 1990 and 1994, your stock fund would have gained 29 percent and 15 percent, respectively.

Over the past 9-1/2 years, a constant dollar investment plan would have served you well. If you invested $1,000 in a growth and income fund and $1,000 in a money fund that earned 4 percent annually at year-end 1985, your investment would have grown to $3,566 by mid-year 1995. If you invested $1,000 in a stock fund and $1,000 in a money fund that earned 4 percent annually at year-end 1985, your investment would have grown to $3,566 by midyear 1995. This example, however, does not assume taxes have been paid on the trades.

You're not going to get rich quick using constant dollar investing. And, of course, keep in mind that past performance is no indication of how constant dollar investing will perform in the future. Nevertheless, a look at the past shows that constant dollar investing works, provided that you invest for at least five years to get results. Even then, if the overall stock market doesn't do that well, neither will your stock fund's constant dollar investment plan.

Sidelines

Want to put some zip in your stock fund's performance? Consider using value averaging instead of constant dollar investing or dollar cost averaging. With value averaging, the investor makes the value of his or her portfolio increase by a fixed amount periodically.

For example, you might determine you want the value of your investments to increase $300 every three months, but the value of your stock fund increases by more than $300. Take out the extra profits and put them in a money fund. If the stock fund fails to increase $300 in value, you must kick in the difference from your money fund.

Value averaging is a more profitable way to invest compared with dollar cost averaging or the constant dollar investment plan, says Michael Edleson, Ph.D., finance professor at Harvard University, and author of *Value Averaging,* International Publishing Corp., Chicago. With value averaging, investors take advantage of relatively short-term declines in their fund's value to invest more money. Then they take greater profits over the longer term.

Although value averaging can be an attractive way to invest in mutual funds, it has drawbacks. You must spend more time with your investments and keep good records. In a bear market, investors must be prepared to kick in a large chunk of money to bring the value of the fund up to the amount the program requires.

The Least You Need to Know

➤ With constant dollar investing, you keep the same amount invested in your stock fund at the beginning of every year.

➤ At the end of the year, take profits in your stock fund and invest it in a money fund.

➤ If you have stock fund losses at the end of the year, take money out of the money fund and invest it in the stock fund.

➤ More aggressive investors can keep a constant dollar amount every six months.

Chapter 20

Keeping an Even Keel: Diversification and Portfolio Rebalancing

In This Chapter

➤ Getting better returns with less risk

➤ An investment program that takes just an hour a year

➤ When to adjust your investment mix

We live in a paranoid society when it comes to money. The result is that most people oversave and underinvest. They sock too much away in the bank and not enough in stocks or bonds.

The reason for this paranoia is that nobody, quite understandably, wants to lose their hard-earned cash. Ironically, years later when that money is really needed to live on, it's the paranoid crew that finds they don't have as much as they'd like. True, they might have succeeded in preserving their principal; but meanwhile, everything they buy costs more. Their low-risk invested money doesn't go quite far enough.

This chapter looks at a low-risk way to invest in mutual funds so that you might avoid this shock later on in life. You'll learn how to manage an investment mix that always matches your tolerance for risk. You'll also learn how to combine dollar cost averaging with the taking of profits to boost the return on your mutual fund investments.

Balancing Your Act

Keeping your investment balanced means diversifying your mutual fund investments by owning different types of mutual funds that invest in different types of assets, such as stocks, bonds, and cash. Stock funds, bond funds, and money funds don't always perform in tandem with each other. So, if a stock fund's total return has declined, the losses may be offset by the total return on the bond fund and money fund. As mentioned earlier in the book, spreading your assets over a variety of different investments is important. If you diversify your mutual fund portfolio, your investment performance should fluctuate less because losses from some investments are offset by gains in others. As a result, you have less risk than if you were to put all the money into one type of investment, such as a stock fund or bond fund.

In addition to lowering the risks, diversification can offer higher total returns than you would expect from investments in only the most conservative types of mutual funds, such as money funds.

We think diversification makes a lot of sense because no one type of mutual fund performs best in all types of economic conditions. No one can predict which fund will register high total returns in the future. That's why it's important to diversify. For example, if you have a diversified portfolio of mutual funds, a decline in the value of your bond fund could be offset by an increase in the total return of an international stock fund that invests overseas.

Diversification alone, however, may not be enough to keep you on a steady course. What happens if your stock fund registers high total returns for a couple of years running? You may find you have too much money in stocks based on your tolerance for risk. That's where portfolio rebalancing comes into play.

Rebalancing Your Act

What is rebalancing? Remember those seesaws at the school playground? The idea was to keep it level. If one kid was too high, the other was too low. The kid on the side closest to the ground had to push up to bring a buddy on the other side down from his or her lofty perch.

Rebalancing your investments works the same way. Sometimes your stock funds shoot up in value and your bond fund or other funds decline in value, so you have to balance things.

In a bull market, such as the first half of 1995, when the average stock fund shot up almost 25 percent in total return, according to Morningstar, you might have found yourself with too much invested in stock funds at the end of the year.

> **Technobabble**
> When you *rebalance* your funds, you periodically adjust the mix of your portfolio to keep targeted percentages of your overall investment dollars in each of your funds, based on your risk tolerance.

If you get into a bear market, you want to keep your losses to a minimum. It's important to take some of your profits and make some readjustments to your mix of mutual funds at least once a year.

In Chapter 6 you learned your risk tolerance, the types of funds you should invest in, and how to slice your investment pie to get the best returns with the least amount of risk.

When you rebalance your funds, you go one step further. You examine your portfolio and make adjustments to ensure your investment mix has remained proportionally the same as when you originally diversified.

For example, suppose you set up your portfolio with 60 percent invested in stock funds and 40 percent in bond funds and/or money funds. You're earning a decent return and are sleeping well at night. Now what happens if stock prices surge into a bull market? At the end of the year, you look at what your investments are worth, and discover that you now have 75 percent of your money in stock funds and only 25 percent in bond funds and/or money funds.

Whoa! That's too risky.

What do you do? You simply adjust your mix so that you have 60 percent stock funds and 40 percent bond funds again. Now you can resume your eight hours of shut-eye every night. When you readjust your mix of funds, you sell some shares of your stock fund and invest the profits in the bond funds. That way you maintain the same percentage of money invested in each stock fund to match your tolerance for risk.

Portfolio rebalancing has some of the same investing characteristics as constant dollar investing, which you learned about in Chapter 19.

What is the difference? With constant dollar investing, you always keep the same amount of money in a stock fund at the beginning of each year. By contrast, with portfolio rebalancing, the value of your investments can go up, but you maintain the same percentage of money that is invested in each fund at the beginning of each year. Both strategies are designed to limit risk; however, portfolio rebalancing is a more aggressive strategy because you will always have more money invested in stock funds each year based on the percentage mix of assets in the portfolio.

The Advantages

There are several benefits to rebalancing your mutual fund portfolio:

➤ You're keeping track of your investments. Rebalancing your portfolio forces you to check the performance of your funds periodically.

➤ You're maintaining a risk level that's comfortable for you. You have evaluated your tolerance for risk and determined that you are an aggressive, moderate, or conservative investor. As a result, you don't want your mutual fund portfolio to get too far out of line. For example, if you are a conservative investor who is comfortable with a 50 percent investment in a stock fund, you don't want to see the value of the stock fund investment become a major proportion of your portfolio. Then you'll have too much money at risk.

➤ You're taking profits in funds that are up. You are readjusting the portfolio mix so that it stays in line with your tolerance for risk.

➤ You're buying low and selling high. Similarly, you are taking profits from funds that have increased in share value.

The Disadvantages

Yes, there really are disadvantages to rebalancing your mutual fund portfolio:

➤ If you rebalance funds outside your retirement plan, you'll pay taxes on your profits. After paying the taxman, your returns may not be that spectacular. Of course, there are ways to minimize your taxes when you invest outside of a tax-deferred retirement savings account. You can invest in stock funds with low portfolio turnover. These funds do not distribute a lot of capital gains to shareholders because they buy and hold the securities in the portfolio. As a result, shareholders may pay less taxes on fund distributions. You also can invest in low-dividend-yielding stock funds. These are funds that primarily invest in small company stocks. Smaller companies plow their profits back into the company and don't pay shareowners dividends. You won't pay much to the taxman if the fund does not earn a lot of dividends.

➤ You could get out of your stock fund too early and miss out on higher returns over the years.

Look Out!
Avoid rebalancing with funds that charge front-end or back-end loads. Every time you exit the fund, you're stuck paying a fee. You wind up just paying your stockbroker or investment company commissions.

Best Types of Funds to Rebalance

Before you start rebalancing, you first need to make sure you select funds that make different types of investments. That way when one is down, the other may be up a bit. It all helps.

Refer back to Chapter 7 for guidelines on the percentages to invest in stock, bond, and money funds. Keep it simple so that it's easier to rebalance your portfolio.

To refresh your memory, younger folks who haven't retired yet probably should pick funds among these categories: aggressive growth funds, growth and income funds, international stock funds, and bond or money funds.

Retired folks should limit their fund categories largely to growth and income funds, bond funds or a utility stock fund, and money funds.

Both groups also might consider a touch of precious metals funds as an inflation hedge.

No matter what age you are, it's important to diversify. By rebalancing, you have an easy-to-use formula of when to buy and sell. It's always best to rebalance your portfolio in a tax-deferred investment such as an IRA, 401(k) company pension, or life insurance policy that lets you invest in mutal funds.

Worst Types of Funds

It is always important to read the prospectus and understand a fund before you invest. You want to invest in mutual funds that have stated in the prospectus that they are always fully invested in either stocks and bonds. That means the fund has very little money in cash.

You want to avoid funds that state in their prospectus that they can use market timing and move between stocks and cash. Funds like this may have lot of money invested in cash. You can check to see how much the fund is invested in cash. If it's a lot, call the fund group and ask the representative whether the fund historically has taken large cash positions when the portfolio is uncertain about the outlook for the financial markets.

If you invest in one of these funds that has a history of holding a lot of cash investments, you can foul up your portfolio rebalancing strategy. Why? Suppose you bring your portfolio back into a 60 percent stock and 40 percent bond mix at the end of the year by moving money out of your bond fund and into your stock fund. Now suppose your stock fund is 30 percent in cash. All you're doing is moving money into an investment with a large cash position. You are not really 60 percent invested in a stock fund and 40 percent invested in a bond fund. That's why its important to own a fund that has an investment philosophy of being fully invested.

Once again, avoid load funds with portfolio rebalancing. If you invest in a front-end loaded fund, you pay commissions every time you add new money into the fund. If a fund has a back-end load, you pay the piper every time you sell fund shares and rebalance.

Getting Started with Your Investment Plan

Once you have determined the percentage of your money to keep in each fund category, the first step is to open accounts with the funds you want to own. It's best to stick with a mutual fund family that has a large number of funds. You also can invest with discount brokerage firms such as Charles Schwab, Fidelity Investments, and Jack White. These brokerage houses have more than 300 funds from numerous fund families under one roof. However, keep in mind that certain important mutual fund families have refused to make their funds available through these rival brokerage house channels.

Next, set up a log book to track your initial investments and year-end values. Suppose you determined originally to have 20 percent of your investments in each of five funds. Your total investment at year-end is worth $5,000, so you must invest $1,000 in each kind of fund.

Finally, tell your fund group or broker how much you want to invest in each fund. Call before 4 p.m. E.S.T., and everything will be readjusted the same day. Call later, and adjustments won't be made until the close of business the next day.

Keep a record of all changes. Always compare them with the changes on the mutual fund's confirmation statement, which you should receive in about a week.

How Frequently Do You Do It?

Nervous Nellies can rebalance their investment mixes every three months. Generally, though, it's best to give it 6 to 12 months for a couple of reasons:

➤ If you make frequent changes, you have to pay taxes on your profitable trades—unless the funds are in an IRA or other kind of tax-deferred investment.

➤ Make frequent changes, and you could get whipsawed. In other words, the funds you're reinvesting might change direction quickly. It's possible to rebalance, take your profits, and reinvest in poorer-performing funds. You could be reinvesting at higher prices than you should.

➤ The longer you wait, the less time you have to spend with a calculator figuring out how much to invest in each fund. You want to limit your time as family money manager to one hour a year, if possible.

➤ The longer you wait, the more time your money has to grow. The average bull market lasts about two years. You want to reap the benefits of rising stock prices without feeling as if you're taking on too much risk. One year, history tells us, seems like a nice compromise.

Technobabble
Whipsaw occurs when your fund's performance sharply changes direction right after you buy or sell.

Getting It to Work

Let's look at how rebalancing worked from 1986 through 1994 based on the performance of Morningstar's average growth fund and the average government bond fund. The hypothetical example assumes that distributions are reinvested. Taxes were not taken.

Suppose you invested $1,500 in a growth fund and $1,000 in a government bond fund at the beginning of 1986. Your mix was 60 percent stocks and 40 percent bonds. You readjusted once a year.

217

You can use more funds if you want an extra layer of diversification, but let's keep it simple. See Table 20.1 for an example of rebalancing your funds, keeping 60% of the dollars in growth funds and 40% in government bond funds.

The table shows how your money will grow if you rebalance at the end of each year, assuming that 60 percent is invested in a growth fund and 40 percent is invested in a bond fund at the beginning of the following year. Fund distributions are reinvested, but taxes are not taken into consideration. Past performance is no indication of future results. This is a hypothetical example to show you how it works. Your total returns may be different in the future.

Column 1 of the table lists the year-end period of the hypothetical study. Column 2 shows the total value at year-end of the growth fund investment, and Column 3 shows the bond fund's total value at year-end. The last column shows the combined total value of both funds.

At the end of each year, you multiply the combined total value of the portfolio by 60 percent to get the amount you should invest at the beginning of the next year in the growth.

Table 20.1 Rebalancing Your Funds

Year Ending	Total Growth Fund $	Total Bond Fund $	Portfolio Total $
1986	$1,725	$1,120	$2,845
1987	1,758	1,149	2,908
1988	2,005	1,244	3,250
1989	2,476	1,456	3,932
1990	2,241	1,698	3,939
1991	3,237	1,795	5,032
1992	3,260	2,133	5,993
1993	3,744	2,407	6,151
1994	3,616	2,361	5,997
Midyear 1995	4,124	2,653	6,339

You did pretty well from 1986 through mid-1995. Your $2,500 investment grew to $6,339 by keeping a mix of 60 percent in a growth fund and 40 percent in a stock fund every year.

Once every year's end, you totaled up the value of both investments. Then you put 60 percent of the total into your growth fund and 40 percent in your bond fund.

Stock and bond funds had some pretty good years since 1986. Your stock fund lost 5 percent in 1990 and 2 percent in 1994. The bond fund lost just 4 percent in 1994. In the future, the returns may be different, so don't count on earning the same amount as the example over the next several years.

Hot Tip
Be sure to check the confirmation statements that are sent to you by the fund group after you make your trades. You want to make sure it follows your instructions to a "T."

It's important that when your investments were up, you took profits. When they were down, you bought more shares at lower prices. The end result was positive. In 1990, for example, your growth stock fund lost 5 percent, and the bond fund gained 8 percent. At the end of the year you remixed. As a result, you invested a few bucks more in your growth stock fund at the start of 1991.

Voila! In 1991, your stock fund gained a whopping 37 percent.

Look what happened by mid-year 1994 following losses in both stocks and bonds in the previous year. Your stock fund lost 2 percent in 1994, but by mid-year 1995—it was up 15 percent.

Your bond fund lost 4 percent in 1994, but by mid-year 1995, the fund was up 11 percent.

How do you keep tabs on your funds so you can rebalance? It's easy. At the end of every year, for example, you look at the combined total value of your mutual fund portfolio. Then you slice the pie appropriately. For example, suppose you keep 70 percent in a stock fund, 20 percent in a bond fund, and 10 percent in a money fund. The total value of your portfolio at the end of the year is $10,000. To rebalance, take 70 percent of $10,000 to get $7,000, or the amount you should have invested in your stock fund. Twenty percent of $10,000 ($2,000) is the amount you should have invested in a bond fund, and 10 percent of $10,000 ($1,000) is the amount you should have invested in a money fund. Once you have the right amounts for each fund, tell your fund service representative or broker how much you want in each fund. The rep or broker will make the exchanges among the funds to bring you into balance.

Sidelines

The installment investment strategy is a little more aggressive than portfolio rebalancing. It works this way. Split your investment equally among several funds. Any new investments are made into the fund that performs the worst. If the stock fund is down, you add money to it after the year has ended. In the next year, if the stock fund is up, you add money to your bond or money fund.

The Least You Need to Know

➤ Diversify your investment mix to match your risk tolerance.

➤ Rebalancing means always replenishing your funds to retain the same percentage mix at the begining of each year.

➤ Rebalancing is a low-risk way to invest.

➤ More aggressive investors can adjust the mix every three months.

➤ Rebalancing lets you take profits in winning investments and dollar cost average into underperforming investments.

➤ Rebalancing works best in retirement savings plans because you don't pay taxes on the trades.

Chapter 21

Retirement Savings Strategies for the Faint-Hearted

In This Chapter

➤ A low-risk way to increase the value of your retirement savings

➤ Best funds for retirement savings

➤ Increasing profits and curbing losses

Most of us want to take no chances with our retirement savings. Does that mean retirement savers should put all their retirement savings in the bank? Nope. There's a low-risk way to build your wealth by gradually investing in a stock fund for growth.

This chapter shows how to use the "Stock Fund Builder" investment plan so you can have more money when you retire. All you need are a well-managed bond fund and a well-managed stock fund, and you're on your way.

Building Slowly but Surely

Cluck! Cluck! Those are the words that best describe most of us when it comes to our retirement savings. Chapter 23 explores the different types of retirement plans you can use. But for now, let's focus on a low-risk way to rack up retirement savings profits.

Chances are you've always saved for retirement in a traditional bank account and you're doing fine. You never lost money. You always received a guaranteed return. The trade-off? You probably won't make as much in low-yielding bank accounts as you might with a mutual fund.

In this chapter, you'll learn about one way to grow your nest egg. You'll learn more about the different kinds of retirement savings plans, such as IRAs and 401(k)s. In the meantime, the Stock Fund Builder investment strategy, which we are about to discuss, works well in any of those plans—provided that you have at least 10 years until your retirement.

"Stock Fund Builder" is a name we've given to an age-old investment strategy that's been used by pension fund portfolio managers for years. People who manage pension funds often invest in bonds and use them as a funding mechanism to invest in stocks. The interest income from the bonds is invested in stocks. It is a low-risk way to invest because you are investing a little bit at a time in the stock market. The pension fund managers are using bond funds to generate income, which is then dollar cost averaged into stocks. You can do the same with a bond fund and a stock fund in your 401(k) company pension plan.

Sidelines

Low-risk investment strategies, such as the Stock Fund Builder, historically have not beaten stock funds over the long term.

Here's how the Stock Fund Builder works:

Step 1. Open an IRA with a mutual fund family so that you can have money switched among funds. It's best to stick with one mutual fund family because you can reinvest your fund's distributions without paying fees. Every year, you invest your tax-deductible contributions into the fund family's bond fund. Because the investment is in a retirement account, the money also grows tax-deferred. You can invest in a long-term, intermediate-term, or short-term bond fund. Consider this your least risky investment.

Step 2. Have the bond fund's distributions, which include income dividends and capital gains, reinvested in the stock fund of your choice rather than back into the bond fund. This is a painless way to invest in stock funds for the long haul.

> **Technobabble**
> With the *Stock Fund Builder*, you invest your bond fund's interest income into a stock fund to build your wealth. By investing, for example, in an IRA, you achieve *tax deferral*, which means you don't pay taxes on the principal you invested or its earnings until you retire.

WHAT?

Step 3. Reinvest your stock fund's distributions into new shares of the stock fund.

Step 4. Every year, invest new retirement plan contributions in your bond fund so that you have even more of your bond fund distributions reinvested in the stock fund.

Now you have a recipe to earn lots more money than with a low-yield bank IRA account.

You don't have to worry about losing a large chunk of money in a stock market crash. By the time you retire, you'll be surprised at how much you're worth. You're investing a little at a time without adding stock market risk to your original principal.

Of course, your bond fund's share value will rise and fall with changes in interest rates. If interest rates rise, you'll see the share value of your bond fund drop. When interest rates fall, the share value of your bond fund will rise. You have to live with the fluctuating bond fund share values because you are using the bond fund as a funding mechanism for your stock fund, but when rates fall, the share value of the bond fund will rise.

> **Sidelines**
>
> Here's a twist on the Stock Fund Builder tactic for those who want to put more into stock funds, but still are chickens. Invest a lump sum in a stock fund for growth, but rather than reinvesting the stock fund's distributions, which include dividends and capital gains, back into the fund, invest them in a money fund or bond fund. This is a lower-risk way to preserve your stock fund's profits. Of course, over the long haul, you make more money reinvesting your distributions into your stock fund. However, more conservative investors may want to sock that extra money away in a less risky place.

No Taxes on Dividends and Profits

The Stock Fund Builder tactic works best with an IRA, 401(k) company pension plan, or tax-deferred annuity that enables you to invest in mutual funds.

You don't pay taxes until you withdraw money from your IRA. Then you pay ordinary income tax on your withdrawals. Tax deferral of your stock fund dividends and capital gains is an important key toward reaping the maximum profits. If you paid taxes on your income, dividends, and mutual funds capital gains, you have a lot less money.

> **Look Out!**
> Avoid bond funds with high expense ratios of more than 1 percent. Fund expenses take a big bite out of your bond fund's distributions. Look for funds with expense ratios of just one-half of one percent. You have more money to invest in your stock fund.

Investing in a tax-deferred IRA makes a lot of sense. Table 21.1 shows you how your money grew tax-deferred compared with the after-tax return at age 65 on the same investment. This is a hypothetical study assuming that the money grows at an 8 percent annual rate and $2,000 is invested annually. The first column shows the age you start investing. Column 2 lists what the investment grew to tax-deferred at age 65, and Column 3 lists what the investment grew to at age 65 after taxes.

For example, a person who begins investing $2,000 a year at 8 percent annually when he or she is age 35 will have almost $225,000 in an IRA at age 65. Outside an IRA, the tax bite slices that kitty to just over $160,000. It pays to invest tax-deferred.

Table 21.1 Value of Investment at Age 65

Age at WhichYou Start Investing	Tax-Deferred Value $	After-Tax Value $
55	$31,291	$27,568
45	$98,846	$75,831
35	$224,692	$160,326

That's a whopping difference of $65,000! Chapter 23 goes into greater detail about saving for retirement. For now, however, you can see the advantage of investing in a retirement account and using this investment strategy.

Watch Your IRA Grow

By using the Stock Fund Builder and sweeping interest income from your bond fund into a growth and income fund, you can increase your wealth without much worry. The illustration in this chapter shows how a $10,000 investment grows using this strategy, compared to a straight growth and income fund, from December 31, 1985 through June 30, 1995. This is a hypothetical example we calculated using Morningstar's data to show you how the strategy works. This is a back-tested study. Keep in mind that past performance is no indication of future results.

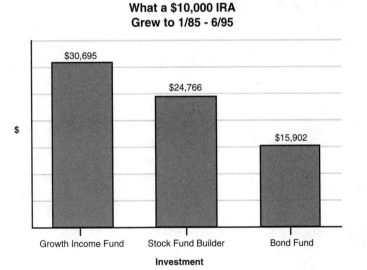

What a $10,000 IRA Grew to 1/85 - 6/95

What a $10,000 IRA grew to from December 31, 1985 to June 30, 1995.

The growth and income fund increased to $30,695. That's pretty good. However, could you have tolerated the 20 percent plunge experienced by growth and income funds in the last three months of 1987, the year of the Black Monday stock market crash?

The Stock Fund Builder was less risky. You earned almost $25,000—and you didn't have to worry about losing.

It's a respectable return, considering that at the beginning of 1987, you didn't have a lot of money invested in your stock fund. Because you invested your bond fund's interest into the stock fund, you were dollar cost averaging and picking up more shares when the stock fund declined.

What if you had left all your money in the bond fund? You would have earned close to $16,000 over the same time frame—$9,000 less than with the Stock Fund Builder.

This is just another way to diversify your investments. You earn an amount somewhere between a stock and bond fund. You can invest a lump sum in a balanced fund that invests about 60 percent in stocks and 40 percent in bonds. However, 60 percent of your money is invested in stocks from the start. That may be too much risk for low-risk-minded investors. The Stock Fund Builder gets you into stocks more slowly. Yet, you build up a nest egg in the stock fund over the years.

What to Do Later

Over 10 or 20 years, you'll probably have a pile of money in your stock fund by using the Stock Fund Builder. Yet, now you're nearing retirement and don't want to risk losing what you earned over the years. You have a couple of options:

Hot Tip
Be sure to invest in stock funds that always stay fully invested in stocks. Otherwise, the Stock Fund Builder investment strategy will not work as well.

➤ **Before Retirement.** Stop moving your bond fund earnings into your stock fund. Then flip back to Chapters 6 and 7 and zero in on your new investment comfort level. Determine the percentages you want in each fund, based on your new risk tolerance level, and practice portfolio rebalancing, which you learned about in Chapter 20.

➤ **After You Retire.** Diversify your money among stocks, bonds, and cash to preserve your wealth and provide retirement income. Chapter 7 discusses the right mix of funds based on your age and tolerance for risk.

Best Funds for Stock Fund Building

Depending on your tolerance for risk, you have a number of fund choices under the Stock Fund Builder. Aggressive investors can use high-yield bond funds and aggressive growth or growth funds. Moderate investors can use high-grade corporate bond funds and growth and income funds. The more conservative should consider a government bond fund and growth and income fund. If you want to add an international component to this tactic, consider a global fund that invests in both U.S. and overseas stocks.

It's best to do business with mutual fund families that have a large variety of well-managed stock and bond funds.

The Least You Need to Know

➤ IRA mutual fund investments grow tax-deferred until you take the money out.

➤ With the Stock Fund Builder investment plan, you increase your earnings with less risk. You invest in a bond fund, then have the bond fund's interest income invested in a stock fund.

➤ You should invest with a mutual fund family that has a wide variety of stock and bond funds.

➤ Even low-risk investment strategies, such as the Stock Fund Builder, historically have not beaten stock funds over the long term.

Part 5
Special Considerations: Taxes, Retirement, College, and Estate Planning

By now, we hope you've grasped some of the basics of mutual fund investing. Despite all we've been through together so far, though, all this information is only the tip of the iceberg. Once you make all this money, you have to deal with the taxman.

Then there are all those reasons you wanted to invest, remember? You need money for retirement and to finance your child's higher education. You also need to plan for your loved ones to be taken care of when you move to the above and beyond.

This part of the book shows you how to deal with all the heavy-duty stuff that comes after you've picked out your mutual funds. You'll learn how to figure out what you owe the taxman, and some good ways to cut your tax bill. You'll also learn how to help get Junior—financially, at least—through the halls of ivy. Then, if there's any money left over, you'll find out how to plan for your own happy and healthy retirement.

The following chapters discuss all these issues as well as the foundation of a good estate plan. You'll learn how to make sure all your hard-earned money goes to the people you really care about. And, in case this book helps put you on the road to accumulating a fortune, you'll also learn some valuable techniques for slashing your estate taxes!

Chapter 22

Mutual Funds and Taxes

In This Chapter

➤ How the IRS taxes your mutual fund earnings

➤ Forms for figuring your taxes

➤ Figuring taxes on selling shares

➤ Cutting the tax bite on your mutual funds

You're off and running with your new mutual fund investments—headfirst, you hope, into a bull market. Everything is going great. That is, until you're faced with the sudden realization that it's time to deal with Uncle Sam. Ugh!

You've now come upon one of the sad truths about mutual fund investing. Unfortunately, we all must pay the taxman on our mutual fund earnings. At the beginning of each new year, you're reminded of this fact when you get those funny-looking tax statements from your investment company.

This chapter examines your mutual fund taxes and suggests ways to cut the tax bite. You'll learn what forms you can expect from your investment company and exactly what they tell you about your profits and/or losses.

Yipes! Taxman's Gonna Get Ya!

There's no getting around it, people. Once you start making some bucks in your mutual fund, the IRS wants a piece of it.

You may pay the taxman on three different sources of income from your mutual funds—dividend and capital gains distributions, plus capital gains when you personally sell your fund's shares at a profit. How do you know what to report on your tax return? You'll pay taxes on the following mutual fund distributions that are listed on the 1099-DIV statement that you receive from your mutual fund every January. There are two types of mutual fund distributions that are taxed:

➤ **Dividend distributions.** This is income from stock dividends and interest from bonds, net of expenses, that the fund's portfolio has earned during the taxable year. Of course, you do not have to pay taxes on exempt interest dividend income that you made from tax-free municipal bond or money funds.

➤ **Capital gains distributions.** This is the net profit that the fund earns from the sale of the mutual fund portfolio holdings. When a fund sells securities that have risen in value, it takes a profit. Any losses from the sale of securities that have declined in value are subtracted from the profits, however.

If your fund sold securities at a net profit, you pay taxes based on whether they are long- or short-term capital gains distributions. Short-term gains are net profits from the sale of securities held for less than a year. Short-term capital gains are lumped with dividend income on the tax form you receive from your mutual fund. Long-term capital gains are net profits from securities held for more than a year. You may also pay long- or short-term capital gains taxes if you sell shares of your fund at a net profit. Don't confuse these capital gains from shares of the fund you sold with capital gains distributions paid to you by your mutual fund. The capital gains from the sale of personally sold fund shares is listed in the 1099-B form that you get from your fund along with the 1099-DIV statement.

How is all this money taxed? Long-term capital gains are taxed at a maximum of 28 percent by the IRS, at the time of this writing. Short-term gains are taxed as ordinary income based on your individual tax rate, which ranges from 15 percent to 39.6 percent.

In January, way before April 15 comes around, you'll begin to get a slew of forms from your mutual fund. Copies, unfortunately, also are sent to the IRS.

The forms tell both you and your favorite Uncle exactly how much you made on your investments. Here are the forms you might expect from your fund:

➤ **1099-DIV.** This tells you how much you made in dividend and capital gains distributions, except from IRAs or other retirement plans. This little exposé reveals the total distributions you received, broken down for dividend income and capital gains.

➤ **1099-B.** This tells how much you got for selling your fund shares. If you own the shares for less than one year, you pay income taxes on the profits, based on your tax bracket, which can range from 15 percent to 39.6 percent. If you own shares for more than a year, you pay a maximum of 28 percent capital gains tax on the profits.

➤ **1099-R.** This tells how much income you received from your IRA or other retirement savings plan. It includes any taxes withheld.

➤ **5498.** This form tells how much you contributed to your IRA during the tax year.

We're sorry to be the bearer of bad news, but first, you owe income taxes on your dividend income and capital gains. Retirees also owe tax on distributions they received from their IRAs or pension plan.

Uncle Sam Takes His Cut

Second, you have to pay tax on any fund shares sold at a profit. Of course, if you lose money on the sale, you may be able to write it off on your income taxes. Keep in mind, though, that losses are subject to the $3,000 annual limit for capital losses ($500 if married, filing separately).

It's advisable to consult with your accountant or tax attorney before you decide on a method for paying taxes on the sale of your mutual fund shares. There are several ways to pay taxes on the sale of your mutual fund:

First In-First Out (FIFO). With this method, as you sell shares of a fund, you assume that the shares you are selling are the first ones you bought. Their cost basis, therefore, is the cost related to the oldest shares of the fund in your portfolio. Here's an example. Let's assume at a point in time, you hold the following 300 shares of a fund: 100 that you bought in January 1993 at $10 a share, 100 that you bought directly or through reinvestment of distributions in January 1994 at $11 a share, and 100 that you bought in January 1995 at $12 a share. Under FIFO, when you go to sell 100 shares, you assume it's the ones you bought in January 1993 at $10 a share.

233

Drawback: With this method, you can pay whopping capital gains taxes when you sell fund shares you've owned for a long time. Of course, if your fund's net asset value declined, this is not the case.

Specifying Shares. Under this method, you designate specific shares to be sold in advance of the sale. In this way, you can select the highest-cost shares to minimize your tax bite.

Drawbacks: Although you pay the lowest amount of capital gains tax on the sale of fund shares with this method, the IRS requires you to keep accurate records of all your mutual fund transactions over the years. So, you must keep much more careful records. If you use this method, be sure that you get a written confirmation from your mutual fund of your instructions to sell specific shares of your fund.

Average Price Per Share. With this method—the most popular—you figure your profits by first factoring the total cost of all the fund shares you bought and dividing that by the number of shares you bought. This gives you the average cost you paid for all your shares. Suppose you paid $8,000 for all your shares and now have 400 shares of the fund. The average cost is $20 a share. If you sold all 400 shares at $22 per share, your capital gain for tax purposes is a $2 per-share gain multiplied by 400 shares. This equals $800. If you sold just 100 shares, you take the same $2 gain and multiply it by 100.

Drawbacks: This is the middle-of-the-road method of figuring taxes due on the sale of fund shares. Unless the value of your shares has decreased, you pay less in taxes than you do under the FIFO method. However, you might pay more to Uncle Sam than if you had sold specified shares. What do you do if you've been socking away $50 to $100 a month into a mutual fund for years via an automatic investment plan? How do you figure the cost of all those shares? Fortunately, many mutual fund groups send you a year-end report that lists the average cost of all the shares you've directly purchased or obtained from reinvestment of distributions. Then you or your accountant can figure any net capital gains based on the sale price of all the fund's shares.

Hot Tip
Many investors overpay their tax on capital gains or profits because they fail to figure accurately the average cost of their shares. Take the time to add up all the shares you bought.

If you don't get a report, you have to go back and calculate the average cost of the fund's shares yourself. Be sure to have all your mutual fund confirmation statements through the years. Most funds have records going back at least 10 years, in case you are missing some statements.

Sidelines

Some fund groups send you a year-end statement that shows the average cost of your funds. If they don't, you've got to keep good records. If you have any questions about your taxes, you can call the IRS toll-free at 800-TAX-1040 for help. To get tax forms and booklets, call 800-829-3676. Publications to ask for are IRS Publication Number 564 on mutual fund distributions, IRS Publication 550 on investment income and expenses, and IRS Publication 514 on foreign tax credit for individuals.

Reducing Your Capital Gains Taxes

There's one upbeat note in this otherwise depressing saga of your mutual fund profits and Uncle Sam. You also can write off any losses from the sales of your mutual fund shares on your income taxes.

This gets tricky—particularly if the fund is a good long-term investment and you really want to keep it.

To qualify for a tax write-off, you can't repurchase the mutual fund for 31 calendar days after you sell it. If you do, the IRS calls it a wash sale and you're dead—tax-benefit-wise, that is. Also remember, as we said before, there is an annual limit on losses you can write off.

You can't be a front-runner either. In other words, you can't buy any security up to 30 days *before* the planned tax-loss sale.

Violate either rule and you lose your capability of writing off your losses.

There are several ways to work around these rules:

Technobabble

A *wash sale* occurs when a security is bought back within 31 days after it is sold, washing out any ability to write off losses on income tax. A *front-runner* occurs if you buy a security up to 30 days before a planned sale to write off losses on your income taxes.

235

➤ **Sell the fund shares at a loss, wait 31 days, and buy them back.** The sale at a loss can occur at the close of trading on the last business day of the year, if you want. This way you realize the loss and can reinvest in your favorite fund 31 days later.

Disadvantage: The fund's price could rise in 31 days and you might be forced to invest at a higher price than when you sold.

➤ **Buy and then sell.** Buy the same amount of mutual fund shares you already own, wait at least 31 days to avoid the wash sale rule, and then sell the original holding. You can use this tactic until the end of November. This way you get to write off your tax loss and still own the fund.

Disadvantage: Because you own more shares, you can be subject to greater losses if the market tumbles.

➤ **Swap funds.** This is a way to avoid the wash sale rule. Sell your fund and invest in a similar fund that sells at about the same price. You can take the capital loss on your taxes and still have an investment that fits your needs.

Look Out!
If you're swapping funds to write off tax losses, make sure the funds you swap are comparable. Otherwise, you can take on more risk than you anticipated.

Suppose you invest $10,000 in the Putnam High Yield Tax-Free Fund at $14.73 and own 678.72 shares. The fund's net asset value drops to $14.10 by the end of June. Your $10,000 is now worth $9,570. Then you sell the fund for a $430 loss. You reinvest the $9,570 in the T. Rowe Price Tax-Free High Yield fund. You now own 823.58 shares at a net asset value of $11.62. As a result, you've realized a loss, but you still own a tax-free high-yield investment.

Other Tax-Saving Tips

The following sections discuss overlooked ways to get a tax break and profit from investing in stock or bond funds.

Loss Carry Forward

Under the tax law, a mutual fund with losses in one year can carry it over until the next year. By selecting funds that have taken advantage of this opportunity, known as a loss carry forward, you can save on your own capital gains taxes in the following year.

Invest in a fund with loss carry forward, and the subsequent capital gains earned by the fund are offset by the capital losses it carried forward.

To make the most of this opportunity, look for well-managed stock or bond funds that have had a bad year. Ask the fund rep whether the fund is carrying forward any losses. If so, you can invest and get a big tax break. You may not have to pay taxes on any capital gains or profits the fund makes in the coming year!

Avoiding Year-End Investments

Uncle Sam has thrown us yet another curve ball when it comes to enjoying our mutual fund profits. You get hit by this one if you happen to invest at the end of a year. It's generally best to hold off on your holiday resolution to step up investing until *after* the ball drops in New York's Times Square.

Why? Guess who pays taxes when a mutual fund distributes its capital gains in December? Usted, vous, and you, that's who. You can avoid this killer of holiday cheer by waiting until after a fund's ex-dividend date to buy fund shares. The ex-dividend date is a fancy word for the date on which the value of the income or capital gains distribution is deducted from the price of your fund's shares.

This sounds pretty complicated, but you can see how it impacts your taxes by looking at what could happen to an unsuspecting investor. This person invests $5,000 in a growth stock fund at the end of November and becomes the proud owner of 312.5 shares of a fund bought at $16 per share. At the end of December, the investor notices that the fund mysteriously dropped in value by $1 per share.

Upon calling the fund to ask why, the investor learns it suddenly decided to pay out $1 per share in capital gains that it had been holding in the fund for a year. This investor now owns more shares of the fund, but the value has not changed.

The investor is in for yet another shock when a 1099-DIV arrives the following January indicating that the investor has $312.50 in capital gains income from the fund. Even though there were no earnings, the investor is forced to pay taxes on capital gains.

> **Technobabble**
>
> A *loss carry forward* is when a mutual fund with losses in one year opts to carry those losses over until the next year, providing investors with a potential tax break in the subsequent year.

> **Technobabble**
>
> A fund's *ex-dividend date* is the date on which the value of the income or capital gains distribution is deducted from the price of a fund's shares. Buying a fund just prior to that date could result in an investor paying taxes for the year on shares that were just bought.

How can that happen? The investor is no idiot, but just bought the fund at exactly the wrong time—before that soooooo important ex-dividend date. As far as Uncle Sam was concerned, the investor might just as well have been a fund shareholder of record for the entire year.

Finding Tax Help

Unfortunately, there's no way to avoid it. Tax season always seems to roll around. Here are a few tips on how to find a good tax preparer who might help you avert some of these bugaboos.

Hot Tip
You can avoid all the tax hassles that Uncle Sam imposes upon us by keeping your money in a qualified retirement savings account. Your money grows tax-deferred in variable annuities, IRAs, Keoghs, SEP Plans, and 401(k) company pension plans until you take your retirement pay. You needn't worry about paying taxes on fund dividends and capital gains distributions or capital gains on the sale of fund shares.

Go to a national tax service if you have a simple return. Tax preparers are required to have at least 75 hours of tax training before they can work for a tax service such as H&R Block.

The Better Business Bureau, however, cautions against using storefront tax return preparers who open for business just for the tax season. You run a greater chance of being audited because a seasonal preparer may not be qualified to do your taxes.

If you are in a high tax bracket, own a business, do a lot of investing, or own property, it's best to seek the help of a Certified Public Accountant (CPA). Better yet: a CPA that's an *enrolled agent* is approved by the IRS to represent taxpayers in the event of an audit.

Questions to ask a tax preparer before you hire:

➤ How many years of experience do you have preparing income taxes?

➤ How many tax returns do you prepare in a year?

➤ How long will it take you to prepare my tax return? You don't want someone to do your return at the last minute. You don't want your tax return arriving at your doorstep by Express Mail on April 14. You need time to review it.

➤ How do you keep updated on changes in the tax laws?

➤ What is your procedure for checking accuracy?

➤ What are your fees? The more complex the tax return, the higher the fee. Most CPAs charge around $75 an hour for their services.

Then take two final steps:

➤ Ask for references.

➤ Check with the local IRS office to be sure no complaints have been filed against the tax preparer.

> **Sidelines**
>
> Here are two other sources of information regarding hiring tax preparers: Send $1 and a self-addressed stamped envelope to the Council of Better Business Bureaus, 4200 Wilson Blvd., Arlington, VA 22203 for publication 24-226, a booklet on how to find a tax preparer. The Ernst & Young Tax Guide 1993, published by John Wiley & Sons, New York, also is an excellent source.

9 Tips On Mutual Fund Taxes

As the scout's motto indicates, it's always best to "be prepared." Here are several ways to make paying taxes on your mutual funds a less frustrating affair:

1. Not all fund distributions are alike. Make sure that you report dividends from the fund as dividends on your tax return. By contrast, capital gains distributions are reported on another line.

2. Avoid paying taxes twice on your fund distributions. If you reinvest in new shares of the fund, you can add the cost of those reinvested shares to your cost basis when you figure gains and losses on shares that you sell. Fortunately, when you automatically reinvest distributions, the cost of the new shares is listed on your fund's statement. Don't forget to save those monthly statements.

3. Just because you sold fund shares or switched funds doesn't mean you *always* owe the taxman. You may be able to offset your capital gains with capital losses.

4. Don't buy fund shares right before the fund's ex-dividend date. The ex-dividend date is the date on which the value of the income or capital gains distribution is deducted from the net asset value (NAV) of the fund's shares. The distribution deducted from the share price (NAV) of a fund you just bought is returned to you or reinvested in new shares.

However, you'll end up paying taxes on this distribution. That's right—you'll pay taxes on money that you just paid out as part of the purchase price of the shares!

5. Keep good records of all your mutual fund transactions. File all your confirmation statements plus your monthly or quarterly statements. You need the information when you file your income taxes.

6. Watch out for nontaxable distributions from your fund. You don't pay any taxes on the return of your own capital. Form 1099-DIV shows how much in nontaxable distributions from your fund.

7. Be sure that your taxpayer identification number is correct when you open a mutual fund account. Otherwise, the mutual fund is required by law to withhold 31 percent of your fund distributions for taxes.

8. Avoid paying double taxes on your international fund's distributions. You are subject to foreign taxes being withheld from your international funds. Be sure you deducted the amount withheld dollar-for-dollar on Uncle Sam's taxes. As mentioned earlier in the chapter, the 1099-DIV lists foreign taxes paid.

9. Don't forget to invest in tax-free bonds and money funds rather than taxable bond funds if you're in a high tax bracket. Individuals with tax rates ranging from 31 to 39.6 percent usually earn higher taxable equivalent yields in municipal bond and money funds than they do in taxable funds.

The Least You Need to Know

➤ You must pay taxes on mutual fund distributions.

➤ You must pay taxes on profitable sales of mutual fund shares.

➤ The investment company sends you forms on the amount you must declare as taxable income.

➤ The average cost method is the most frequently used method to compute taxes on the sale of mutual fund shares.

➤ Take advantage of tax strategies you can use to cut your tax bite. Consult a CPA or tax advisor, if necessary.

Chapter 23

Saving for Important Life Goals

In This Chapter

➤ Saving for your child's college education

➤ Investing your college savings kitty

➤ Calculating how much you need to retire

➤ The *right* way to invest for retirement

It's tough enough to meet your everyday living expenses. Meanwhile, staring you straight in the face is a double whammy—saving for a child's higher education and your own retirement.

Unless you're lucky enough to be born into wealth, or you just happen to pick the right numbers in the lottery, there's only one other way to meet these challenges: Save, Save, Save! Make the wrong investment decisions, or shun the idea of investing altogether, and you could wind up short of money.

This chapter looks at how to save and invest to meet these two important financial commitments in your family's life. You'll learn to figure out what these two luxuries are apt to cost. Then you'll learn some savvy investment strategies for meeting these two very important goals.

The Cost of the Kids' College Education

The quality and level of your child's higher education may well depend upon how soon you begin saving—so might your retirement.

You've probably already heard the stories. College expenses could double in 10 years. Four years of public college now costs about $38,000 to $45,000. Private schools cost twice that much. And by the time your child is ready for a higher education, assuming costs rise 7 percent annually, four years at a public college could cost almost $120,000.

All this means that you need to save $344 a month over the next 15 years to cover the full cost of a future college education, assuming you can earn 8 percent annually from that investment.

Suppose your Little Lord or Lady Fauntleroy wants to be a Harvard student or attend another Ivy League school? You'll have to save $677 a month earning 8 percent to pay for an estimated $238,000 for four years. Table 23.1 shows how much you'll have to save if your child begins college in 2000, 2005, or 2010. This table assumes that college costs are rising 7 percent annually and your investments earn 8 percent annually.

Table 23.1 College Costs and How Much to Save

Year Beginning College	Public Cost	Monthly Savings	Private Cost	Monthly Savings
2000	$ 65,000	$885	$130,000	$1,770
2005	91,000	498	182,000	995
2010	119,000	344	234,000	677

How Much to Save

All this might sound a little intimidating, but actually, it merely involves a little planning. Take a few minutes and fill out the College Costs Worksheet in this chapter on estimating the cost of a higher education. Answer each question to find out how much you must save to cover the full cost for one year of college. Once you calculate how much you need to save to cover one year of college, multiply that number by four to get the amount you need to cover four years.

COLLEGE COSTS WORKSHEET
Fill in the blanks

1. Enter your child's age. _____
2. Enter the number of years before your child enters college. _____
3. Enter the annual cost of college from table 1. $_____
4. Multiply #3 by an inflation factor selected in table 2. $_____
5. This equals your child's future annual college cost. $_____
6. Multiply #5 by 2 for a two-year college or by 4 for a 4-year school. _____
7. Your child's estimated total future college cost. _____
8. Select from table 3 the investment factor for the investment return you expect to achieve (after taxes). _____
9. Multiply the amount in #7 by #8 (the investment factor). This is the amount you need to set aside each year to fund your child's education. Divide this amount by 12 to achieve the monthly figure; by 52 for the weekly amount.

YEARLY SAVINGS NEEDED = $_____
MONTHLY SAVINGS = $_____
WEEKLY SAVINGS = $_____

TABLE 1: ANNUAL COLLEGE COSTS
(Based on 7% inflation rate/year)

ENTRANCE DATE	PUBLIC	PRIVATE
1992	$9,007	$19,350
1993	$9,638	$20,704
1994	$10,313	$22,154
1995	$11,034	$23,704
1996	$11,807	$25,364
1997	$12,633	$27,139
1998	$13,518	$29,039
1999	$14,464	$31,072
2000	$15,476	$33,247
2001	$16,560	$35,574
2002	$17,719	$38,064
2003	$18,959	$40,729
2004	$20,287	$43,580
2005	$21,707	$46,630
2006	$23,226	$49,894
2007	$24,852	$53,387
2008	$26,592	$57,124
2009	$28,453	$61,123

TABLE 2: COLLEGE COST INFLATION FACTORS

YEARS TO START OF COLLEGE	INFLATION FACTOR			
	4%	6%	8%	10%
1	1.04	1.06	1.08	1.10
2	1.08	1.12	1.17	1.21
3	1.12	1.19	1.26	1.33
4	1.17	1.26	1.36	1.45
5	1.22	1.34	1.47	1.61
6	1.27	1.42	1.59	1.77
7	1.32	1.50	1.71	1.95
8	1.37	1.59	1.85	2.14
9	1.42	1.69	2.00	2.36
10	1.48	1.79	2.16	2.59
11	1.54	1.90	2.33	2.85
12	1.60	2.01	2.52	3.14
13	1.67	2.13	2.72	3.45
14	1.73	2.26	2.94	3.80
15	1.80	2.40	3.17	4.18
16	1.87	2.54	3.43	4.59
17	1.95	2.69	3.70	5.05
18	2.03	2.85	4.00	5.56

TABLE 3: ESTIMATED INVESTMENT RETURNS

YEARS TO START OF COLLEGE	INVESTMENT RETURN, AFTER TAXES OF:		
	4%	6%	8%
1	.981	.971	.962
2	.481	.471	.463
3	.314	.305	.296
4	.231	.222	.213
5	.181	.172	.164
6	.148	.139	.131
7	.124	.116	.108
8	.106	.098	.090
9	.093	.085	.077
10	.082	.074	.066
11	.073	.065	.058
12	.065	.058	.051
13	.059	.051	.045
14	.054	.046	.040
15	.049	.042	.035
16	.045	.038	.032
17	.041	.034	.029
18	.038	.031	.026

Source: Alan Lavine. Printed with permission of Consumer's Digest.

Sidelines

Overwhelmed? Don't let it get to you. You may not need to save 100 percent of the cost of a four-year college education. For families who make between $20,000 and $60,000 a year, financial aid might pay for 20 to 99 percent of the cost of college, depending on your income and family's net worth and whether your child attends a public or private school. About 25 to 30 percent of the cost of college is covered by financial aid, reports the Department of Labor. Other sources include bank loans, home equity loans, and life insurance loans against cash value policies. In addition, your child may receive a scholarship, grandparents may give money to children for college, and your teenager might work part-time and contribute to the education kitty. By the time you figure in all those options, you may need to save only 50 percent or less of the total cost.

Building a College Savings Kitty

Once you've got a fix on how much you need for college savings, you can invest to reach your goal. As you learned in earlier chapters, the more time you have, the more you should invest in stock funds. You can invest 100 percent in aggressive stock funds to save for your child's future education. As the child approaches college age, though, it's generally best to go with the low risk and invest in fixed-income funds. Four or five years before a child enters the halls of ivy, it's best to keep about 60 percent of the stash in intermediate and short-term bond funds. CDs, Treasury securities, and money funds are also good investments to protect your profits. The rest may be invested in a growth and income fund or balanced fund. Table 23.2 provides some examples of how you might allocate your mutual fund dollars, depending on the child's age.

The table shows you the historical annual average total return on stocks as an estimate of what you may expect to earn in aggressive stock or growth stock funds. Remember, there are no guarantees. But on average, this is the kind of return these funds have generated.

Table 23.2 Mutual Fund Investments for College*

Type of Fund	Child's Age	Risk You Can Tolerate
Aggressive or Growth Funds	1-12	High

Comments: These funds invest in growth stocks. Expect to average 10 to 12 percent total return per year, earning between -11 and +31 percent per year (a typical range). After age 12, substitute growth and income or balanced funds.

High Yield Bond Funds	1-8	High

Comments: These yield 10 percent, but are risky. Put only a small portion of college savings in this type of fund. They have an interest rate and credit risk. Parents in high tax brackets can consider municipal bond funds.

High Grade Corporate Bond Funds	1-18	Moderate

Comments: Funds invest in A to AAA rated bonds. The yield is 7 percent as of this writing. There is an interest rate risk. Parents in high tax brackets can consider municipal bond funds.

Short-Term Bond Funds	1-18	Low

Comments: Funds invest in U.S. Treasury and corporate bonds. They are less risky than long-term bonds, but yield up to 6 percent as of this writing. Parents in high tax brackets can consider municipal bond funds.

Money Funds	1-18	Low

Comments: Funds invest in short-term money market instruments. They yield 5% as of this writing. Parents in high tax brackets can consider tax-free money funds.

Source: Alan Lavine. Printed with permission of Consumer's Digest.

Once you establish your college investment plan, it's up to you to change to more conservative funds as the child nears college age. Parents, though, can avoid this burden with special college savings plans offered by Fidelity

Investments College Savings Plan (800-544-8888) and Twentieth Century College Investment Program (800-345-2021). With these programs, you use dollar cost averaging in one of the fund group's stock funds. Then, money automatically is moved into the fixed-income fund of your choice when your child nears college age. One hundred percent is invested in a lower-risk money fund or bond fund when your child is ready to enter school.

Sidelines

One thing you don't need when you're investing for your child's college education is more taxes! There are a couple of ways, besides investing in tax-free bond funds or money funds, to reduce the tax bite of saving for your child. Probably the easiest and most common method is merely to put the investment in the child's name.

It's generally best to set up a custodial account with a financial institution using the Uniform Gift To Minors Act (UGM) or the Uniform Transfer To Minors Act (UTMA). Grandparents also may give the child money for college using this tactic. The IRS allows an annual gift of $10,000 per adult without charging gift taxes. However, if you take this route, the money becomes the child's when he or she turns 18, or whatever age your state considers adulthood.

There are several free sources of information on saving for college that may help you get started:

➤ "12 Tips for College Savers," published by Neuberger & Berman Management Inc., 800-877-9700.

➤ The Federal Student Aid Information Center fields your questions at 800-433-3243.

➤ "Paying For College: A Step-by-Step College Planning Guide," T. Rowe Price Investment Services, 800-225-5132.

Start Saving for Your Retirement Now

Now that you've gotten your college savings plans under way, you probably want to start working on your own retirement. Most of us have to work past age 65 to be able to retire. Don't expect things to get any cheaper by that time, either. In fact, just the opposite is likely to happen.

If inflation grows 3.5 percent a year, $60 worth of groceries today should cost $120 in 20 years. "I don't have to worry because I pay Social Security out of my paycheck," you say.

Unfortunately, no one knows for sure what's going to happen to Social Security by the time the baby boomers head south to Florida to live out their golden years. As of mid-1995, it was projected that the Social Security system would be paying out more than it would be taking in by the turn of the century.

You might have to work longer, and/or Congress might be cutting back on Social Security benefits over the next couple of decades.

Today, Social Security replaces about one-third of a worker's income. Unfortunately, you probably need about 70 to 80 percent of your annual current income when you retire to maintain your standard of living.

Look Out!
Don't jump the gun and start dumping all your money into a retirement account before first evaluating your insurance needs. You might need disability insurance to protect your income in the event you become ill or injured. Your family also may need permanent income protection in the event of an untimely death.

The Pot of Gold

Fortunately, the government might be taking it away with one hand, but it's giving it back with the other. Although you can't necessarily bank on Social Security, you can put money into an IRA or other type of retirement savings account to build a worry-free retirement. In fact, more tax incentives, encouraging people to save for their retirement, are under consideration by Congress as this book is being written (mid-1995).

The best thing about retirement savings accounts, such as IRAs, is that contributions may be tax-deductible. If you have no other pension plan, or, if you earn under a certain level, you might be able to save twice: once by paying less in taxes to Uncle Sam, and twice, by deferring taxes on your IRA earnings until you retire.

If you can't make tax-deductible contributions to your IRA because you have a company pension plan and a high salary, it still makes sense to have an IRA. The $2,000 a year in the IRA grows tax-deferred until you take distributions at age 70-1/2. In the following section, you'll learn about the income limits for IRA tax deductions.

Your Personal Retirement Fund: IRAs

With an IRA, you control your investments. You can invest IRA money into your choice of bank CDs and savings accounts, stocks, bonds, mutual funds, and American Eagle gold coins. Before you consider any of these investments, check with your bank, broker, or investment company to make certain they have the capability of setting up your desired investment as an IRA. Because many financial services providers view IRAs as long-term relationships with their customers, it's possible some might require less to open an account if it's being used as an IRA.

Fortunately, Uncle Sam allows any taxpayer who has earned income and is not covered by a company pension plan to make tax-deductible contributions to an IRA. Single taxpayers can put $2,000 annually into an IRA and get a dollar-for-dollar deduction on their income taxes. Married couples without company pension plans that file joint returns can salt away a maximum tax-deductible contribution of $4,000. However, the deduction is phased out or eliminated entirely, based on income, for taxpayers who already have a pension plan.

Even with pension plans, single taxpayers and heads of household can deduct their full $2,000 annual contribution if they make $25,000 or less annually. Married couples can deduct their maximum $4,000 if both work and if they, combined, make $40,000 or less a year.

But, at this writing, with a pension plan, no IRA deduction is permitted for singles or heads of households whose annual income is over $35,000, or for married couples filing jointly who make more than $50,000 annually.

Singles and heads of households that make between $25,000 and $35,000 and married couples who make between $40,000 and $50,000 are subject to a phase-out schedule on their deductions if they have pension plans.

Even if you have a company pension plan and are over the IRA income limits, that doesn't mean you should ignore this valuable tax shelter. You can make nondeductible after-tax contributions to an IRA, and the money still grows, tax-deferred, until you retire. When you withdraw the money from the IRA, you pay no taxes on the principal—just on the IRA's earnings.

For the Self-Employed: SEPs

A Simplified Employee Pension Plan (SEP) is an expanded IRA for the self-employed. As with IRAs, SEP plan holders can invest in bank accounts, stocks, bonds, and mutual funds and deduct their contributions on their taxes. If you own your own business, you can sock away more into a SEP than an IRA. Your employees also have the option of saving through the SEP plan.

This plan is called "simplified" because it's easy to set up. You fill out a form similar to that for an IRA. As with IRAs, you control the investing. Each year, you can contribute up to 13.0435 percent of net earnings or $30,000, whichever is less, into this tax-deferred retirement savings plan. Unlike an IRA, all contributions to a SEP-IRA are tax-deductible.

Keogh Plans

A Keogh is a more flexible retirement plan for the self-employed than a SEP. You can contribute more to a Keogh than either a SEP or an IRA. Depending on how it is set up, you can contribute 25 percent of your income annually to a maximum of $30,000. As with other retirement plans, Keogh contributions are tax-deductible. A Keogh can be set up as a profit-sharing plan or a plan that pays a specified income after you retire.

To start a Keogh, though, you may have to hire a lawyer to file a written plan with the IRS. There also is a lot of record keeping to do. Annual IRS forms must be filled out, and the IRS requires a lengthy report every three years.

401(k), 403(b), and 457 Plans

These are all known as salary reduction pension plans because your taxable wages are reduced by your contribution—so you have less wages to report to the IRS. The 401(k) plans typically are used by people employed in private industry. The 403(b)s are used by those who work for nonprofit organizations, and 457s are for state and municipal employees. Depending on the plan, workers usually agree to put up to 10 percent of their wages into their mutual fund pension plan investments. Employers also are permitted to make matching contributions. Typically, employers pay from 25 cents to 1 dollar for every 1 dollar a worker invests.

Hot Tip
Call the IRS for free publications on retirement savings rules (800-829-1040, and press 2). Ask for publication number 560, Retirement Plans For the Self-Employed and 590, Individual Retirement Arrangements.

Your Own Tax Shelter

In all of the retirement programs just mentioned, even if your investments are not tax-exempt, you always have the advantage of tax deferment. In other words, your retirement account is your very own tax shelter. The savings that tax deferment brings is staggering. For example: Suppose you're in the 28 percent tax bracket and you put $2,000 annually in a tax-deferred account for 20 years and earn 8 percent annually. You end up with $98,846.

If you save the money outside an IRA in a taxable investment, you have just $54,598. That's a big difference!

How Much for Retirement?

Once the rest of your financial house is in top shape, you must figure out how much income you'll need when you retire.

As mentioned earlier, you'll probably need about 70 to 80 percent of your current annual income after you retire. That may sound like you're taking a pay cut, but nearly 25 percent of your wages goes to job-related expenses. You'd be surprised how much you spend to look sharp and feel sharp!

Of course, you'll also have to consider your current age and how far away you are from retirement. Add to your current income less 50 percent an inflation factor for each year away from retirement you are.

The Savings Gap

What you might run up against is a gap between your Social Security income and what your pension will pay. It's important to make that up somewhere. Social Security doesn't cover that much. As of mid-1995, the maximum amount a wage earner at age 65 could receive monthly was $1,022. A widow or widower got the same. If, however, you began to withdraw your money early—at age 62 to age 64-1/2—you got a lot less. The most a 62 year-old wage earner could get from Social Security was $818 a month. A widow or widower got $847.

To have an extra $100,000 at retirement, assuming the investment grows at an annual rate of 8 percent, you should save $575 a month over 10 years, $307 a month over 15 years, $219 a month over 20 years.

Sidelines

It's a good idea to obtain an advance estimate of your benefits by calling the Social Security Administration at 800-937-2000 and requesting form SSA-7004. You also can get a copy at your local Social Security office.

Achieving Your Goals

Mutual funds can help you reach your retirement goals. The plan is to have 70 to 80 percent of your current income when you retire. Social Security will pick up some of that. Here are a couple of benchmarks to give you an idea of how much you need and how much you must save. This assumes your retirement savings earns 8 percent and pays you 8 percent annually when you retire.

➤ If you currently make $30,000 a year, you need to accumulate $225,000 in a retirement kitty earning 8 percent a year to pay you $22,500 annually when you reach age 65. Over the next 20 years, if you earn 8 percent annually you must save $4,917 a year to reach that goal.

➤ If you make $50,000 a year, you need to amass $374,000 to provide you with an annual income of $37,500. Over the next 20 years, you have to save $8,173 a year.

➤ If you currently make $70,000 a year, it will take $523,000 to reach your target annual income of $52,500. Over the next 20 years, you have to save $11,429 a year.

What to Invest In

The longer you have to invest, the more you should invest in stock funds. When you approach and hit retirement, however, you need to save your money.

➤ If you're just starting out in the work world, go for the gusto. You'll be investing for 25 to 30 years, so put 100 percent of your investment dollars in stock funds. Split it up among a small company stock fund, growth and income fund or growth fund, and an international fund.

➤ When you are in your peak earning years and have about 15 years to retirement, you need to think in terms of lower risk. A stock market plunge could put a serious dent in your nest egg, and it may take a longer time to recover. Keep a mix of about 60 percent in a stock fund and 40 percent in a bond fund. On the stock side, invest in a growth fund, growth and income fund, and international fund. On the bond side, split your investments among an intermediate-term bond fund and a money fund.

➤ When you hit those retirement years, keep about 30 percent in a well-managed growth and income fund or growth fund and an international growth and income fund. Invest 55 percent in an income fund that pays high dividend yields and a bond fund. The rest should be invested in a money fund in case you need the cash.

The Least You Need to Know

➤ The earlier you invest, the better.

➤ The longer you have to invest, the more you should invest in stock funds.

➤ The shorter the time until your child goes to college, the more you should invest in lower-risk bond and money funds.

➤ The closer you are to retirement, reduce the money you have in stock funds and increase the money you have in bond and money funds.

➤ Financial aid may cover more than 50 percent of college expense.

➤ To make up for the shortfall between what your savings will be worth when you retire and the money you need, start investing now.

Chapter 24

Managing Your Estate

In This Chapter

➤ Strategies for setting up an estate plan

➤ Leaving money to your loved ones

➤ Reducing estate taxes

➤ 10 steps to a good estate plan

If you think estate planning is only for the rich, think again. Anyone who has a family or business responsibilities needs some type of plan for their surviving loved ones. Besides, once you start applying the principles in this book, you'll be amazed at how your money will grow over the years!

You might already own a house, a car, jewelry, and—we're willing to bet—at least one collectible. What about those marbles or the Monopoly game you used to play when you were a child? Those items still lodged in your attic all are starting to add up in value.

Estate planning may be beyond the scope of this book, but you certainly want your loved ones to reap the maximum benefits of your newly acquired investment prowess. This chapter reviews what to do so that your loved ones have the income and property they need when you're not around. Just think how much further ahead they'll be if you take the time to plan!

Where There's a Will...

The most common estate planning tool is a will. A will is a legal document that determines who will manage your estate, who will get your property and belongings, and who will become guardian of your minor children when you die.

If you die without a will, which is called *intestate*, the state determines who gets what and who takes care of your children when you are not around.

It's important to register the ownership of your mutual fund and other investments the right way, so consult a lawyer or financial planner.

When you invest the family's mutual funds, as well as other securities, there are several ways to set up the accounts. Ownership of the investment is an important consideration. If you do it the wrong way, your heirs will end up paying income taxes that could have been avoided. Later on in the chapter, you'll learn about estate taxes.

There are three ways to own property—whether it's a mutual fund or a piece of real estate (please note, however, that in addition to the methods listed, mutual funds may be registered with a sole owner as a custodian, guardian, or a trust under a court order):

➤ Outright ownership

➤ Joint tenancy with right of survivorship

➤ Tenancy in common

In the first method, you own all of it. Suppose you have $50,000 sitting in a mutual fund in your name. You can stipulate in your will, for example, that

Hot Tip
All you might need in your estate plan is a simple will. However, if you own property and investments, you could need more. It's always a good idea to consult an attorney or financial planner about your estate plan.

you want your son or daughter to have the mutual fund. After your will is probated, the executor of your estate will transfer the fund to the person designated in the will. The person who inherits the mutual fund does not have to pay income taxes on the inheritance. If he or she sells the mutual fund later on, the cost of the investment for income tax purposes is based on the fair market value at the date of your death. Suppose Lorain left her brother Bob a no-load mutual fund worth $50,000 in her will. Bob's cost for tax purposes is $50,000. If he sells the fund a few years down the road for $55,000, he will owe taxes on the $5,000 long-term capital gain.

Sidelines

Please note that accountants refer to the *basis* of an investment. Basis is the original cost of the investment, which is its purchase price, plus out-of-pocket expenses that must be reported to the Internal Revenue Service when an investment is sold. If a no-load mutual fund was purchased for $2,000 and is sold today for $3,000, the basis is $2,000.

The basis is used when calculating the taxes due on long- and short-term capital gains. Long-term capital gains or losses are based on investments that are held for one year. Short-term capital gains or losses are investments that are held for less than one year.

With the second method of owning property, you own all the property with someone else. If you own a mutual fund jointly with your wife, husband, or child, the ownership automatically passes to the surviving spouse. You don't have to go through probate court as you do with a will. The ownership automatically transfers to the joint registrant of the mutual fund. See the discussion on setting up a custodial account for your child later in this chapter.

When you die, the surviving owner will not pay income taxes on the inheritance. When he or she sells the mutual fund, however, capital gains taxes on the sale of the mutual fund at a profit will be owed. The capital gain is based on the appreciation in the value of the mutual fund according to your cost of purchasing the fund. Suppose Bill invested $10,000 in a no-load mutual fund with his wife Betty as joint owner 20 years ago. When Bill died this year, the fund was worth $40,000. Betty automatically became sole owner. The investment had appreciated $30,000 in value. If Betty sells the fund, she'll have to pay long-term capital gains taxes of 28 percent on $30,000, or $8,400.

With the third method, owning something as tenancy in common, you own part of it and can give, sell, or leave your part of the property to others when you die. If a person owns a mutual fund under this form of ownership, he or she can designate in their will who gets their portion of the investment. No income taxes are paid on the inheritance. If the individual that inherits the deceased's share of the mutual fund sells those shares, the cost of the investment for income tax purposes is based on the fair market value at the date of the death.

Technobabble
Probate is the procedure by which state courts validate a will's authenticity. Once the will is approved, the property can be given to the heirs. By giving someone you trust *durable power of attorney*, you're legally giving that person authority to manage your affairs if you become ill or incapacitated. A *living will* is a legal document prepared in advance of a serious illness that details your wishes about future health care.

It's a good idea to have your lawyer prepare a durable power of attorney and a living will. The durable power of attorney delegates the power to handle your business and financial affairs should you become disabled or incapacitated.

By selecting a trusted person to exercise this power, you may avoid interruptions of your business and financial matters. Without it, no one will be able to access your bank account, securities, or any other property in your name without resorting to lengthy legal proceedings.

An executor is the person named in the will to handle the estate, distributing funds, paying taxes, and carrying out other duties stated in the will.

Going One Step Beyond a Will

Trusts, which attorneys say are a bit more flexible than wills, have been gaining popularity as estate planning tools.

Some types of trusts enable you to save money by foregoing probate and letting you leave money directly to your heirs. You can transfer your existing mutual funds in a trust once it is set up. The trustee, the individual responsible for managing the trust, may also invest in new mutual funds. When you go to the above and beyond, your estate will pass to your beneficiaries, based on the terms of the trust agreement. Other kinds of trusts can reduce your estate taxes and provide income to your spouse or children. However, these goals also might be accomplished by a will, and a trust is not always the right answer. A trust, like a will, is a written legal document. You have your money and other assets managed by a trustee so that your heirs get your assets when you die.

Technobabble
A *trust* is a legal document similar to a will that does not have to be approved by probate court before your loved ones can inherit your wealth.

Trust and estate tax laws are complex, so before you act, seek the advice of an experienced attorney that specializes in trusts and estates.

Sidelines

For more information on estate planning, write to the American Association of Retired Persons at 1909 K St., NW, Washington, D.C. 20049. You might check with your insurance agent or accountant for free information on estate planning. Also contact your state's Bar Association for a list of lawyers that specialize in estate planning.

Types of Trusts

A trust can be set up as either revocable or irrevocable.

Here's how the more popular trusts work:

➤ **Revocable Living Trust.** With a revocable living trust, you can avoid the costly process of probate, which, depending on the size of the estate, can cost several thousand dollars. You control a revocable living trust and can change the terms of the trust at any time. You can manage the assets or hire someone to manage the money based on the trust's instructions. In addition, you can distribute the assets in the trust to your loved ones, or you can keep the money in the trust for as long as you want.

There are drawbacks to living trusts. Not all of your assets can be put in a living trust. You might have to have a will for other property such as cars, household items, and jewelry. You can't get a mortgage from some lenders if the home is included in a family or living trust. Plus, although you avoid probate cost when you have a revocable living trust, the assets in the trust are considered part of your taxable estate. You could be in for a large tax bill if your estate is sizable.

Technobabble
There are two kinds of trusts. A *testamentary trust* is created within a will and takes effect when you die. A *living trust* or *inter vivos trust* operates when you are alive.

Look Out!
Living trusts are expensive to set up. You can pay as little as $50 to $100 for a will, but it can cost over $1,000 for a living trust.

257

➤ **Irrevocable Trust.** You *can* reduce the tax bite in addition to avoiding probate with an irrevocable trust, but the terms of an irrevocable trust can't be changed. A trustee manages and distributes the assets of the trust based on the trust document. You give up ownership of any asset you placed in this type of trust. That's why you save on taxes. Legally, the assets are considered gifts to your beneficiaries.

There are also drawbacks to irrevocable trusts. They are expensive to set up. It may cost a few thousand dollars in legal fees. Once you establish an irrevocable trust, you can't change the terms of the trust. You're stuck.

➤ **Testamentary Trust.** Testamentary trusts are a different ballgame altogether. They're used for special situations. For example, say you want to establish a fund to pay for your grandchildren's education, but believe they might squander the money. With a testamentary trust, you can see to it that they're taken care of. The will, containing instructions, goes to probate, and the trust is set up. A trustee then takes control of the assets. Assets in a testamentary trust are considered part of your taxable estate because you've had control of the money during your lifetime.

Tax Planning For Naysayers

You could be very wrong if you think you'll never have enough money to worry about estate taxes.

The number of taxpayers subject to estate taxes was expected to grow to almost 45 percent by the close of this century—from 80 tax filings per thousand taxpayers to 115 per thousand in 1999.

When you factor in your home and personal belongings, chances are you're worth a lot more than you think—or, at least, you could be worth a bundle *sooner* than you think.

Under the rules as of mid-1995, taxes were required to be paid on estates worth more than $600,000. The inheritance tax ranged from 37 percent to 55 percent on estates worth more than $3 million. On top of that, there also may be state inheritance taxes.

Could you and your loved ones ultimately get socked with a big estate tax bill? Yes! The value of your assets could increase substantially, particularly if you've got a good 10 years to retirement. So, sit down with your accountant or financial advisor and look at the numbers now.

Ten Steps to Estate Planning

You have to have a game plan. Here are a few things to help you and your loved ones handle the transition:

1. Take your financial inventory. Review your net worth, or your total assets less your total liabilities.

2. Meet with an experienced CPA, financial planner, and attorney to help you set up an estate game plan.

3. Review your financial goals. Make sure you're saving for retirement and have adequate life insurance and disability insurance coverage.

4. Decide who should inherit your money and property when you die. Ask yourself how much you want to leave your spouse, children, relatives, or friends.

5. Determine the cost of probating a will versus establishing a revocable or irrevocable living trust.

6. Review the tax ramifications. Estimate how much your estate will be worth by the time you die.

7. Look into ways you can cut the size of your taxable estate.

8. Make provisions to pay any estate taxes due. You might not think your heirs will owe the estate taxman, but over time, your assets could grow to more than $600,000.

9. Evaluate the cost of life insurance, which can be used to pay estate taxes.

10. If you set up a trust, make sure that it is valid. A trust agreement should include the following items: how the trust is managed and how the assets should be distributed, identification of the property in the trust, names of beneficiaries or those who will receive your assets, name of a trustee to manage the trust assets, and the terms of when the trust will end.

The Least You Need to Know

➤ You must have a will to make sure that the ones you love inherit what you want them to have.

➤ Give someone you trust durable power of attorney. Then you know someone is available to manage your financial and medical affairs in the event you are seriously incapacitated.

➤ If you and your family are worth a few hundred thousand dollars, having a living trust may be better than a will. Living trusts avoid probate.

➤ Use irrevocable trusts to reduce your estate tax bill.

Glossary

Accredited Personal Financial Planning Specialist (APFS)   Financial planning designation indicating that a Certified Public Accountant (CPA) has passed a tough financial planning exam administered by the American Institute of Certified Public Accountants.

Administrative operational expense   Charge for maintaining your mutual fund account.

ADV form   Form on file with the Securities and Exchange Commission that contains important financial information about a registered investment advisor.

Advisor (Adviser)   1. Person or company responsible for making mutual fund investments. 2. Organization employed by a mutual fund to give professional advice on the fund's investments and asset management practices. Also known as investment advisor.

Aggressive growth funds   Mutual funds that strive for maximum growth as the primary objective.

Annual report   Updates that detail performance for the year.

Annual return   The percentage of change in a mutual fund's net asset value over a year's time, factoring in income dividend payments, capital gains, and reinvestment of these distributions.

Asset-allocation fund   Balanced fund in which changes are made in the stock and bond percentage mix, based on the outlook for each market.

Automatic investment plan   Program that allows you to have as little as $50 a month electronically deducted from your checking account and invested in the mutual fund of your choice.

Average price per share   Most popular method of paying taxes on mutual fund sales, in which you calculate gains or losses by first figuring an average cost per share. You calculate the total cost of all the fund shares you own and divide that by the number of shares you own.

Balanced funds   Mutual funds that invest in both stocks and bonds, typically in relatively equal proportions.

Bankers Acceptance (BA)   Short-term loan to companies that export worldwide. It is secured by goods that are to be sold.

Bear market   Period during which the stock market loses more than 10 percent of its value.

Beta value   Measure of a fund's volatility. The lower the beta value, the less risky the fund.

Blue-chip stocks   Stocks issued by well-established companies that pay dividends.

Bond   A debt instrument issued by a company, city, or state, or the U.S. government or its agencies, with a promise to pay regular interest and return the principal on a specified date.

Bull market   Period during which the stock market moves higher for a couple of years straight.

Callable   Debt that may be redeemed before it matures.

Capital appreciation funds   Mutual funds that strive for maximum growth. Although these funds can earn the greatest gains, they also can rack up the heaviest losses. Also known as aggressive growth funds.

Capital gains   Profits on the sale of securities.

Certificates of Deposit (CDs)   Debt instruments issued by banks and thrifts.

Certified Financial Planner (CFP)   Financial planner that obtains a license issued by the College of Financial Planning. The designation shows that the financial planner has had training in budgeting, taxes, savings, and insurance.

Charitable lead trust   Legal document used to avoid estate taxes, in which the charity receives the investment income and the principal goes to the trust beneficiaries when you die.

Charitable remainder trust   Legal document set up with a charity, in which the charity pays you income for life. When you die, the money goes to the charity, tax-free.

Chartered Financial Consultant (ChFC)   Designation issued indicating completion of a program in financial, estate, and tax planning, in addition to investment management.

Chartered Life Underwriter (CLU)   Designation issued indicating training in life insurance and personal insurance planning.

Check-a-month plan   Program through which money is automatically taken out of your checking account and invested in your mutual fund.

Closed-end funds   Funds whose shares are traded on an exchange, similar to stocks. The price per share doesn't typically equal the net asset value of a share.

Commercial paper   Short-term loans to corporations.

Common stock   Unit of ownership in a public corporation with voting rights, but with lower priority than either preferred stock or bonds if the company is ever liquidated.

Constant dollar investing   Investment strategy that preserves profits by periodic evaluation and adjustment of a portfolio. You maintain the same amount in your stock fund each year by channeling funds from and to a bond or money market fund.

Convertible bond funds   Mutual funds that invest in bonds that can be converted into stocks.

Corporate bonds   Debt instruments issued by corporations.

Custodian   Bank or other financial institution that safeguards mutual fund securities and may respond to transactions only by designated fund officers.

Distributions   Dividends income and capital gains generally paid by mutual fund companies to their shareholders.

Diversification   Act of investing in different kinds of investments to lessen risk.

Diversified   Spread out, as among a variety of investments that perform differently.

Dividends   Profits that a corporation or mutual fund distributes to shareholders.

Dollar cost averaging   Strategy of making regular investments into a mutual fund and having earnings automatically reinvested. This way, when the share price drops, more shares are bought at lower prices.

Dow Jones Industrial Average   Model for the overall stock market that tracks the performance of 30 U.S. blue-chip stocks.

Equities   Investments in stocks and other assets.

Equity income funds   Mutual funds that favor investments in stocks that generate income over growth. As a result, they can be less risky than other types of stock funds.

Eurodollar CDs   CDs issued by U.S. banks that have branches in other countries. These tend to have higher yields than domestic CDs.

Ex-dividend date   Date on which the value of the income or capital gains distribution is deducted from the price of a fund's shares.

Face value   Value of a bond or note as given on the certificate. Corporate bonds are usually issued with $1,000 face values, municipal bonds with $5,000 face values, and government bonds, $1,000 to $10,000 face values. Also known as the principal.

Financial planner   Individual who helps establish a financial game plan. Although a financial planner may have certain licenses or designations indicating the extent of his or her training, there is no requirement that a financial planner have a license. Financial planners carry professional designations, such as CFP and ChFC.

First In-First Out (FIFO)   Basis for calculating the tax impact of mutual fund profits and losses that assumes shares sold are the oldest shares owned.

Fixed-income fund   Another term for a mutual bond fund.

Front-end loads   Sales commission paid to purchase shares of mutual funds.

General purpose money funds   Mutual funds that invest largely in bank CDs and short-term corporation I.O.U.s called commercial paper.

Global funds   Mutual funds that invest in both the U.S. and foreign countries. Also known as world funds.

Government-only money funds Mutual funds that invest in Treasury bills and short-term loans to the U.S. government. These are the least risky money funds because their investments are backed by Uncle Sam.

Growth funds Mutual funds that invest in the stocks of well-established firms that are expected to be profitable and grow for years to come.

Growth and income funds Mutual funds that own primarily blue-chip stocks of well-established companies that pay out a lot of dividends to their shareholders. These funds generally develop stock portfolios that balance the potential for appreciation with the potential for dividend income.

Hedging Strategy of investing in one or more securities to protect yourself from potential losses in other investments.

High-quality corporate bond funds Mutual funds that buy bonds issued by the nation's financially strongest companies.

High-yield bond funds Risky bond mutual funds that invest in high-yield bonds of companies with poor credit ratings. The bonds are rated below triple B by Standard & Poor's and Moody's. Also known as junk bond funds.

Income Periodic interest or dividend distributions obtained from a fund.

Income funds Mutual funds that invest in higher-yielding stocks, but may own some bonds. You get income first along with some growth. These funds usually invest in utility, telephone, and blue-chip stocks.

Inflation Rise in prices of goods and services.

Inflation hedge Term describing an investment that performs well when inflation heats up.

Installment investment strategy Investment strategy in which you divide your investment among several mutual funds and make any new investments into the fund that performs the worst.

Insurance agent Individual licensed to sell insurance.

Insured municipal bond funds Mutual funds that invest in insured bonds issued by cities, towns, states, toll roads, schools, water projects, and hospitals. The interest income is tax-free, and the bonds are insured against default by large private insurance companies, such as American Municipal Bond Assurance Corp. (AMBAC) and Municipal Bond Insurance Association (MBIA).

Interest income Earnings received, often from bonds.

Intermediate-term bond funds   Mutual funds that invest in bonds that mature in about 5 to 10 years.

International bonds   Debt instruments issued by foreign governments or corporations.

International funds   Mutual funds that invest in stocks or bonds of world-wide companies.

Investment banker   Firm that sells stocks or bonds to brokerages which, in turn, sell them to investors on a securities exchange.

Investment company   Firm that, for a management fee, invests pooled funds of small investors in securities appropriate for its stated investment objectives.

Investment objective   Description, included in a fund prospectus, of what a mutual fund hopes to accomplish.

Irrevocable trust   Legal document that allows you to avoid probate and reduce the tax bite. You give up ownership of any asset you placed in this type of trust, and it can't be changed.

Junk bond funds   Mutual funds that invest in bonds issued by companies or governments that are rated below BBB by Standard and Poor's or Moody's. Also know as high-yield bond funds.

Long-term bond funds   Mutual funds that invest in bonds that mature in more than 10 years.

Management fee   Charge for running the fund.

Market timing   Strategy by which investors attempt to buy low and sell high by buying when the market is turning bearish and selling at the end of a bull market.

Maturity date   Date that a bond is due for payoff.

Money market mutual fund   Mutual fund that invests typically in short-term government and company loans and CDs. These tend to be lower-yielding, but less risky than most other types of funds. Also known as money market funds or money funds.

Municipal bond funds   Mutual funds that invest in tax-exempt bonds is-sued by states and local governments.

Net asset value   Per-share value of your fund's investments. Also known as share price.

No-load mutual fund   Mutual fund that is sold without sales commission.

Note   Another word for short-term bond.

No-transaction fee account   Brokerage firm account that allows customers to purchase a selection of mutual funds with no charge or a limited charge.

Open-end funds   Funds that permit ongoing purchase and redemption of fund shares (mutual funds are open-end funds).

Over-the-counter market   Market that uses a network of brokers to buy and sell securities rather than an exchange.

Portfolio manager   Person responsible for making mutual fund investments.

Precious metals mutual fund   Mutual funds that invest in precious metals and mining stocks.

Preferred stock   Type of stock that takes priority over common stock in the payment of dividends or if the company is liquidated.

Principal   Original investment.

Prospectus   Legal disclosure document that spells out information you need to know to make an investment decision on a mutual fund or other security.

Rebalancing   Investment strategy in which you adjust your mix of investments periodically to keep the proper percentages of money in each fund, based on your tolerance for risk.

Regional funds   Mutual funds that invest in one specific region of the globe.

Registered representative   Person licensed to sell stocks, bonds, mutual funds, and other types of securities.

Repurchase agreements   Generally, overnight loans secured by U.S. Treasury securities.

Risk   In relation to a mutual fund, chances of losing money.

Risk tolerance   Amount of money you can stomach losing in a given year.

S&P 500 index   Measure of the performance of a large group of blue-chip stocks in the U.S.

Salary reduction plan or 401(k) plan   Retirement plan that allows employees to have a percentage of their salaries withheld and invested prior to the payment of federal taxes. Often, the employer might match the contribution, and earnings are tax-deferred until retirement.

267

Secondary market   Market wherein bonds, stocks, or other securities are bought and sold after they're already issued.

Securities   Stocks, bonds, or rights to ownership, such as options, typically sold by a broker.

Securities exchange   Tightly regulated marketplace where stocks, bonds, and cash are traded.

Securities and Exchange Commission (SEC)   U.S. government agency in charge of regulating mutual funds and other securities.

Share   Unit of ownership.

Shareholder   One who owns shares. In a mutual fund, this person has voting rights.

Short-term bond funds   Mutual funds that generally invest in bonds that mature in less than three years.

Simplified Employee Pension Plan (SEP)   Retirement plan that permits tax-deferred investments for self-employed individuals.

Single-country funds   Mutual funds or closed-end funds that invest in one country.

Single-estate municipal bond funds   Mutual funds that invest in the bonds of a single state so that investors avoid paying both state and federal taxes on their interest income.

Small company stock funds   Volatile mutual funds that invest in younger companies whose stocks are frequently traded on the over-the-counter stock market.

Socially responsible funds   Mutual funds that invest in companies that don't pollute the environment or sell arms. They will not own tobacco or alcohol stocks, nor invest in companies with poor employee relations.

Specialty funds   Funds that invest in one specific industry or industry sector.

Speculation   Gambling on a risky investment in hopes of a high payoff down the road.

Stock   Investment that buys ownership in a corporation, in exchange for a portion of that company's earnings and assets.

Stockbroker   Person licensed to sell stocks and other types of securities. Also known as a registered representative.

Stock fund builder   Investment strategy in which you invest your bond fund's interest income into a stock fund to build your wealth.

Swap   Switch, as in what bond fund managers do to obtain higher-yielding bonds that have credit ratings similar or equal to their existing bonds.

Taxable bond funds   Bond mutual fund in which interest income is taxed by Uncle Sam.

Tax-deferred investment   An investment that is not taxed until money is withdrawn, usually at retirement.

Tax-free bond funds   Tax-free mutual funds that invest in municipal bonds issued by states, cities, and towns.

Testamentary trust   Legal document set up by a will when a person dies that is used for special situations, such as to establish a fund to pay for a child's education.

Total return   The rate of return on an investment, including reinvestment of distributions.

Transfer agent   Entity that maintains shareholder records, including purchases, sales, and account balances.

Treasury bills   Short-term I.O.U.s to the U.S. Treasury.

Trust   Legal document that does not have to be approved by probate court before your loved ones can inherit your wealth.

12b-1 fee   Fee deducted from the earning of your mutual fund to cover a fund's sales and marketing expenses.

Uniform Gift to Minors Act (UGMA)   Law adopted in most states that sets rules for distribution of an investment to a child.

Uniform Transfer to Minors Act (UTMA)   Law in some states that governs how a child takes custody of an asset.

Uninsured high-quality municipal bond funds   Mutual funds that invest in the least risky municipal bonds. These bonds are rated single A to triple A, but they are not insured.

Uninsured high-yield municipal bond funds   Mutual funds that pay the highest tax-free yields but invest in states or municipalities with lower credit ratings.

U.S. government agency bonds   Debt instruments issued by federally sponsored agencies of the U.S. government.

U.S. Treasury bond funds   Mutual funds that invest in U.S. Treasury bonds and notes.

U.S. Treasury bonds   Debt instruments directly backed by the U.S. Treasury.

U.S. Treasury-only money funds   Funds that invest in Treasury bills, or T-bills, which are short-term I.O.U.s to the U.S. Treasury. These funds typically pay the lowest yields but are considered the least risky money funds.

U.S. Treasury securities   Generally, Treasury notes, bills, or bonds issued and guaranteed by the U.S. government.

Value averaging investing   Investment strategy in which you always make sure that the value of your fund increases by a specific amount over a specific time period.

Variable annuities   Insurance program that allows you to direct your investment in a choice of mutual funds. Meanwhile, you get tax deferment of your earnings and a death benefit guarantee, and you are able to obtain periodic checks for life.

Wash sale   Strategy in which a security is bought back within 31 days after it is sold, "washing out" any capability of writing off losses on income taxes.

World funds   Mutual funds that invest in both the U.S. and foreign countries. Also known as global funds.

Yankee dollar CDs   Debt instruments issued by some of the largest foreign banks in the world that have offices in the United States. They often yield slightly more than U.S. bank CDs.

Yield   Interest or market earnings on a bond or other investment.

Zero coupon Treasury bond funds   Mutual funds that invest in a certain type of Treasury securities that provide no monthly income, but, instead, pay the investor accumulated income and principal at the bond's maturity.

Mutual Fund Newsletters and Investment Regulatory Agencies

Mutual Fund Newsletters

Dow Theory Forecasts
7412 Calumet Ave.
Hammond, IN 46324

Fabians' Investment Resource
P. O. Box 2538
Huntington Beach, CA 92647

Fidelity Insight
Mutual Fund Investors
Association
P. O. Box 9135
Wellesley Hills, MA 02181

Fund Exchange
1200 Westlake Ave. N.
Suite 700
Seattle, WA 98109

Focus: Market timing

Growth Fund Guide
Growth Fund Research Building
Box 6600
Rapid City, SD 57709

Income Fund Outlook
The Institute for Econometric
Research
2200 SW 10th St.
Deerfield Beach, FL 33442

Income Investing
290 Eliot St.
P. O. Box 9104
Ashland, MA 01721

InvesTech Mutual Fund Advisor
2472 Birch Glen
Whitefish, MT 59937

Jay Schabacker's
Mutual Fund Investing
7811 Montrose Rd.
Potomac, MD 20854

Moneyletter and Income Investing
290 Eliot St.
P. O. Box 9104
Ashland, MA 01721

Mutual Fund Forecaster
The Institute for Econometric
Research
2200 SW 10th St.
Deerfield Beach, FL 33442

Mutual Fund Letter
Investment Information
Services, Inc.
680 North Lake Shore Dr.
Suite 2038
Chicago, IL 60611

Mutual Fund Performance Reports
CDA/Wiesenberger
1355 Piccard Drive
Rockville, MD 20850

No Load Fund Analyst
300 Montgomery St.
Suite 621
San Francisco, CA 94104

No Load Fund Investor
P. O. Box 318
Irvington-on-Hudson, NY 10533

NoLoad Fund X
235 Montgomery St.
Suite 662
San Francisco, CA 94104

Focus: Best performing funds to buy

Sector Funds Newsletter
P. O. Box 270048
San Diego, CA 92198

Focus: Market timing with sector
funds

Stockmarket Cycles
P. O. Box 6873
Santa Rosa, CA 95406

Focus: Market timing with
mutual fund advice

Investment Regulatory Agencies

State Securities Agencies

Alabama Securities Commission
334-242-2984

Alaska Dept. of Commerce &
Economic Development
Division of Banking, Securities &
Corporations
907-465-4242

Arizona Corporation Commission
Securities Division
602-542-4242

California Dept. of Corporations
213-736-2495

Colorado Division of Securities
303-894-2320

Connecticut Department
of Banking
203-240-8230
800-831-7225

Delaware Department of Justice
Division of Securities
302-577-2515

District of Columbia Services
Commission
Securities Division
202-626-5105

Florida Office of the Comptroller
Division of Securities
904-488-9805
800-848-3792

Georgia Office of the Secretary
of State Securities Division
Information: 404-656-2695
Complaints: 404-656-3920

Hawaii Dept. of Commerce &
Consumer Affairs
Securities Commission
808-589-2730

Idaho Dept. of Finance
Securities Bureau
208-334-3684

Illinois Office of the Secretary
of State
Securities Department
217-782-2256
800-628-7937

Indiana Office of the Secretary
of State Securities Division
317-232-6681
800-223-8791

Iowa Department of Commerce
Insurance Division
Iowa Securities Bureau
515-281-4441

Kansas Securities Commission
913-296-3307

Kentucky Dept. of Financial
Institutions
Division of Securities
502-573-3390
Requests for information must
be in writing:
Department of Financial
Institutions
477 Versailles Rd.
Frankton, KY 40401
Attn: David Ashley

Louisiana Securities Commission
504-568-5515
Requests for information must
be in writing:
Louisiana Securities Commission
Energy Centre
1100 Pydras St. Suite 2250
New Orleans, LA 70163

Maine Dept. of Professional &
Financial Regulation
Bureau of Banking, Securities
Division
207-582-8760

Maryland Attorney General's
Office
Division of Securities
410-576-6360

Massachusetts Secretary of
the Commonwealth Securities
Division
617-727-3548

Michigan Dept. of Commerce
Corporation and Securities Bureau
517-334-6200

Minnesota Dept. of Commerce
Information: 612-296-2283
Complaints: 612-296-2488

Mississippi Office of the Secretary
of State
Securities Division, 601-359-6364
800-804-6364

Missouri Office of the Secretary of
State
Securities Division
314-751-4136
800-721-7996

Montana Office of the State
Auditor
Securities Department
406-444-2040
800-332-6148

Nebraska Dept. of Banking &
Finance Bureau of Securities
402-471-3445

Nevada Office of the Secretary
of State
Securities Division
702-486-2440
800-758-6440

New Hampshire Bureau of
Securities Regulation
603-271-1463
800-994-4200

New Jersey Dept. of Law and
Public Safety
Bureau of Securities
201-504-3600

New Mexico Regulation &
Licensing Dept.
Securities Division
505-827-7140
800-704-5533

New York Dept. of Law
Bureau of Investor Protection and
Securities
212-416-8200
Requests for information must
be in writing
Attn: Alice McInerney
New York State Department of
Law
Bureau of Investor Protection and
Securities
120 Broadway 23rd Floor
New York, NY 10271

North Carolina Office of the
Secretary of State
Securities Division
919-733-3924
Complaints: 800-668-4507

North Dakota Office of the
Securities Commissioner
701-328-2910
800-297-5124

Ohio Division of Securities
614-644-7381

Oklahoma Dept. of Securities
405-235-0230

Oregon Dept. of Consumer &
Business Services
Division of Finance & Corporate
Securities
503-378-4387

Pennsylvania Securities
Commission
717-787-8061
800-600-0077

Rhode Island Dept. of Business
Regulation
Securities Division
401-277-3048

South Carolina Securities Division
803-734-1087

South Dakota Division
of Securities
605-773-4823

Tennessee Dept. of Commerce &
Insurance
Securities Division
Information: 615-741-3187
Complaints: 615-741-5900

Texas State Securities Board
512-305-8332

Utah Dept. of Commerce
Division of Securities
801-530-6600
800-721-3233

Vermont Dept. of Banking,
Insurance & Securities
Securities Division
802-828-3420

Virginia State Corporation
Commission
Division of Securities & Retail
Franchising
804-371-9051

Washington Dept. of Financial
Institutions
Securities Division
360-902-8760

West Virginia's State Auditor's
Office
Securities Division
304-558-2257

Wisconsin Office of the
Commissioner of Securities
800-472-4325

Wyoming Secretary of State
Securities Division
State Capitol Bldg.
Cheyenne, Wyoming 82002
307-777-7370

National Regulators

Commodity Futures Trading
Commission
202-254-3067 (enforcement
division)

National Association of Securities
Dealers
202-728-8000 (main)
800-289-9999 (information about
brokers and firms)

National Futures Association
Disciplinary Information Access
Line (DIAL)
200 W. Madison St. Ste. 1600
Chicago, Illinois 50505
800-621-3570 (national)
800-572-9400 (in Illinois)

U.S. Securities and Exchange
Commission
202-942-7040 (main)
800-SEC-0330 (complaints/
consumer information)

Authors' Picks: Mutual Funds that Have Withstood the Test of Time

Although past performance is no guarantee of future results, there is something to be said for mutual funds that have withstood the test of time. Here are a list of load and no-load growth and income funds and balanced funds that have done well for more than five decades ending in mid-year 1995, according to CDA Wiesenberger. These funds are also rated as above average for return and below average for risk by Morningstar.

Stock Funds

➤ **Investment Company of America.** Over the 54 years ending in 1994, this growth and income fund grew at an annual average total return of 12.31 percent. By mid-year 1995, the fund's total return was 16.22 percent. Over the past three years, the fund grew at a 10.4 percent annual average total return. The fund is rated above average for return and below average for risk by Morningstar, Inc. It invests in large company stocks for the long term. The fund has a 5.75 percent front-end load.

➤ **Fidelity Fund.** Over the past 54 years, this growth and income fund grew at an annual average total return of 11.78 percent. By mid-year 1995, the fund's total return was 15 percent. Over the past three years, the fund's annual average total return gained 14.3 percent. It is also rated above average for return and below average for risk by Morningstar. Stocks held by the fund include IBM, Scott Paper, Tyco International, and Viacom. The fund is no-load.

➤ **Safeco Equity Fund.** Over the past 54 years, this growth and income fund grew at an annual average total return of 11.43 percent. By mid-year 1995, the fund's total return was 12.44. Over the past three years, the fund grew at an annual average total return of 22.84. This fund rates high for return and average for risk. Presently, the fund is invested primarily in mid-sized companies that are either undervalued or have strong earnings growth. Stocks in the portfolio include GTE, US West, Motorola, and Salomon Brothers. The fund is no-load.

➤ **Fundamental Investors.** Over the past 54 years, this growth and income fund grew at an annual average total return of 10.93. By mid-year 1995, the fund's total return was 18.9 percent. Over the past three years, the fund has grown at a 15.9 percent annual average total return. Its return is rated above average. Its risk is rated below average. The fund focuses on companies that should benefit from changing economic conditions. Holdings include Capital Cities/ABC, Intel, Federal Express, and Walt Disney. The fund has a 5.75 percent load.

➤ **Lexington Corporate Leaders.** This growth and income fund grew at a 10.3 percent annual average total return over the past 54 years. By mid-year 1995, the fund's total return was 19.1 percent. Over the past three years, the fund's annual average total return was 11.1 percent. The fund is rated above average for return and below average for risk. The fund has invested in the same 30 blue chip stocks for over five decades. Holdings include Eastman Kodak, Mobil, Exxon, Sears Roebuck, General Electric, and AT&T. The fund is no-load.

Balanced Funds

➤ **Delaware Fund.** This balanced fund has grown at an annual average total return of 10.8 percent since 1940. By mid-year 1995, the fund's total return was 12 percent. Over the past three years, it has grown at an annual average total return of 9.7 percent. The fund invests in larger companies that are expected to increase their dividends. The fund invests about 40 percent in intermediate-term bonds rated A or above by Standard & Poor's and Moody's. For these reasons, this fund typically pays a higher dividend yield than similar funds. There is a 5.75 load.

➤ **American Balanced Fund.** This balanced fund has grown at an annual average total return of 9.65 percent since 1940. By mid-year 1995, the fund's total return was 13.7 percent. Over the past three years, the fund has grown at an annual average total return of 10.52 percent. The fund buys undervalued blue chip stocks and intermediate-term investment grade bonds. There is a 5.75 percent load.

➤ **CGM Mutual.** This balanced fund has grown at an annual average total return of 9.44 percent since 1940. By mid-year 1995, the fund's total return was 15.2 percent. Over the past three years, it's grown at an annual average total return of 11.4 percent. This is an aggressive balanced fund that can invest up to 75 percent in stocks. The fund looks for undervalued blue chip or smaller company stocks. The fund is no-load.

➤ **George Putnam Fund.** This balanced fund has grown at an annual average total return of 9.38 percent since 1940. By mid-year 1995, the fund's total return was 14.65 percent. Over the past three years, it's grown at an annual average total return of 9.54 percent. The fund can invest up to 75 percent of its assets in stocks. The fund wants to own undervalued stock in large companies that should show improved earnings. On the bond side, it invests in higher-yielding corporate bonds. The fund has a 5.75 percent load.

➤ **Dodge & Cox Balanced.** This balanced fund has grown at an annual average total return of 9.2 percent since 1940. By mid-year 1995, the fund's total return was 16.5 percent. Over the past three years, it's grown at an annual average total return of 13.5 percent. The fund may invest up to 75 percent of assets in stocks. It also invests in longer-term government and investment grade corporate bonds. The fund buys undervalued stocks with the potential of registering strong earnings growth. This is a no-load mutual fund.

➤ **Vanguard Wellington.** This balanced fund has grown at an annual average total return of 9.02 percent since 1940. By mid-year 1995, the fund's total return was 17.74 percent. Over the past three years, the fund has grown at an annual average total return of 12.01 percent. The fund can invest 60 to 70 percent in stocks. The fund invests undervalued large company stocks that pay high dividends and should appreciate in value. On the bond side, the fund sticks with government securities and high-grade corporate bonds. The fund is no-load.

The 10 Most Popular Funds: How Have They Done?

You can see why people like these funds. In recent years, they've all had double-digit returns. In addition, they all have performed well historically. The following table summarizes the performance of the 10 most popular funds (*Source: Lipper Analytical Services*):

Fund Name	Assets (Billions)	Objective	Annual Return, 3 Years Ending June 30, 1995
Fidelity Magellan	$45	Growth	18.1%
Investment Company of America	$22	Growth & income	11.7
Washington Mutual Investors	$15	Growth & income	12.8
Fidelity Puritan	$14	Balanced	13.8
Vanguard Windsor	$13	Growth & income	15.1
Income Fund of America	$12	Income	10.5
Twentieth Century Ultra	$11	Aggressive growth	20.1
Janus Fund	$11	Growth	11.8

continues

continued

Fund Name	Assets (Billions)	Objective	Annual Return, 3 Years Ending June 30, 1995
Fidelity Growth & Income	$12	Growth & income	15.2
Vanguard Index 500 Portfolio	$13	Growth & income	13.1
Other Indexes			
S&P 500			13.2
Lehman Brothers Aggregate Bond Index			7.5
Treasury Bills			3.9

Mutual Fund Problem Solver

You know the old saying, "If things can go wrong, they will." When it comes to your hard-earned cash, any mistakes can wind up being more expensive than you'd like.

Fortunately, some of the most common mutual fund problems can be nipped in the bud by taking a few simple steps up front. Here's how to handle some of the most common headaches you might experience with your mutual fund:

➤ **Problem:** You need to sell your mutual fund and the fund group's toll-free numbers are tied up.

Avoid this situation by taking these steps when you first open your account. Always get a non-toll-free number for the mutual fund. Also get the fund's street address where fund transactions are handled—not a post office box number. Then, have an overnight express mail letter ready to send the fund group in the event you want to sell. Before you send out express mail, however, try calling the fund's non-toll-free phone number. It may cost you a few dollars, but it's cheaper than express mail.

➤ **Problem:** The fund service representative made a mistake on your order.

Again, take some advance action while you're conducting the transaction. Make it a practice to keep a record of the time, date, and name of the person who handled your order. Most mutual fund groups record your transactions. Next, find the name of the service representative's supervisor. Speak to the supervisor *and* put your request in writing. If you have access to a fax machine, zip him or her a letter with your problem. Your problem should be resolved.

➤ **Problem:** You are supposed to receive a check from your fund and it gets lost in the good old U.S. mail.

Call the toll-free number listed on your mutual fund statement. This will put you in touch with a service representative, who, upon hearing of your problem, should be able to stop payment on the check and issue a new one. Be sure to verify that they have your correct address.

➤ **Problem:** You change your mind about a trade.

Yes, you can do it—if you call the fund before 4 p.m. E.S.T. the same day. That's the time the fund group settles its transactions.

➤ **Problem:** You've transferred your IRA or retirement plan to a mutual fund family from another financial institution. It's delayed.

This happens frequently. Sometimes it can take a few weeks for a transfer to be completed due to misplaced instructions or computer foul-ups. If it's been more than five business days and you haven't heard from your new fund group confirming completion of the transaction, call and ask what the problem is. Your new fund group should call the other institution, and then call you back.

What if nothing happens? Call your old fund group and ask to talk to the supervisor of the department that handles transfers. Explain your problem. Then follow up with a letter. It may take some time, but paperwork problems should be solved.

➤ **Problem:** You've lost some of the mutual fund statements and you need the information on shares you bought in the past for tax purposes.

Call your fund. Most groups have at least 10 years' worth of data about your investments. It may take time to fish it out of the computer or other records, so be patient and don't wait until the last minute to do your taxes.

➤ **Problem:** You need to stop payment on a money fund or bond fund check.

Just call the fund. Be sure you have the date, check number, and amount of the check. The fund family either will do it for you or give you the toll-free number of the mutual fund's custodian bank. Some funds charge $10 to stop payment on a money fund or bond fund check. Others will stop payment free of charge.

➤ **Problem:** You've got a beef with your broker or financial planner. Perhaps the financial advisor put you in unsuitable mutual funds, funds that don't fit your investment objective or tolerance for risk. Or an advisor keeps switching you from one fund to another to make fat commissions.

Again, avoid this problem from the beginning by conducting all your transactions in writing. Note dates and times of your trades. Keep copies. Complain to your broker or financial planner briefly in writing, documenting the precise trades and times and solicit a written response. If you get no relief, try the person's supervisor. Explain the situation. Still no satisfaction? File a complaint with your state's securities division.

If you're still not satisfied and your dispute is with an individual licensed by the National Association of Securities Dealers (NASD), there's more hope. You can arbitrate with the NASD. Call 212-480-4881 to obtain an arbitration kit. This material shows you how to file a legal complaint with a securities arbitration committee, which will hear your case and determine whether you should be compensated. The cost of arbitration depends on the amount of your claim. It's also a good idea to consult with an attorney before you act.

Index

Symbols

J-K-L

M

R

S